TAIWAN LIVES

TAIWAN AND THE WORLD

William Lavely, Madeleine Yue Dong, James Lin

SERIES EDITORS

TAIWAN LIVES

A Social and Political History

NIKI J. P. ALSFORD

University of Washington Press
Seattle

Taiwan Lives was made possible in part by funding from the Taiwan Studies Program, a division of the Henry M. Jackson School of International Studies at the University of Washington.

Additional support for this publication was provided by the Chiang Ching-kuo Foundation for International Scholarly Exchange.

This book will be made open access within three years of publication thanks to Path to Open, a program developed to bring about equitable access and impact for the entire scholarly community, including authors, researchers, libraries, and university presses around the world. Learn more at https://about.jstor.org/path-to-open/.

Copyright © 2024 by the University of Washington Press

Design by Mindy Basinger Hill / Composed in Adobe Caslon Pro
Maps by Ben Pease

All rights reserved. No part of this publication may be reproduced or transmitted in any form or by any means, electronic or mechanical, including photocopy, recording, or any information storage or retrieval system, without permission in writing from the publisher.

UNIVERSITY OF WASHINGTON PRESS *uwapress.uw.edu*

Library of Congress Cataloging-In-Publication Data

Names: Alsford, Niki J. P., author.

Title: Taiwan lives : a social and political history / Niki J. P. Alsford.

Description: Seattle : University of Washington Press, [2024] |
Series: Taiwan and the world | Includes bibliographical references and index.

Identifiers: LCCN 2023037512 | ISBN 9780295752150 (hardcover) |
ISBN 9780295752167 (paperback) | ISBN 9780295752174 (ebook)

Subjects: LCSH: Taiwan—Biography. | Taiwan—History.

Classification: LCC DS799.6.A57 2024 | DDC 951.2490922—dc23/eng/20231024

LC record available at https://lccn.loc.gov/2023037512

♾ This paper meets the requirements
of ANSI/NISO Z39.48-1992 (Permanence of Paper).

COVER PHOTOGRAPHS *front* A gathering of people among the Paiwan
Indigenous group. PCE/FMC/6/12/26. United Reform Church, PCE Collections.
back Tsai Ing-wen, August 30, 2008, by MiNe (sfmine79) / Flickr CC BY 2.0 DEED LICENSE

To all the people of Taiwan

Contents

ACKNOWLEDGMENTS *xi*

NOTE ON TRANSLITERATION *xiii*

INTRODUCTION *1*

Part One **A SOCIAL HISTORY**

Background

1 A Sojourner's Tale JOHN DODD *21*

Becoming Japanese, 1895–1930

2 A Merchant's Tale KU HSIEN-JUNG *31*

3 A Settler's Tale LIN SHIH *39*

4 A Colonialist's Tale SHIMIZU TERUKO *47*

Pathways to War, 1930–1945

5 A Hunter's Tale: Ro'eng *59*

6 A Miner's Tale: Jack Edwards *71*

7 A Child's Tale: Chen Pi-Kuei *81*

White Terror, 1945–1987

8 A Diplomat's Tale: George H. Kerr *93*

9 A Preacher's Tale: Shoki Coe *100*

10 An Exile's Tale: Su Beng *109*

A New Hope, 1987–Present

11 A Writer's Tale: Sanmao *119*

12 An Activist's Tale: Fan Yun *125*

13 A Pop Star's Tale: Tzuyu *134*

Part Two **PIVOTAL EVENTS**

Establishment of the Taiwan Cultural Association, 1921

14 A Doctor's Tale: Chiang Wei-shui *145*

15 A Philanthropist's Tale: Li Chunsheng *154*

The 228 Incident, 1947

16 A Hawker's Tale: Lin Chiang-mai *163*

17 A Refugee's Tale: Jin Su-qin *171*

Martial Law, 1947–1987

18 A Tangwai's Tale: Huang Hsin-chieh *183*

19 A Prisoner's Tale: Chen Chu *190*

Part Three **BEING TAIWAN**

20 An Anthropologist's Tale: Arthur P. Wolf *199*

21 A Businessman's Tale: Chang Yung-fa *203*

22 An Epidemiologist's Tale: Chen Chien-jen *211*

23 An Indigenous Tale: Icyang Parod *217*

24 A President's Tale: Tsai Ing-wen *226*

A Conclusion *232*

Glossary *235*

References *245*

Index *267*

Acknowledgments

The most challenging part of any book is ensuring that the acknowledgments adequately recognize all of those who have played a role in bringing the project to life. Realistically, I cannot thank every person who has been a part of this journey, and I apologize to anyone who is absent here.

I simply could not have completed this project without the expert feedback of Jo-hsuan Wang, Jacques Rouyer Guillet, and Dean Karalekas, who read this work in its various incarnations.

A supportive working environment is essential, and I am blessed to be surrounded by wonderful colleagues at the University of Central Lancashire, including Sojin Lim, Ed Griffith, Lara Momesso, Ti-han Chang, Adina Zemanek, Moises de Souza, Rowann Fitzpatrick, Daniel Waller, and Helen Martin.

Nothing can be accomplished in this field without collaboration and cooperation beyond one's own institution. Gratitude is owed to Futuru Tsai at National Taitung University, as well as Dafydd Fell and Chang Bi-yu at the Centre of Taiwan Studies at the School of Oriental and African Studies, the University of London (SOAS). Learning from and alongside these giants of the field is a privilege.

I owe extraordinary appreciation to Mariama Sekloawu, Olivia Sekloawu, and Summer-Grace Williams. Having their infectious enthusiasm and diligent support has unquestionably benefited this project.

Academics need a wide range of assistance and support to tackle projects such as this one. The North American Taiwanese Professors Association (NATPA) generously provided sponsorship for the research project that resulted in this book. Extra-special thanks go to Shyu-tu Lee, Ching-Chih Chen, and Peter Chow for their guidance and patience. I will be eternally grateful for their gift of spending their precious time on my work and providing me with their invaluable insights.

Bringing this work into the printed realm took a great number of people who collectively constitute the team at the University of Washington Press. I am also thankful for the comments provided by two anonymous reviewers. Lorri Hagman, Marcella Landri, William Lavely, and James Lin, in particular, deserve special mention for their hard work.

Lastly, I would like to be clear that any errors or failings in this work are mine and mine alone.

Note on Transliteration

Place-names: I have tried to provide a clear codification of Taiwanese place names. Wherever possible, I include the current-standard alternative that is officially used in Taiwan. Since the Hanyu Pinyin (HP) system has become the international norm for Chinese romanization, I use this as the standard in all other circumstances.

"Formosa" is used interchangeably with "Taiwan," depending on context. This book uses "Qing," for the imperial dynasty in China and Taiwan and "Manchu" for the ethnic group that led that dynasty.

Personal names: Individuals' preferred romanization, sequence of family name and given name, and hyphenation of their own names is honored.

Other Chinese terms: For consistency, all other romanization of Chinese words uses HP.

Other languages: Romanized terms from other written language systems are indicated, when not obvious from context, with the following abbreviations:

TH · Taiwanese Hokkien (Tâi-gí; HP Taiyu)

J · Japanese (standard Revised Hepburn system)

K · Korean (standard Revised Romanization transcription)

TAIWAN LIVES

Introduction

Taiwan stands on the front lines of democracy
worldwide. As long as the people of Taiwan remain
united and uphold our core values while responding
prudently to regional developments, we can overcome
the challenges posed by authoritarian expansion.

TSAI ING-WEN · 2021

In the late fourteenth century, a narrator joins a company of twenty-nine pilgrims at the Tabard Inn in Southwark, near London. The band of men are traveling to Canterbury, to the shrine of the martyr Saint Thomas à Becket. Geoffrey Chaucer's narrator provides a descriptive account of the pilgrims, who each tell their own stories, twenty-four of which make up *The Canterbury Tales*. Those descriptions of characters paint a critical portrait of English society. Although fictitious, they offer insights into the customs and practices of the period. The *Tales* were written during a tumultuous and complex period in English history. In spite of a split within the Roman Church, Catholicism remained the sole Christian authority throughout the country even though it was faced with significant scrutiny (Cooper 1991). The *Tales* offer the reader diverse views of England following the Black Death. They reflect the conflict among social classes (those who pray, fight, and work) and are interlinked through common themes. Liminality figures prominently. Their space, both geographic as well as spiritual, transforms concepts of place between the "real" or absolute landscape and the "imagined" or relative landscape.

Exploring a sociopolitical history of Taiwan offers similar interpretations. Each of the twenty-four nonfictitious tales told here is liminal, not only covering the life of a single person but also connecting, thematically, to the landscape. Each tale offers a document on life and action, and how they are interpreted in a contemporary society. The complex colonial history of Taiwan is layered, beginning with the arrival of the Dutch in the seventeenth century, and each form of colonization has influenced the sociopolitical makeup of the island. The first is a hybrid form of colonization, where the settler colonists were Chinese but the administration and military structures were Dutch. The second layer consists of a more integrated settler colonial period, one that is much more complex and interwoven with the expansion of the Qing dynasty on the Chinese mainland. This form of colonization mirrors that of other settler colonial expansionisms, such as the United States, Canada, Australia, and New Zealand, and involved the systematic replacement of Indigenous populations with an invasive and violent settler society. Over time, these communities would develop a distinct identity shaped by this relationship.

This colonization is distinct from traditional "metropole" forms of colonization in that the settlers stayed, unlike sojourning agents in the form of traders, governors, or missionaries. Its form is structural rather than confined to a single event. It is a persistent, ongoing elimination and subjugation of native populations. In Taiwan, this was characterized by a marked increase in volatile Chinese settlement. Toward the end of the nineteenth century, the island's semicolonial condition, which followed its inclusion in the treaty port system (1858–95), would bring waves of settler colonists while having a long-lasting effect on the geopolitical and economic importance of the island. This was further extended during Japan's imperial colonization. The Japanese colonial government practiced a divide-and-rule policy by pitting the multiple ethnicities of Taiwan against one another. While there may have been one Japanese Empire, there was no single Japanese imperial experience. The hardline position toward specific ethnicities led to systematic resistance among different groups. This resistance was countered by many in Japan and others who had begun to settle on the island, who wished to know more about the Japanese Empire, thus fueling a civilizing project to document and understand its colonial acquisitions.

It is clear that throughout the colonial periods in Taiwan, there was (and continues to be) no single narrative: no unified form of imperialism and, consequently, no common experience. Instead, conflicting narratives of

TABLE 1. *A colonial historical timeline*

COLONIAL PERIOD	DATES
Dutch	1624–62
Spanish	1626–42
Zheng Family (Koxinga)	1662–83
Qing	1683–1895
Japanese	1895–1945
Republic of China (ROC)	1945–present
White Terror	1947–87

identity would continue in the postwar period with the arrival of the Chinese Nationalist government-in-exile. Each period of colonization demonstrates a complex narrative of Taiwan, and this has influenced how the meaning and perception of identity is both demonstrated and interpreted. Attention to this layered, complex, and interwoven fabric of colonialism is important to any discussion of whether Taiwan has moved beyond the bounds of colonization and into a postcolonial narrative. If indeed it has, the question, then, is, Of what layer of colonization is it now *post*colonial?

TAIWAN IN HISTORY

Taiwan, although among the closest of the Pacific islands to the continental mainland, remained relatively obscure and remote from continental Asia for most of its history prior to colonization in the seventeenth century, despite having a critical role in the spread of Austronesian languages and cultural practices to maritime Southeast Asia. One factor for this obscurity was geographical. To understand this, it is best to start with some definitions.

Landscape can be either absolute (fixed) or relative (changeable). The absolute here is its latitude and longitude—its "fixed" geographical positions. Taiwan straddles the Tropic of Cancer and is divided through the middle by a range of rugged mountains with 268 peaks over 3,000 meters; the highest, Yushan, stands majestically at 3,952 meters, the largest peak on the Asian continent east of the Himalayas and the third highest of the Pacific islands after Puncak Jaya in New Guinea and Mauna Kea in Hawai'i. The island sits on one of the most seismically active zones in the world. Known as the Pacific Ring of Fire, it is a forty-thousand-kilometer horseshoe-shaped ring of oceanic trenches and volcanic arcs, home to roughly 75 percent of the world's active and dormant volcanoes. Almost 90 percent of the world's earthquakes occur along this ring, with at least 80 percent of them being among the largest. Taiwan, whose geological topography is scarred by this violence, has forty-two known active fault lines.

The relative landscape, on the other hand, has been and continues to be influenced by humans through population size and density, as well as land use and settlement patterns. The absolute influenced what people grew, farmed, and fished, which in turn influenced their relative belief systems. This relative landscape has led to multiple interpretations of what Taiwan is and what it is not. Yet, among the relative, there are also absolutes. Passage to Taiwan for early colonial settlers, for example, posed both relative and absolute dangers. The criminality often centered on the island, such as smuggling, piracy, and illegal immigration, resulted in significant relative danger. At the same time, the crossing from the Chinese mainland to Taiwan at certain times of the year was extremely treacherous; this absolute danger, referred to colloquially as the Black Trench (Heishuigou), made the passage not only dangerous but also extremely expensive (Itō 2004, 56–59). The journey across the strait was so hazardous that there was a saying, "Six in ten die, three stay, and one is sent back" (*Liusi, sanliu, yihuitou*; Gu 1999, 24). Yet it was not just in this passage taken by the colonial settlers that the sea or ocean posed absolute dangers. For coastal Austronesian-speaking peoples, oceanic spaces are not barriers; they act as highways and reservoirs of critical natural resources. Changes in the nature of these seascapes are continuously expressed in a range of historical, cultural, and political contexts. Oceanic pasts are a shared heritage. They are the linkages among the peoples of the world and have been used, and continue to be used, in the spread of ideas, trade, and migration. They reinforce expressions of entanglement and have given rise and clarity to its dangers, expressed through deities, maritime myths, and sea shanties. For Taiwan, pre-Sinitic deities were later adapted by Fujianese seafaring peoples and subsequently entered into their pantheon of gods, including the Maternal Ancestor, Mazu, whose cult arose along the central coast of

Fujian but soon spread throughout the maritime region. People carried these interconnected systems of beliefs on seacraft in much the same way as Islam, Christianity, and sects of Buddhism entered Taiwan. Yet, as with all settler colonial nations, Taiwan's history is framed in reference to its land: who oversaw and cultivated it, who invaded it, who stole it, and how it was commodified, broken into pieces, and sold.

The eighteenth century saw the height of settler immigration to Taiwan. It was also a high period, beginning in the seventeenth century, when maritime East Asia was woven into the fabric of international trade, each thread delicately intertwined into zones of exchange. The traffic in enormous quantities of silver followed the market for Chinese silk and pottery and Southeast Asian tropical goods. This cargo was collectively carried on Chinese junks, Japanese *shuinsen* (abolished in the seventeenth century), and Southeast Asian jongs, which in turn mapped and navigated the river courses and sea-lanes. The vessels thus connected the export-oriented harbors to the Spanish galleons, the Indian dhows, and the Dutch and English men-of-war (at the turn of the nineteenth century), who in turn brought this trade to the thriving economic systems of the Indian Ocean, Europe, and the Americas. By the nineteenth century Taiwan was firmly situated within this network as a hub of exchange. It was a site of entanglement of the desires of the West and the products of the East. This historical reality continues to situate Taiwan today. Taiwan matters to the United States because it is a significant economic force as a major supplier of semiconductors. What is more, due to its strategic location in the Western Pacific, it holds a crucial geopolitical position. In this context, Taiwan's importance to the United States in the present period is no different than it was to the Dutch, Spanish, Manchus, British, and Japanese in the past. What is more, this "desire" is mirrored by the island's unremitting importance to China.

Most of Taiwan's population consists of ethnically Han Chinese speakers of a Sinitic language. This is a product of settler colonialism. In the United States, a significant portion of the population is of European descent and comes from Indo-European-speaking backgrounds, including English, Spanish, French and German. This is also true of Canada, Australia, and New Zealand. Yet each of these nations has a statehood that is clear and separate from their European forebears. They have shared cultural and historical heritages, and although this sits within their nation-building

INTRODUCTION *5*

narratives, seldom is there a call for their incorporation into a European-area study program. More often than not, it is the history of others in the makeup of the nation that guides their academic dialogue. Whether Native Americans, African Americans, First Nations Peoples, Aborigines, or Māori, they form an important dialogue in positioning colonial settlers within nation-building discourses. So, in the case of Taiwan, what is missing? There is a clear expression of Taiwanese nationalism articulated by the population. For example, according to an Election Study Center survey conducted by National Chengchi University in December 2021, 62.3 percent of respondents saw themselves as solely Taiwanese, with only 2.8 percent seeing themselves as Chinese. A major factor calling Taiwan's notion of statehood into question is its postwar history and other stories about what people perceive Taiwan to be. Taiwan lives in a state of ambiguity that has persisted since the Allied powers entrusted stewardship over Taiwan and its offshore islands to the Chinese Nationalist leader Chiang Kai-shek as a wartime ally. This decision denied Taiwan the post-Japanese colonial construction that is visible on the Korean peninsula, and to a certain degree on the Chinese mainland in the Communists' consolidation of power following establishment of the People's Republic of China (PRC) in 1949.

As in all consolidated national histories, there is a need for continuity. The nation-state based on ethnicity is a recent concept. Yet for national governments, particularly those that break away from colonialism, there is a need to create a story: a national story. For China, this story includes a supposedly unbroken history that extends back five thousand years, irrespective of the fact that the Manchu dynastic rulers of the Qing and the Mongol rulers of the Yuan were not ethnically Chinese. In the PRC's narrative, the remnants of the Chinese Nationalists on Taiwan are a disconnect. The problem is less that Taiwan is an unsolved issue than that the Republic of China (ROC) continues to exist on Taiwan. When one speaks of independence in present-day Taiwan political affairs, it is independence from the ROC rather than the PRC, which has never held jurisdiction over the island. Taiwan is now synonymous with the ROC, and as such it is written into the national history of China. To the PRC, the existence of the ROC legitimizes its claim over the island, and this narrating of Taiwan as a part of the history of China was equally used by Chinese Nationalists as they sought to justify their colonial control over the island. This ultimately led to the ideas espoused in the so-called 1992 Consensus, which claimed that both mainland China and Taiwan belong to "one China," but the two sides of the Taiwan Strait differ in their interpretation of what this means.

The history of Taiwan thus has many layers. Taiwan was put on the world map, so to speak, in the seventeenth century with the arrival of the Dutch. As the Dutch began to settle in what is today Tainan, they opened up the island to Chinese settlers. This hybrid form of colonialization would frame Taiwan in new forms of power and legitimacy (Andrade 2009, 118). Following the Dutch defeat in 1662 by Ming loyalist Zheng Chenggong (also known as Koxinga), power shifted once again, moving into an extensive period of "settler colonialism" under the Manchus. This layer of colonization would characterize Taiwan for much of the eighteenth and early nineteenth centuries. Throughout this period, Taiwan was being cut from the same transnational colonial fabric seen elsewhere, where land was seen as a resource for overseas expansion (Shepherd 1995). In the mid-nineteenth century the gaze of the British Empire (as well as other Europeans and Americans) fell on the island, and Taiwan again witnessed a shift in power, as a new semicolonial layer enveloped the island, connecting it to the wider treaty port system that spread throughout the region following the signing of treaties at the end of the opium wars. This semicolonial situation extended from 1858 to 1895, when Taiwan was colonized by the Empire of Japan, which retained control until 1945. Unlike other nations, such as Korea, which shed the Japanese colonial yoke after the war, a modern postcolonial nation was not birthed in Taiwan. Instead of being liberated from colonialism, the island was recolonized under the ROC (in exile) in a form of "exiled colonialism." The full impact of colonization became evident on 28 February 1947, when the Chinese Nationalist government, led by Chiang Kai-shek, responded to widespread protests following an incident with a cigarette vendor and a government official (see "A Hawker's Tale"). The government's response was characterized by brutal force, including the killing of innocent civilians, arbitrary arrests, and torture. In the aftermath of what became known as the 228 Incident, the Nationalist government declared martial law in Taiwan, suppressing dissent and tightening control over the island. This incident marked the beginning of a prolonged period of authoritarian rule and rekindled a fervor for self-determination, a start-again nationalism that would finally bear fruit in 1987 with the lifting of martial law and the island's first steps toward democracy. This journey would mark other shifts as Taiwan moved to self-identify through a postcolonial lens that came to a head between 18 March and 19 April 2014 with the Sunflower Movement and a visible shift from ethnic forms of nationalism to a civic national outlook.

AN INDIGENOUS POSITION

To narrate an Indigenous peoples' perspective in this book of tales requires rethinking a consensual national story that is deficient not in its facts, dates, or details, but rather in its essence. It is a national story informed by an inherent myth that has urged Taiwanese to accept and embrace their settler colonial past. This story persists solely to prevent challenges to the orthodoxy and not from a desire to nativize the past.

The complexity of Taiwan's past challenges our understanding of who is Indigenous or an Austronesian speaker. In Taiwan the term *Indigenous* is widely used, yet there remains no exact consensus on its precise meaning. After all, numerous unrecognized Indigenous groups in Taiwan are fighting for formal designation. Self-identity alone is not enough to warrant recognized Indigenous categorization. This is complicated further by the difficulty of identifying markers of unique identities or specific cultural groups. The Japanese designations of Indigenous groups in Taiwan, starting in 1897, were primarily based on linguistic families. Since then, additional Indigenous groups have been identified and formal designations made consisting of multiple groupings within these initial categorizations. The difficulty in describing cultural practices, particularly among smaller groups, continues to be debated (John Hsieh 2021, 239). In Taiwan, Indigenous status conveys particular legal and political rights. Falling outside this categorization has considerable implications for both individuals and communities. To better understand this situation, it is important to define the term Austronesian.

In the pre-Columbian world, Austronesian speakers were the most widely dispersed ethnolinguistic population (Bellwood 2009, 336). Their languages spread south from Taiwan through the Philippines, into Indonesia and Malaysia, across the Pacific islands, and as far west as Madagascar. Taiwan is widely accepted as the cradle of this Austronesian expansion. It is home to nine languages in the Austronesian language family, one of which is widely acknowledged to be the progenitor of all subsequent spread. Rather than a single mass-migratory event, this migration was a process, a combination of several push-pull factors converging over thousands of years (Alsford 2021). Contemporary models of Taiwan's prehistory assume human settlement around thirty thousand years ago. The movement of this settlement, likely via a land bridge, fits other models of human migration that followed longitudinal migration. The motivation for migration remains unknown, like much else about those peoples, who appear in archaeological records only in the form of chipped-pebble tools, as human remains, and in origin myths of some present-day Indigenous cultures. The first archaeological record, 5,500 years ago, belongs to the Dapenkeng culture and is representative of a Neolithic people; sites of settlement are recorded along the shores of Taiwan. This is important because it is commonly accepted that these peoples, or the languages they spoke, were the forebears of the Austronesian linguistic family and that any proto-Austronesian language can thus be reconstructed to represent the primary diversification of the language among these settlers.

Today, Austronesian speakers in Taiwan make up 2.38 percent of the island's total population. Taiwan is the only colonial Chinese-speaking Pacific island. Most Pacific Islanders, including those in Taiwan, practice Christianity, with a minority following animistic belief systems. The multiple layers of colonization have had a lasting effect on the complexity of the Indigenous peoples' relative landscape. Each period of colonization adds layers to how they are categorized. During the Manchu colonization, Indigenous peoples were classified as either *shengfan* (raw), so named due their seminomadic way of life, or *shufan* (cooked), or "civilized," as they had either been converted to Christianity by early Europeans or had later submitted to Chinese settler culture.

The systematic categorization of the island's people, coupled with fluctuations in Qing policy, generated a complicated history, revealing the government's inability to utilize Taiwan's assets. This lack of direction ultimately led the economy of Taiwan in the eighteenth and early nineteenth centuries to become largely restricted to cross-strait trade. A prohibition on the migration of families gave rise to an unstable society of male migrant laborers. Yet those colonists who had braved the dangerous strait came to Taiwan precisely because they wanted to pursue economic self-interest without strict interference from the state (Henry Tsai 2009, 9). This ultimately caused the Taiwan frontier to frequently oppose bureaucratic restrictions. There were 159 major uprisings between 1684 and 1895, with a particularly violent period in 1768–1887, which saw fifty-seven armed confrontations between settlers and authorities (Henry Tsai 2009, 9). This led to the Qing government's famous observation, "Every three years there was an uprising and every five years a rebellion" (*Sannian yixiaofan, wunian yidafan*; Itō 2004, 66).

In spite of the frequent violence, the settler colonists continued to plow their land and grow rice, sugar, and other important crops for the purpose of exporting them across the strait (Gates 1987, 35; Lin Yuju 1995). The settlers were firmly embedded in a capitalist economic system and were signified by the localization of their regional factions, namely the Hakka, Zhangzhou, and Quanzhou kin networks (Chiukun Chen 1999, 147). Forms of social conflict continued as more urban centers in northern and central Taiwan began to form in the mid-nineteenth century (Gardella 1999, 178–79). Economic expansion and opportunity may have aided in the stabilization of Han ethnic violence as cooperation on the frontier became necessary (Lin Man-houng 1979, 18–31). This was followed by settler colonization of the Ilan plain early in the nineteenth century, when migration expanded rapidly and on a large scale (Jacobs 2008, 40).

The Qing colonial authorities' repeated attempts to prohibit migration across the strait resulted in a gender imbalance, as the limited permitted migration did not include families. The result was that the majority were seasonal male workers. Some who were loyal to filial obligations returned. Among those who returned during off-seasons, some maintained families on both sides of the strait, taking Indigenous wives in addition to those on the mainland. Others simply defied limitations and remained in Taiwan, either marrying into local existing communities or taking Indigenous brides into the new settlements. Accordingly, "There were only Chinese grandfathers, not Chinese grandmothers" (*You tangshangong, wu tangshanma*; Tai 2007, 52).

Frontier settlements in Taiwan influenced not only the absolute landscape (its geography) but also its folklore and cultural expressions. The eras of colonization and mass migration would see many of the settlers adapt a manifest destiny approach to concepts of identity. They would consider their virtues to be divinely accepted through their worship of Mazu (goddess of the sea) and Tudi Gong (tutelary deity of locality and human communities). Their mission to "civilize" the Indigenous population led them to redeem and remake the landscape in an imagined duplicate of the mainland. Taiwanese identity would thus be a Han identity. Yet the interconnectivity of the peoples and the relationalism that functioned within their realities resulted not in a consolidated Han identity but rather in constructions of new, Taiwanese identities.

THE STRUCTURE OF THIS BOOK

Taiwan Lives is structured in three thematic parts that run chronologically, allowing the reader to interlace the many threads of Taiwan's past. This organization avoids a rigid and compartmentalized evolution of history, instead accentuating the island's interconnectivity and cultural complexity. The book starts with a social history that focuses on the view from below rather than the usual top-down approach to understanding complex historical narratives. This is a people's history—one that presents accounts of historical events from the perspective of the common people.

The book opens with a background story about a British resident living in Taiwan in the late nineteenth century to provide context for the people, or lives, presented in this volume. Although the stories start in 1860, the history of Taiwan includes many influential figures from before this time. Rather than an incomplete history, I see it as an invitation for further discoveries. The stories in the first part are organized into four main subject areas. The first focuses on the beginning of Japanese colonialism in 1895 and its profound impact on Taiwanese society. The following three tales explore the history of a merchant, a settler, and a colonial person to provide a comprehensive understanding of the period. The second section, "Pathways to War, 1930–45," starts with Indigenous resistance and the tale of an Indigenous person joining the Japanese Army during the Pacific War. This is followed by the stories of a British POW and Taiwanese child laborers during the war. The third section, "White Terror, 1945–1987," looks at the post-Japanese colonial period and the arrival of the Chinese Nationalists, including the story of a diplomat and two tales of exile. The final section, "A New Hope, 1987–Present," covers the period from the lifting of martial

INTRODUCTION *11*

law in 1987 to the present day, with tales about a writer, an activist, and a pop star. The second part of the book focuses on events that have shaped the discourse of Taiwan's identity since the early twentieth century, starting with the Taiwan Cultural Association in the 1920s and moving on to the 228 Incident in 1947. For the 228 Incident, there are two contrasting tales that highlight the formation of Taiwanese identity and the differentiation between shared historical narratives in Taiwan and China. This portion of the book provides an intellectual history of Taiwan and delves into the early stages of nation-building on the island.

The next section, "Martial Law, 1947–1987," provides a deeper analysis of the formation of Taiwanese identity and the journey toward democracy. This section includes the Tangwai's Tale and the Prisoner's Tale, respectively following the story of Taiwanese politician Huang Hsin-chieh and dissident Chen Chu, one of the "Kaohsiung Eight" (Meilidao Shijian).

The final part, "Being Taiwan," traces the development of Taiwan's social and political history through its past, present, and future. "An Anthropologist's Tale," focusing on Arthur P. Wolf, starts by analyzing Taiwan's global perception and interpretation. This is followed by "A Businessman's Tale," examining the story of Chang Yung-fa and the Evergreen Company. The impact of COVID-19 on Taiwan in 2020 is explored in "An Epidemiologist's Tale," which focuses on the highly praised epidemiologist Chen Chien-jen, who managed both the pandemic and the 2002 SARS outbreak. "An Indigenous Tale" delves into the Council of Indigenous People's role and the significance of Indigenous activism in Taiwan. The book concludes with a focus on President Tsai Ing-wen in "A President's Tale."

The twenty-four tales that make up this book are but a snapshot of the roles various men and women have played in the formation of modern Taiwan. This set is not intended to be definitive. Some readers may think that some tales should not have been included. This is also okay, as it reflects the struggle to define what Taiwan is and what Taiwan isn't. Taiwan is the product of a geopolitical scuffle with a long historical legacy. From a cradle of Austronesian expansion to the dynamic economic powerhouse and successful democracy it is today, Taiwan is layered in colonial histories. The Taiwanese fight for democracy occurred when the world turned its back on the island. The 1 May 2021 edition of *The Economist*, whose headline called Taiwan "The Most Dangerous Place on Earth," ran an article that mentioned the "exercise of high-caliber ambiguity," between the United States and the People's Republic of China but remained ambiguous on what the people of Taiwan actually think. Taiwan is not dangerous; those who advocate for conflict to change its course are dangerous. In spite of all that has been gained, Taiwan continues to be framed as a shrimp between two whales. The importance of this book thus lies in the study of that shrimp—not to ignore the whales but to give the shrimp center stage. To truly understand Taiwan, one must study Taiwan as a thing-in-itself. I hope this book achieves that objective.

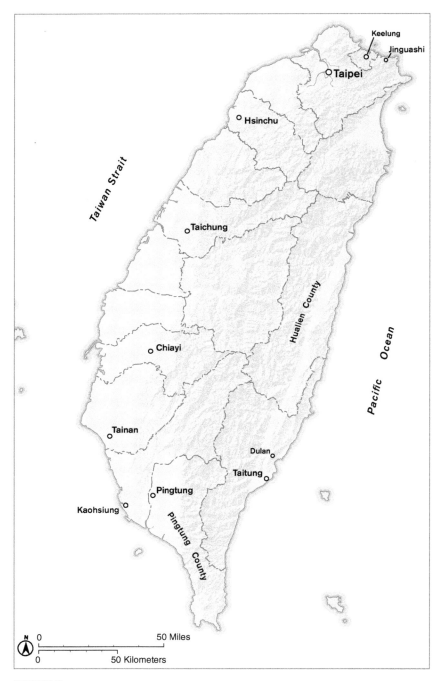

TAIWAN

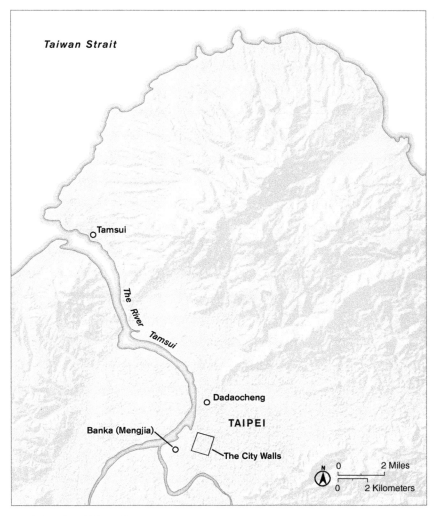

NORTHERN TAIWAN

PART ONE

A Social History

BACKGROUND

1

A Sojourner's Tale

JOHN DODD

[Transnational history] is the study of the ways in which
past lives and events have been shaped by processes and
relationships that have transcended the borders of nation
states. [It] seeks to understand ideas, things, people, and
practices which have crossed national boundaries.

ANN CURTHOYS AND MARILYN LAKE · 2005

Taiwan's story is a narrative of settler colonialism. It is a tale of violence
and conflict as ethnic groups maneuvered for better position. This process
took on multiple layers of coloniality. Taiwan is strategically situated and
plays a vital role in big-power dynamics. As different hegemonic powers
sought to gain influence, Taiwan was often used as a launching pad to
gain better access to economic markets. For Europeans, this began with
the Dutch in the seventeenth century, who used Taiwan as a strategic hub
in their efforts to balance power. The Spanish, competitors of the Dutch
in the seventeenth century, set up their colony on the northern shores of
the island. Following the eviction of both, the island was used as a staging
post for rebellion against the Manchu invasion of China proper. Following
its incorporation into the Manchu Empire (the Qing), the island was a
principal site of settler colonialism. In the nineteenth century, the British
used it as a treaty right; the French, in the same century, blockaded it in

their war with China. And for the Japanese, in the twentieth century it was to be an opportunity to showcase their colonial achievements.

In 1894–95, Japan went to war with the Manchus. To reprise the question posed by historian Robert Eskildsen, if the Sino-Japanese War was fought mainly on Korean territory, why did Japan colonize Taiwan as an outcome of the conflict?" (Eskildsen 2005, 281). Taiwan, as "a territory at the periphery of the dominant powers in nineteenth-century East Asia," disrupts two essential historical narratives of the period: nationalism and imperialism, both used exhaustively to explain the modern history of the region. By analyzing these macro-level "isms," Eskildsen attempts to illuminate Taiwan's sense of space in an East Asian historical narrative (Eskildsen 2005, 281–82). Yet if one wants to truly understand how Taiwan both positioned itself and was positioned by the powers that surrounded it, one must first view this intervention through multiple interconnected colonial processes. The immediate colonization of Taiwan, in the Taiwan War of 1895, was not peaceful in a homogenous sense, nor was it necessarily a continuation of the Sino-Japanese War (Alsford 2018). This, of course, is not to say that the turbulence and violence which persisted throughout 1895 was necessarily a by-product of the arriving Japanese military. Taiwan's violent and turbulent past stems from the multiple layers of different forms of colonization, the most immediate and transformative of which was the opening of the island in the nineteenth century to international trade and the establishment of the treaty port system.

The treaty port community, which was predominantly British, arrived and settled on Taiwan from the 1860s. Their settlement transcended the bounds of a British society, and the locality of each of these ports (Tamsui, Keeling, Tainan, and Kaohsiung) represented a shared inner-social environment of local and foreign communities. From this a complex system emerged, with a distinctive set of institutions. The governing institutes of the Qing authorities were now coupled with the foreign-run Imperial Chinese Maritime Customs, the British consulate and its military garrison, and the Protestant mission. Situated within, and between, these structures were the agents, with their own motivations for being there, whether these involved trading firms and their support staff, mission stations, or simply leisure or scholarly purposes.

For the British community in Taiwan, the motivation was first and foremost trade, followed closely by the complexity of missiology. The two were often indistinguishable, with missions frequently located in areas in which international trade had become localized—even in areas outside the immediate perimeters of the treaty port, such as Changhua in central Taiwan and Xindian in the north, which were already interconnected through the growth of international trade that radiated out from the treaty port towns (Rubinstein 1991b, 18–19). Thus, the system of interaction that arose between communities and environments could not exist independently of human agency, and it was subsequently these human protagonists who fundamentally began to shape, or rather domesticate, the landscape of nineteenth-century Taiwan (Knapp 1999).

Since the arrival of the Dutch, the southern city of Tainan had been the capital of the island. As demographics, trade, and migration shifted northward as a result of the treaty port system, there were calls to relocate the capital. Following the confirmation of Taiwan as a province of the Qing Empire (as opposed to a prefecture of the province of Fujian) in 1887, representatives of the political tradition wanted the surrounding areas of present-day Taichung, a central location with a milder climate, to become the provincial new capital. However, since an emerging gentry that had established its wealth on the banks of the River Tamsui had, thanks in part to their private donations, built a new walled city in 1884 close to the market towns of Banka (Mengjia) and Dadaocheng, Taipei was chosen to be the new provincial capital. This, achievement was arguably largely informed by gravitational shifts (economic, political, and social) from the south to the north due in part to the establishment of the treaty port on the mouth of the River Tamsui, where in 1861 British vice-consul Robert Swinhoe had been given the task of establishing British trade on Taiwan. Swinhoe claimed that trade in the south was negligible and sought permission to move north (Swinhoe 1864, 7–8).

Foreign merchants were initially enthusiastic about the opening of Taiwan at Tamsui and Dadaocheng since it was less strictly segregated from the local population compared to other treaty ports. Though some greeted the opening of the port in 1862 with great hostility toward a foreign presence, others within the local community had a more positive response to the new challenges and opportunities related to trade and infrastructural modernization (Alsford 2018, 10–11).

In 1864, John Dodd settled in Taiwan. This, however, was not the first time he had visited this island. Four years earlier, he had sailed into the quiet and sleepy harbor of Tamsui (Otness 1990, 42). This small port would transform Taiwan in the mid-nineteenth century into a significant site of industry.

Although earlier scholarship mentioning John Dodd had him originating from Scotland, he was born in Preston, Lancashire, a county in northwest England, on 25 October 1838. John Dodd Sr. worked as a local butcher in Preston, but by 1841 he was a pub landlord. By 1861, the Dodd family, now including a younger daughter, Margaret, had moved fifty-eight miles north to the ancient village of Crosby Ravensworth in Penrith, Cumbria. However, the family went without John, who by 1859 had settled in Hong Kong (Alsford 2010a).

In 1860, Robert Swinhoe disclosed in a report to the British authorities that the north of the island of Taiwan offered potential tradable commodities. He concluded that rice, indigo, camphor, coal, grass-cloth fiber, tea, and sulphur, among other products, were suited for exploitation. Although Swinhoe felt that the quantity of tea growing in the vicinity was adequate for domestic consumption, the quality was inferior to tea grown on the Chinese mainland. Nonetheless, during one of his many ventures in China, Swinhoe saw that Chinese tea dealers in the Fujian treaty ports of Amoy (Xiamen) and Fuzhou were purposely mixing Formosan tea with quality tea grown on Fujian's mountain ranges. Swinhoe deduced that the tea could be exported profitably to other Chinese ports but was not suited for the international market except possibly the Chinese market in Singapore and Australia. Shortly after filing his report to the Royal Geographical Society, Swinhoe was visited by John Dodd. Swinhoe gave Dodd his opinion on the commercial opportunities that northern Taiwan offered. He proposed camphor or coal as being the most profitable and advised against tea.

John Dodd began researching the environment and paid particular attention to the camphor forests growing on nearby hills. On one occasion in 1865, while exploring the forests, Dodd noticed that cinnamon trees were growing between wild tea bushes (Dodd 1895, 569). Collecting a few samples, he sought out advice on cinnamon trading upon his return to Tamsui. He was informed that not only was the cost of the trade too high, but also the process of separating the bark was too expensive and involved a lot of skilled labor. Despite Swinhoe's advice, Dodd decided that tea was his best option and started to make inquiries. He encountered small patches of tea being cultivated in the gardens of farmers for domestic consumption and local trade between Keelung and Banka, a small local market town on the River Tamsui. With his personal comprador, or middleman, Li Chunsheng, Dodd bought all the tea he could afford and shipped it to Macao. The tea was well accepted and fetched a good price on the market (Alsford 2010a, 10). Dodd immediately made loans to the farmers for the purpose of extending cultivation and with Li Chunsheng was able to entice the local farmers to increase production. Taking the grading of tea into account, he imported tea plants from Ankoi in the Amoy District and mixed it with local tea to improve its quality.

John Dodd understood that establishing a small-scale tea factory in northern Taiwan would be a risky investment, especially since the competition in other ports was deep-rooted and organized. Initially Dodd had to rely on the large trading company Jardine Matheson and Company for shipping tea from Tamsui to Amoy, where it could be re-exported for the international market. In addition, he encountered the difficulties of establishing a new industry in tightly formed and heavily factional communities. In 1868, he began searching for suitable property in Banka. This bustling market town made up predominately of Chinese settlers was one of the most populous northern towns in the mid-1800s (Pickering [1898] 1993, 34; Allen 1877, 259; Collingwood 1867, 168). Its narrow streets were often filled with the melody of numerous workmen and traders. There was no sound of machinery, just the clanking and hammering of tools from the blacksmiths and carpenters along with the chipping sounds of the stonecutters and masons. Dust filled the air from the limestone deposits and charcoal burners. The smell of fish and livestock blanketed this marshy, muddy district. In spite of the difficulties, Dodd rented a small shop, for tea processing, from Mrs. Huang, the widow of a camphor merchant. The widow, an elderly lady, had no influential family and was often squeezed for imaginary tariffs by the local Chinese officials. She quickly accepted the fee of fifty dollars as a down payment for the humble property left to her at her husband's death (Davidson 2005, 199). However, this caused numerous problems among other local residents, especially as it was the first time a foreign resident had moved into the district. To settle the dispute, the local officials seized the widow's shop with the excuse that her husband had not paid off loans made for camphor trading prior to his death, and they nailed the doors shut. Dodd demanded that the British vice consul, Henry Holt, intervene, and following extensive negotiation with the local authorities, Holt was able to secure the property for Dodd. In 1870, Dodd began to bring men in from Fuzhou to commence firing tea in the district. Fuzhou, during this period, was the principal location in China for obtaining tea, and its treaty port housed numerous premises where tea was processed for an international market (Gardella 1994, 56).

In the United States, John Dodd found a market for his teas, and this market would play a vital role in the subsequent development of the Formosan tea industry. As his company grew, Dodd needed larger premises and decided to move farther upriver to the market town of Dadaocheng. By 1872, Dodd and Company had attracted rivals from other British trading companies. The competition in the area began to raise the cost of tea, and in a short period, Formosa oolong tea had become a valuable export. Dodd was keen to extend his position in society beyond the stereotypes often associated with merchants—in particular, the notion that the merchants were often without wit or knowledge of the world beyond the treaty port (Murphy 2003, 163; Boehm 1906, 83). Dodd frequently spent time among the Indigenous communities in the surrounding areas. During his visits he listened to and recorded several Formosan languages, and he published his research with the Royal Asiatic Society in Singapore in 1882 and 1895 (Dodd 1882a; Dodd 1882b; Dodd 1895).

Following a brief experiment with petroleum extraction and trade, John Dodd left Taiwan on 3 March 1890. After returning to Britain, he moved to Atcham in Shropshire, where on 7 August 1893 he married Mary Lloyd, the daughter of a Welsh cabinetmaker. In the 1901 census, John Dodd is referred to as "a retired merchant from China" living with his wife in the mountainous regions of northern Wales. Dodd remained in Wales for the rest of his life, dying in the peaceful hamlet of Trefriw on 15 July 1907 after two days in a coma following a brain hemorrhage. His brother-in-law, John Lloyd, was present at his death. Dodd is buried at Saint Mary's Church in Llanrwst.

The treaty port system in Taiwan, evidenced in John Dodd's story, is an important beginning in the ideological shifts on the island. The arrival of international trading networks would establish Taiwan's regional geostrategic importance, whereas trade prior to this time was largely limited to cross-strait traffic with the occasional route to Japan (though this was often done via one of the larger ports on the Chinese mainland). The transition in Taiwan would occur at a time of rapid standardization, such as the widespread adaption to new technological systems, including the telegraph and railways, and the extensive industrialization that would mark the so-called Second Industrial Revolution (1870–1914). This synergy, facilitated by processes of social interaction, resulted in alternative constructions of Taiwanese identity and the experience of being in Taiwan. From this point onward, the identity of the settler communities began to converge towards a Taiwan-centered identity.

BECOMING JAPANESE

1895–1930

2

A Merchant's Tale

KU HSIEN-JUNG

Merchants have no country. The mere spot they stand
on does not constitute so strong an attachment as
that from which they draw their gains.

THOMAS JEFFERSON · 1814

Taiwan has been shaped by migration. The development of urban areas from the mid-nineteenth century was a process of redeveloping older farmsteads. Construction techniques featuring single-story houses that ribbon-developed along narrow streets were being replaced by two-story shophouses. With the interaction of inhabitants from neighboring areas, streets were built on a larger grid system connected by a main thoroughfare—an interurban linkage. These connections were based on lineage corporations that were either agnatic or diasporic (Sangren 1984, 391; Shepherd 1999, 128). They were designed and built to aid trade and build community, intended to develop both domestic and international markets through various forms of corporations. This peculiar mix of associations largely came into existence after the ports of Tamsui, Keelung, and Kaohsiung opened in the nineteenth century, highlighting an upward turn in economic growth that led more families to migrate to urban centers. The entrepreneurial spirit of these settlers resulted in many very wealthy merchants becoming important local notables (Chiukun Chen 1999, 159).

Temples constructed as public spaces via this new wealth, communally built by neighborhoods, guilds, and other associations, were key to the acceptance of these new categories of notability. Funding this type of project established authority in a local community. Merchants desirous of converting their wealth into status and moving into the literati class contributed to building official temples. In the absence of official temples, they sponsored the building of temples to gods or spirits included in the official cults. An example of this effort to enhance social reputation, surpassing the significance of building temples for popular deities like Tudigong and Mazu, who enjoyed popularity across all social classes, was the construction of temples known as *wenwu miao* (temple of literature and martial arts). These temples were dedicated to both Confucius and Kuan-ti (Guandi) and were often established near private schools (Feuchtwang 1977, 584).

Christian converts' efforts in building churches, such as Li Chunsheng's church on Jinan Street in Taipei, followed similar principles (Alsford 2010a, 313). Public space in nineteenth-century Taiwan was therefore clearly important. Yet it was the synergy in such spaces that characterized the development of the region. As urban centers shifted from *old networks* into new *modern spaces*, aspects of society also began to change and localize.

The increasingly urban environment in Taiwan became a place where people, most notably the gentry elite, expressed the importance of their culture (Meskill 1979, 200). In pursuing respectability, they often put their efforts on display through public works, such as marketplaces, recreational parks, and temple compounds (Xu Yaxiang 2013, 19–20). For many Taiwanese residing in developing harbor towns, that expression frequently reflected a multicultural entanglement. It was an interconnected and predominantly transnational phenomenon, with mutual influences convoluting across boundaries. It was fueled by the enclaves of the treaty port system. In many ways these expressions of culture were unique to their respective urban centers. Cultural expression in Dadaocheng was different from Keelung, and Banka was unlike Zongli. They were all junctions of contact and exchange between a burgeoning domestic economy and a developing international market.

Taiwan during this period was therefore "a creation of its settlers [and] not an emanation of the [Manchu] state" (Meskill 1979, 257), although the establishment of Confucius temples (*wen miao*) in Taiwan indicates that certain aspects of Taiwanese culture were shaped by the state. The Taipei

Confucius Temple in Dadaocheng, for example, was built in 1879, after the Taipei Prefecture was established in 1875. The reorganization of trade networks correlated strongly with changing settlement patterns among the Han elite, and although the period witnessed a surge in the number of nouveau riche families, the dilution had little impact on privilege status and social ethos. Instead, what tended to change was the way status was practiced and performed.

The strong economic attraction to Taiwan led to a growing settler population. Monopoly traders figured predominantly, later followed by land-hungry farmers. Merchants and craftsmen tended to concentrate in coastal townships, and fishermen and salt producers exploited resources along the coastline. The farmers clustered around fertile plains that were suitable for agriculture and easily irrigated. Increasingly, as the Chinese settlements encountered Indigenous resistance, pioneering families tended to band together in fortified villages. This bound them into cohesive communities that were based on either regional or agnatic kinship.

The regular exchange of cross-strait goods was further enhanced in 1725 with the establishment of a guild-type organization known as the *jiao* system. Members of the guild (*jiao shang*) were categorized by the type of guild (*jiao pu*) to which they belonged. The Quan *jiao*, for example, traded with Quanzhou, and the Xia *jiao* with Xiamen (Amoy). They were also known by the location of resident members; Qian *jiao* in Zhuqian (present-day Hsinchu) is a good example of this. At times, the guilds were industry-based, such as the *tang jiao* (sugar guild).

Early settlers began to cluster culturally with others in an imagined, or affinity, kin network. They were divided according to the area of the Chinese mainland from which they came. On arrival, they brought with them their cultural practices and customs. Most of the coastal-dwelling settlers hailed from either Quanzhou or Zhangzhou prefectures in Fujian. Government restrictions on the movement of people had a profound effect on settlement patterns as they prevented any migration of large lineages or village groups. This frequently led to violent clashes between factional clans. Yet, amid all this, the settler farmers continued to plow their land and grow their rice, sugar, and other important crops for export across the strait. The settlers were firmly embedded in a capitalist economic system, and this was symbolized by the localization of their regional factions. Forms of social conflict continued to exist as more urban centers began to emerge in northern and central Taiwan. Economic expansion and opportunity, rather than disruption of cooperation, in fact aided in the stabilization of Han ethnic violence as collaboration on the frontier became necessary (Lin Man-houng 1979). The narrative of Taiwan's urban settlement is thus closely integrated into the history of Han Chinese pioneer settlement and the establishment of the *jiao* system.

By complying with the rules laid down by the Ministry of Revenue (Hubu), all land under Qing jurisdiction in Taiwan could now be legally settled. Migration to the north beginning in 1725 met with little Indigenous resistance. With only four designated Indigenous village settlements, known as *she*, land was abundant. In addition, initial interaction resulted in small-scale trade, agricultural cooperation, and intermarriage (Knapp 1980, 58).

Houses had ancestral tables recording statements of succession of continuity. As in the south, the first batch of reclamation migrants were single males (in the case of northern Taiwan, also Hakka), and without formal grounding, these early migrants were quasi-transients who either returned home (sojourners) or formed a foothold in the area by creating a nuclear family (settlers). Once moored, they bonded into a community structure and were dependent on both the social and natural environments. The speed of land reclamation was largely contingent on the type of natural environment: the climatic and geophysical features (absolute landscape) as well as the type of resources available. Although this was not a hurried process, the cultivation of land became a precondition for transient males to adopt a more stable and settled role in the landscape. The social features consisted of networks, with the formation of conjugal units and extended links to other regions both on Taiwan and on the mainland, where more substantial and permanent village structures were established.

Stability became an important factor in developing land in the north. Associated organizations fostered the newly founded farmsteads; predominant among these was the *baojia* system, an arrangement that emphasized the influence of the Qing state on social organizations in Taiwan, which featured mutual surveillance and registration of all individuals by household. Knapp writes that each household received a placard to write down the names of all its male members. Transient males were recorded as lodgers in monasteries and temples, and these sites expressed territorial hierarchy where the gods acted as a metaphor for the civic system of authority (Knapp 1976, 56).

For this reason, many temples became large, elaborate, and comprehensive meeting grounds (Alsford 2018, 91). As the temple foreground space became associated with market areas, the level of social interaction expanded, and new networks and associations began to form. With no clear imperial administrative regulation and intermittent migration of northbound pioneering families in the eighteenth century, market town development in the north appeared haphazard. Aside from Banka, developed on the Tamsui riverbank by Quanzhou settlers in 1723, and farther south, Zhuqian, a former Indigenous village settled in 1711, there were no large settlements. Instead, sporadic farmsteads sprang up, and small markets were established in 1747 in Humaozhuang (present-day Taoyuan City) and 1765 in Zhongli. The opening of the treaty ports in the nineteenth century and the shift toward globally desired agricultural commodities such as tea and camphor caused the north to develop more rapidly and in a manner that was significantly different from what took place in the south. It was here that merchants, such as Ku Hsien-jung, made a name for themselves.

When Ku Hsien-jung was born on 2 February 1866 in Lukang, central Taiwan, Lukang was the island's second largest city and the principal harbor through which trade between central Taiwan and the Chinese mainland was conducted (DeGlopper 1995, 67). Ku's father, Ku Chin, was from Huian in Quanzhou. He passed away when Ku was only a year old. Ku had an older brother, Ku Hsien-chung, and their mother raised both boys single-handedly. Life was difficult, and Ku was unable to attend school. He did, however, manage to learn occasionally from a local *jinshi* (an imperial scholar or recipient of the highest imperial exam) named Huang Yu-shu (Wu Wen-hsing 2012).

At the age of nineteen, Ku went to Taipei. He found employment as a manual laborer but soon set up his own business selling groceries. At twenty, he traveled to China to trade in sugar. In 1888, he received a level 5 military title for assisting the imperial government in fighting off a mob of landowning farmers and militia members in what came to be known as the Shih Chiutuan Incident (Shi Jiuduan Shijian) in Changhua. In 1891, Ku married Chen Hsiao from Lukang, and the couple moved to Taipei, where Ku continued to build his sugar business. The following year, he began trading in coal out of Keelung. With the arrival of the Japanese in 1895 and in the absence of any governing authority in Taipei, Ku, along with a diverse group of elite men, formally surrendered the city to the Japanese (Alsford 2018, 174). In August of that year, Ku traveled south with the Japanese military to suppress resistance. The Japanese colonial government rewarded him for his efforts.

Under the Japanese, Ku's business grew rapidly. In 1896, he had established the Dahe Company (Dahehang), and over the next couple of years, he obtained monopoly rights to sell camphor and salt. By 1900, he had attained significant status and wealth in Taiwan (DeGlopper 1995, 114). He was able to set up sugar plantations and factories in his hometown of Lukang and in Erlin, a short distance south of Lukang. By the end of the decade, Ku had been given the rights to sell opium, and four years later he obtained permission to trade in tobacco in Taichung. As Ku's wealth increased, he began to participate in philanthropic causes, such as donating money to build Taichung's First Boys' High School and a Confucius temple in Taipei. His efforts did not go unnoticed, and he received numerous honorary titles from the Japanese government.

Since banking would become a defining feature of the merchant-gentry class that formed in nineteenth-century Taiwan, Ku Hsien-jung would become a prominent figure, as is clear in the position his descendants have in contemporary Taiwan. Although these merchants amassed significant wealth, the landed gentry, such as the Banka and Wufeng Lin families, also invested heavily in various industries. At times, these different classes worked together. In 1905 Ku Hsien-jung and Lin Hsien-tang, along with other wealthy merchants in the area, established Chang Hwa Bank (Zhanghua Yinhang). By 1920, Ku owned 11,000 shares as the bank's largest shareholder, with Lin Hsien-tang second with 4,480 shares, and Lin Cheng-tang, also from the Wufeng Lin family, among the top ten shareholders with 1,200 shares.

In 1919, Lin Xiong-zheng, from the Banka Lin, established Hua Nan Bank (Huanan Yinhang). Ku and Lin Hsien-tang took on consultant positions within the firm. When the Southern Warehouse Company (Nanyang Cangku Zhushi Huishe) was established in 1920, out of the total 50,000 shares, the Wufeng Lin family owned 2,200 shares, Ku owned 1,000, and the Banka Lin owned 4,100. The links between the families would continue into the postwar period. In 1954, for example, when the Ku family started the Taiwan Cement Corporation, the Wufeng Lin family became significant shareholders. Despite their cooperation, the two families disagreed politically. Lin Hsien-tang was a leading figure in the 1921 Petition Movement and a close associate of Chiang Wei-shui, whose tale is narrated in chapter 14.

Politically, Ku was known to cooperate with the Japanese colonial authorities. He was publicly against the Petition Movement for the Establishment of a Taiwanese Parliament, and as a response to the movement he, along with the Banka Lin family in 1923, set up an association known as the Gongyihui to oppose the movement (Chou Wan-yao 2011, 4). According to a statement made by Ku in 1923, Taiwan had progressed dramatically over twenty years, and this was a result of the colonizing efforts of the Japanese (He 2009). Moreover, Ku often used China as a comparison. He regularly highlighted the political chaos occurring in China during this period as evidence of the stability of the Japanese. He, along with members of the Gongyihui, regularly posted articles in various newspapers (in both Taiwan and Japan) claiming that the petition movement did not truly reflect the opinion of the majority of Taiwanese people. As a result, Ku was highly praised by the Japanese authorities but disliked in many segments of Taiwanese society, where he was described as the "gentleman hired by the Japanese emperor" (*yuyong shenshi*; Chou 2011, 4).

In 1934, Ku was selected to be a member of the House of Peers, or the Upper House of the Japanese Diet [J. Kizoku-in]. As the first Taiwanese to sit in the House, he was described in the Japanese press as "the most patriotic person of the island" (He 2009, 102). The following year, Ku traveled to China to meet Chiang Kai-shek. There he proposed a closer relationship between China and Japan. In 1937, Ku died in Tokyo from heart disease. He left behind six wives, eight sons, and four daughters. Following his death, the Ku family remained among the top five wealthiest families in Taiwan. Some of the family's business is still active in Taiwan today, including the Koos Group (KGI), a pan-Asian business conglomerate that deals in petrochemicals, cement, and manufacturing, and the CTBC Financial Holding Company (Zhongxin Jituan), led by Jeffrey Koo Sr., the grandson of Ku Hsien-jung.

The narrative of the merchant class and the wealth they obtained from trading is an integral part of the story of pioneering settlement. The establishment of the *jiao* system and the legalization of migration across the Taiwan Strait between 1732 and 1740 would significantly influence how these settlements formed. Yet it was the opening of treaty ports and access to an international market that had the most profound impact on the direction these wealthy families would take, although many of these elite families amassed their wealth under Japanese rule. Thus, the differing colonial layers, although oppressive on many levels, facilitated remarkable stories of economic influence and social position. Individuals, such as Ku Hsien-jung, learned how to navigate the colonial authorities. He, like many other pioneers in Taiwan, was able to adjust his identity to fit his environment, whether this was social, natural, or most importantly, political and economic.

3

A Settler's Tale

LIN SHIH

The forest is so deep and the bamboo thickets so dense
that you cannot see the sky. Brambles and vines are so
tangled that you cannot lift a foot. Since the Chaos
of Creation, no axe has ever entered here.

YU YONGHE · 1959

In 1697, Yu Yonghe, a traveler from China's eastern coastal province of
Zhejiang, was tasked with leading an expeditionary party to Taiwan, which
had only "entered the map" (*ru bantu*) fourteen years prior and became part
of the Manchu Empire. Yu wrote, "In the past dynasties there were no links
[from Taiwan] to China: the Chinese did not know that this piece of land
existed. Even geographic maps, the Imperial Comprehensive Geographies,
and other such books that contain records of all the barbarians, do not
include the name Taiwan" (Yu Yonghe 1959, 32).

Yu Yonghe was one of a number of early pioneer writers to enthusias-
tically document the natural and social environs of Taiwan. Ji Qiguang,
one of Taiwan's first county magistrates; Lin Qianguang, Taiwan's first
Confucian school instructor; and the literati Xu Huaizu and Wu Zhenchen
had all written on their experience in the newly acquired colonial territory
(Emma Teng 2004, 47). Early knowledge of the island had developed
slowly as the Manchus began to consolidate their power in the areas they
governed, and attempts were made to restrict access to areas where they

did not have control, namely Indigenous territories. In 1688, Jiang Yuying began compiling the island's first gazetteer, which Gao Gongqian completed and published in 1696.

Taiwan, for its early pioneers, would prove to be an island of dichotomies. Writers such as Gao and Yu alluded to benefits as well as risks, to both the fertility of the land and its barren wastelands. Yu encouraged settlement, stating that the poor in China should "just grab a bag and run over" (Emma Teng 2004, 64). Gao wrote that "people [in Taiwan] don't suffer even without much to wear.... Fruit and vegetables grow well, even in winter; flowers always bloom and the leaves of the trees stay green year round" (Gao 1987, 189). Another contemporary wrote, "[The island] is full of naked tattooed savages, who are not worth defending, is a daily waste of imperial money for no benefit" (Gao 1987, 2). The Manchu annexation of Taiwan was one event within a broader narrative of Qing expansionism, as the regime moved to consolidate power and eliminate external threats and rivalries. In the case of Taiwan, this threat came from the remnants of the former Ming dynasty, while for the central Eurasian steppes, it was the Mongols and Russians. By 1760, the Manchu Empire had doubled its size, with its frontiers encompassing both areas of exclusion and inclusion. Moreover, these frontiers were subject to fluctuation. The Manchu colonization of Taiwan differed from the consolidation of power in the former Ming territories and the westward expansion into present-day Xinjiang and Tibet. In other words, the Manchus were not unlike other colonial powers, which governed territory differently depending on local factors and the needs of the metropole. This is important, because the way Taiwan was shaped and domesticated by the frontier settlers has not been repeated elsewhere. Taiwan was different from other Manchu colonial frontiers. The landscape—both natural (absolute) and social (relative)—shaped the people we now know as Taiwanese.

After incorporation of the island into the Manchu colonial project, the patterns and processes of Han migration to Taiwan varied depending on changing Manchu migration law. Without making any attempt to address the Malthusian problems facing inhabitants of the southern coastal provinces of China—rice deficiency and overpopulation—the Qing authorities regularly imposed imperial decrees that prevented migration. But attraction to the island did not abate, and Chinese settlement continued.

Unregulated migration and unofficial settlement patterns displaced many lowland Indigenous communities, as settler farmers illegally cultivated traditional Indigenous hunting grounds. The first response of the government was to impose a heavier punishment on illegal immigration and to segregate Indigenous territory by limiting Han settlement. Between 1684 and 1788, the Manchus changed their policy on migration no fewer than seven times. Such fluctuations demonstrated that the hallmark of early Manchu policy toward Taiwan was maintenance of an existing status quo. Nonetheless, migrants flocked to the island to take advantage of the double harvest facilitated by the island's subtropical climate and the high price its commodities fetched on the mainland market (Shepherd 1995, 137).

Fueled by fears that the island could be used as a base for antigovernment resistance, the Qing authorities imposed numerous restrictions not only on immigration but also on communication between the island and the mainland. Crossing between Taiwan and China was allowed only via the ports of Xiamen and present-day Tainan. Furthermore, cargo restrictions were put in place and shipments of commodities such as rice from Taiwan were not allowed to exceed 60 *shi* per ship. In addition, because the limited migration permitted by the government did not include wives or families, many of the new immigrants were transient male seasonal workers (Mazumdar 1998, 210). Due to filial obligations observed by many Chinese families, the government felt that through male-only migration, they could not only control permanent settlement in Taiwan but also hold families responsible if the migrant worker became wayward (Shepherd 1995, 143; Yu-Wei Hsieh 1967). Although strict in theory, this was often difficult to police, and as a consequence many of these seasonal workers opted for permanent settlement (Itō 2004, 56–59). As well as seeking permanence, many took Indigenous wives in addition to those they had left behind.

This fluctuating policy on immigration was not dissimilar to the Ming ban on overseas trade (*haijin*), which was never really accomplished, and both were counter to the needs of the coastal populations (Meskill 1979, 27; Goddio and Casal 2002, 43–54). Thus, in spite of Taiwan's relative physical proximity to the Chinese mainland, the island existed in a wilderness that was both culturally and politically outside the cosmographic center of Chinese civilization (Emma Teng 2004, 43). Prohibitions on ocean trading heavily restricted Chinese overseas trade in spite of their proven shipping industry and the hardiness of the Chinese junk, and private trading thus became synonymous with smuggling and piracy (Vermeer 1999, 69).

Passage to Taiwan was dangerous. It was risky. The criminality of smuggling, piracy, and illegal migration significantly added to the relative danger. The predominant risk was piracy; the coastline of southern China, throughout the Ming-Qing transition, harbored a core group of Chinese pirates with a larger number of press-ganged men and boys (Anthony 2009, 10; Anthony 2003). In addition to these were the Japanese *wakō* who harassed the Taiwan Strait as early as the thirteenth century. Crossing the strait at certain times of the year was extremely treacherous. Yu Yonghe, writing in his journal at Penghu on 14 March 1697, recounts, "During storms or on a restless sea, whirlpools would form and drag ships to their doom.... Legend says that their spirits haunt the strait, demanding from fishermen a human sacrifice every three years. 'If you don't comply then the spirits will haunt you for another three years,' the fishermen say" (Keliher 2003, 39).

Passage across the Taiwan Strait, known colloquially as the Black Trench, was not only treacherous but also extremely expensive (Itō 2004, 56–59). Settlers who were caught were punished, which included branding with a five-by-five-centimeter character on their cheeks (*cizi zhushui*) and submission to eighty lashes before being sent back (Xu Xueji 2005; Wu Micha 2005, 106). For those involved in human trafficking, the leader was either permanently enlisted into the military or ordered to serve as an indentured laborer, depending on their age (Wu Micha 2005, 106). The huge cost of passage and the illegality of smuggling shepherded in a criminal syndicate. The price of punishment led a number of captains to simply sail to other islands scattered along the China coast, informing their passengers that they had arrived safely in Taiwan. In other cases, the captain would load as many migrants as possible into the ship's hull before nailing the entrance shut. Under cover of darkness, the ship would set sail. If it arrived safely, it would anchor offshore at a sandbar to avoid unwanted exposure. Many drowned in the unpredictable tides while wading ashore. Those who reached dry land still had to avoid detection; if caught they were fined and forced to return to China, where they would await punishment.

For many early pioneers, the economic advantages outweighed the risks. The huge demand for rice in the southern provinces brought significant economic gain from the double-harvested rice grown on Taiwan. By 1717, the Chinese population in Taiwan had exceeded that during the preceding colonial periods (Dutch, Spanish, and Zheng). The ebb and flow of the Qing administrative policies toward the island created a similar ebb and flow in the economy. The social and economic balance of the early pioneering society thus bore a strong resemblance to that in the provinces of southern China, where most of Taiwan's settler population had originated (Gates 1987, 32–33). As the population expanded, most of the crops harvested on the island were used for domestic consumption. Exceptions were rice and sugar, due to their high value on the mainland market. During the early pioneering years, these commodities became the island's chief export in the cross-strait junk trade.

As profits increased with the demand for both rice and sugar, the total area under cultivation expanded substantially in the early years. During the reign of Emperor Kangxi (r. 1662–1722) maritime trade between China and Taiwan was largely encouraged. A number of junks took advantage of this opportunity, carrying raw materials from Taiwan to numerous ports on the Chinese coast. Rice, peanut oil, and indigo found markets in China, while deer hide was exported to Japan. The Taiwan-bound vessels carried cotton cloth, silver, ironware, and herbal medicine—though the vessels frequently returned with just ballast.

Life for the early pioneers was arguably more comfortable than for those on the mainland. Narratives of the island's richness and the lavish lifestyle of its people began spreading across the coastal regions of southern China. Taiwan thus became the new world for the Chinese in much the same way as their European migratory counterparts saw the Americas. The major factor marring this analogy was the weak and fluctuating enforcement on immigration imposed by the Manchus. Still, strong economic attraction to Taiwan led to a growing Chinese population by the end of the seventeenth century. Monopoly traders figured predominantly in the early years of economic penetration into areas settled by Indigenous communities. These were later followed by the land-hungry Chinese farmers who extended the Chinese settlements and spread out southward toward Fengshan and northward towards Zhuluo (Shepherd 1995, 168).

The increase in the amount of land recorded on tax registers reflects the spread of Han settlement. Commercialization, changing trade patterns, and population expansion would help frontier settlements push the Indigenous border farther into the mountainous interior.

———

Lin Shih was the first of the Wufeng Lin family to migrate to Taiwan. Born in 1729 in Zhangzhou, Fujian, Lin Shih was raised by his grandmother, as both of his parents had died between his tenth and twelfth birthdays. In 1746, at the age of seventeen, he joined some friends and crossed the Black Trench to Taiwan. He did not stay long, returning to the Chinese mainland after receiving a letter from his grandmother calling him back. He spent the next few years avoiding all his grandmother's attempts to tie him down. This included refusing marry (Meskill 1979, 57). In 1754, the year after his grandmother passed away, he moved to Taiwan to settle. He ordered his brothers to guard the family tomb, but following another return visit he fetched his brothers and his parents' bodies for reburial, returning to Taiwan in 1757. He settled in present-day Dali (Taichung) due to its location, as it was close to the mountains and therefore had an abundant water supply. The land he settled was in the gray area between the Han frontier settlements and Indigenous land. He therefore did not purchase it but was able to obtain it by tilling new ground. Within a few years, Lin Shih had grown wealthy and was chosen to be the head of the Lin clan around his village.

He fathered six sons with his wife, Ms. Chen—and likely a number of daughters, but these are not recorded. To have so many surviving children and a wife who had birthed such a large family in a frontier settlement testifies to the position of privilege Lin Shih had obtained. The Lin family considered the period between 1760 and 1770 their golden years. During this time he acquired enough land to rent to tenant farmers and to withdraw from the fields himself (Meskill 1979, 60). In spite of his success, life on the frontier was hard and factionalized. Tension between the prominently Zhangzhou lineal families in Dali and the neighboring Hakka communities was incessant. In 1782, this erupted in an armed confrontation outside a known gambling spot near Changhua. The Manchu authorities responded, announcing that if armed violence were to persist, those caught up in the conflict would be branded rebellious. To prepare themselves and avoid losing everything in Taiwan, Lin Shih asked his eldest, Lin Sun, to take money back to their ancestral home to buy land. On route, Lin Sun, at twenty-one, suddenly fell ill and died. This was devastating for Lin Shih, who had favored Lin Sun. What is more, four years later, Lin Shih's concerns about being involved in an altercation were realized.

Records show that in 1786, during the Lin Shuangwen rebellion, Lin Shih tried to stop the rebels (Lin Ching-hu 2011, 233). He was concerned, as he himself was also a Lin, though reputedly unrelated, and the head of the Dali Lin clan. He failed, and the following year Manchu authorities arrested him for participating in the rebellion and confiscated all his belongings. He was imprisoned in harsh conditions in Lukang. He was not executed, likely because he convinced the Manchu officials that he was not related to Lin Shuang-wen despite coming from the same village in Zhangzhou (any relationship would have been removed from the record, so it is impossible to know for sure). It was only in 1788 that he was able to clear his name, and he died shortly after being released. As Lin Sun had died on the voyage to China, his wife, Huang Jui-niang, along with their sons, Lin Chiung-yao and Lin Chia-yin, moved to Ataabu in present-day Wufeng in 1789. Ataabu was much closer to Indigenous territory than Dali, but as Han settlers had pushed farther inland, places like Ataabu became a connecting point—an interurban linkage—and trade in the district saw a sudden boom. Lin Chia-yin had started his trade in groceries, but gradually he was able to buy land and became a landowner.

Lin Chia-yin's first son, Lin Tin-pang, along with his descendants, became known as the *xiacuo*, or lower mansion family. His second son, Lin Tien-kuo, and his line would be referred to as the *dingcuo*, or upper mansion family. The *xiacuo* and *dingcuo* would form the two main sections of the Wufeng Lin family mansion (Hsu Hsueh-chi 1998, xii–xxi). In the early years, the *xiacuo* line was much more successful, as some of its members became military leaders. Lin Wen-cha (1828–64) helped suppress various rebellions against Manchu colonial rule. He died in battle in Fujian. Lin Wen-ming (1833–70), like his brother Lin Wen-cha, joined the military and earned the rank of level 2 vice general. He was instrumental in helping the Manchus suppress the Tai Chao-chuen Incident (Daichaochun Shijian; 1862–65), and as a reward the Manchus granted the Lin family the right to

A SETTLER'S TALE   45

trade in camphor—a key commodity following the opening of the treaty ports in the 1860s. Thus the Lin family became the richest landowning family in central Taiwan.

Lin Wen-cha's son Lin Chao-tung fought in the Sino-French War, and because of his contribution, he earned a level 3 rank. He was also instrumental in establishing the Taiwan Republic in 1895 (Alsford 2018, 159). As the Republic began to crumble, it was reported that Lin Chao-tung had left with other prominent families from Keelung in early May 1895. However, this report is likely false, since it was also reported that Lin Chao-tung was present in Changhua and had assembled his troops to resist the Japanese. As the Japanese began to advance south in June 1895, Lin Chao-tung eventually conceded, acknowledging that resistance in central Taiwan would be futile. He asked his cousin Lin Chao-hsuan, the son of Lin Wen-ming, and Lin Wen-chin, the head of the *dingcuo,* to remain in Wufeng. In late June, Lin Chao-tung left Taiwan to join his family, who had left Taiwan on a boat bound for Quanzhou in June 1895. Lin Chao-tung died in Shanghai in 1904.

With the evacuation of most of the *xiacuo*, the *dingcuo* line became the prominent family line. The most famous figure in this line was Lin Hsien-tang, a close friend of Chiang Wei-shui who was crucial in the Petition Movement for the Establishment of a Taiwanese Parliament.

The Japanese consolidation of power in 1895 positioned Taiwan on a completely different trajectory. The main river thoroughfares and harbors of Taiwan started to choke with traffic as many families with their belongings sought passage out of Taiwan. Of 2.7 million residents, 6,466 (0.24 percent) had left by the 8 May 1897 deadline (Wu 2005, 20–21). This migration to the Chinese mainland would prove to be an important filtering system in the development of a Taiwan-centered identity. Japanese colonialism became a necessary other in ending factionalized identity among the Chinese frontier settlers and drawing together a Taiwanese selfhood.

4

A Colonialist's Tale

SHIMIZU TERUKO

Formosa was transformed into a modern island
by the Japanese. The economic role of Japan in Korea,
on the other hand, is still disputable and many Koreans
remain unconvinced of any significant Japanese
contribution. Such awareness (and lack of it) is an
explanation itself for the varied sentiment of the two
people toward their colonial rulers.

EDWARD I-TE CHEN · 1973

Colonization has shaped Taiwan to such an extent that there is no identifiable noncolonial period, at least in the sense of how people identify what it means to be from Taiwan or in Taiwan in the present period. Whether Indigenous or non-Indigenous, migrant or sojourner, the colonial layers of Taiwan's past inform how the self is performed. The notion of *becoming* and not of *being* is written into the history of what Taiwan is and what it is not. For Leo Ching, a postcolonial theorist, in *Becoming "Japanese,"* coloniality in the Japanese context is best understood in the encounters between Taiwan indigeneity and Japanese nationalism (Ching 2001, 5). Taiwan's Indigenous soldiers, who fought and died for Japan, are enshrined at Yasukuni. They died as Japanese (J. Nihonjin), but their descendants and those soldiers who survived are denied this identity. They have no access to *being* Japanese. They became Japanese only in the concealed notions of *dōka* (assimilation) and *kōminka* (imperial subjects) that were engineered for colonial control. Identity in Taiwan can be seen as a consciousness in contradistinction to two nationalisms: Japanese and Chinese (Dawley 2019, 21). The presence of China in Taiwaneseness is crucial in understanding the Japanese colonial period, not least as a sociocultural and political imaginary. For Leo T. S. Ching, "China loomed large in the consciousness of Taiwanese intellectuals throughout the colonial period" (Ching 2001, 7). This notion of political and social imaginary also informs Ann Heylen and Scott Sommers's *Becoming Taiwan,* where they present an argument that colonial Japan was compelled to make concessions (Heylen and Summers 2010, 10). The foundation of this argument rests on the types of social organizations that existed in Taiwan prior to Japanese colonization. Systems such as the *baojia* were purposely adopted by Japanese colonial authorities to manage centralized planning of colonial development outside of key urban areas.

The process of social engineering through incorporation of Japanese colonial policy, while upholding specific community-based social practices, would produce an ethnogenesis concentrated in the port city of Keelung but with resonance throughout the island (Dawley 2019). The Japanese colonial period holds significant importance. The nostalgic view of the Japanese empire, prevalent among many in Taiwan today, is rooted not in the colonization by the Japanese, but rather in the Taiwanese national awakening that occurred during the period of Chinese Nationalist rule, which followed the Japanese colonial era. This said, there is another factor. The transition of power in 1895 was for the most part considered simply a power shift in distant empires. Very soon, the people in Taiwan recognized that the Japanese were more invasive than the Manchus. They fashioned and reshaped everyday life in Taiwan. Unlike most European colonial expansions, the Japanese Empire began in a regional propinquity. It focused its initial expansion on countries (Taiwan and Korea) with a recognizable shared cultural heritage. This affinity shaped how Japan governed its colonies.

Officially, Taiwan became a dependency of Japan when, as a stipulation in the Treaty of Shimonoseki, the Manchu Empire ceded the island after its defeat in the Sino-Japanese War (1894–95). However, the preceding events on Taiwan spoke of an undeclared war, which can be understood as the Taiwan War of 1895 (Alsford 2018, 22–29). The rationale for this argument was that the immediate colonization of Taiwan was neither peaceful in a standard sense nor a continuation of the Sino-Japanese War. The resistance, although led differently by Tang Jingsong, Qiu Fengjia, and Liu Yongfu, was a disconnect from the Sino-Japanese War in that it took place after the signing of the treaty, the departure of the Qing army and government, and the proclamation of the Republic of Formosa on 23 May 1895. The treaty went into effect on 17 April 1895, followed by an imperial edict ordering all civil authorities and military to leave for the mainland on 20 May 1895. Tang Jingsong, the former governor of Taiwan province and then elected president of the republic, issued an edict that the people of Taiwan (Taimin)—the first time that term would be used—would resist Japanese rule and become an independent country. The Manchus responded to foreign inquiries by officially stating that they no longer had jurisdiction over the island and as such were not involved in any of its affairs (Alsford 2018, 24). The resistance was in fact a separate, undeclared war. The Japanese, not wishing to be embroiled in another conflict, would refer to this resistance as the Taiwan Campaign. Although the republic was short-lived, ending with the capitulation of Tainan on 21 October 1895, it exemplifies a beginning in Taiwan's journey to selfhood and the starting point of a national consciousness as the people began to come together in an act of resistance.

Kobayama Sukenori, the first governor-general, reported back to Tokyo on 21 October 1895 that the island had been secured and began to administer the island. In spite of the collapse of the republic, resistance continued in the form of quasi-monthly anti-Japanese uprisings. By 1902, most anti-Japanese activities among the Han ethnic groups began to fade, the most notable exception being the 1907 Beipu Incident (Beipu Shijian), an armed local uprising that also included ethnic Hakka- and the Saisiyat-speaking peoples in what is now Hsinchu. This was followed by the Tapani Incident (Jiaobanian Shijian) in 1915, one of the largest armed uprisings involving Han Chinese settlers. This incident was seen as a nationalist uprising against the Japanese, and the millenarian and folk religious language used by leaders of the resistance, such as Yu Qingfang, led Japanese authorities to make comparisons to the Righteous Harmony Society of the Boxer Rebellion in China (Katz 2005, 3–4). The colonial authorities, as a result, paid closer attention to Taiwan's popular religious movements, and temples and places of worship were managed more carefully. Following the Tapani Incident in 1915, Han resistance all but stopped. However, Indigenous resistance persisted as the Japanese continued to encroach upon Indigenous territories. A crisis ensued in 1930 with the Musha Incident (Wushe Shijian; Berry 2022). Faced with internal and external criticism of the unprecedentedly harsh military response, the colonial authorities began to bolster periods of Japanization with education and social programs among Indigenous communities.

Taiwan was governed under both military and civilian authorities. Each period emphasized different policies.

In total, nineteen governors-general oversaw Taiwan in the Japanese colonial period, with an average of 2.5 years of service (see table 2). Japanese colonization can be divided into three distinct periods that begin and end in military rule, with a seventeen-year high period of civilian rule that occurred at roughly the same period as the Taisho democracy in Japan. This high period focused mainly on social and economic development. The change to military rule in 1936 was related to the Japanese war effort in China.

During the colonial period many people from the Japanese home islands migrated to and settled in Taiwan. This settler colonialism can be divided into four stages: (1) early privately run immigration projects, (2) early government-run immigration projects, (3) later privately run immigration projects, and (4) later government-run immigration projects (Lin Chengjung 2006). Government-run migration projects differed from privately run ones in that the former were not run for profit, while the latter were. Sale and purchase of land resulted in a migration of people to Taiwan. The occupation of the immigrants varied and can be divided roughly into four key industries: agriculture, labor, fisheries, and commercial. Not all of those who immigrated settled permanently, as some occupations were seasonal.

The first phase of government-led immigration projects followed the Russo-Japanese War (1904–5). In Japan proper, victory brought vigorous growth in enterprise. To avoid stagnation, the Japanese government encouraged migration to Taiwan by granting permission to develop and build on arable land. In total, the Japanese colonial authorities allocated thirty-eight pieces of land to immigrants. The early stages of the project saw the sale of only nine pieces of land, and a few of the immigrants either returned to Japan or changed to a different occupation. During the second phase, the

TABLE 2. Japanese governor-generals (1895–1945)

NAME	PRECEDING OCCUPATION	MILITARY OR CIVILIAN	DATES
Kabayama Sukenori	Admiral (Imperial Japanese Navy)	Military	10 May 1895–2 June 1896
Katsura Tarō	Lieutenant General (Imperial Japanese Army)	Military	2 June 1896– 14 October 1896
Nogi Maresuke	Lieutenant General (Imperial Japanese Army)	Military	14 October 1896– 26 January 1898
Kodama Gentarō	Lieutenant General (Imperial Japanese Army)	Military	26 February 1898– 11 April 1906
Sakuma Samata	General (Imperial Japanese Army)	Military	11 April 1906–1 May 1915
Andō Teibi	General (Imperial Japanese Army)	Military	1 May 1915–6 June 1918
Akashi Motojirō	Lieutenant General (Imperial Japanese Army)	Military	6 June 1918– 24 October 1919
Den Kenjirō	Member of Motojirō Cabinet	Civilian	29 October 1919– 6 September 1923
Uchida Kakichi	Member of House of Peers	Civilian	6 September 1923– 1 September 1924
Izawa Takio	Member of House of Peers	Civilian	1 September 1924– 16 July 1926
Kamiyama Mitsunoshin	Literary figure	Civilian	16 July 1926–16 June 1928
Kawamura Takeji	Member of House of Peers	Civilian	16 June 1928–30 July 1929
Ishizuka Eizō	Member of House of Peers	Civilian	30 July 1929– 16 January 1931
Ōta Masahiro	Director of Kwantung Leased Territory	Civilian	16 January 1931– 2 March 1932
Minami Hiroshi	Member of House of Peers	Civilian	2 March 1932–26 May 1932
Nakagawa Kenzō	Undersecretary of Education	Civilian	26 May 1932– 2 September 1936
Kobayashi Seizō	Admiral (Imperial Japanese Navy)	Military	2 September 1936– 27 November 1940
Hasegawa Kiyoshi	Admiral (Imperial Japanese Navy)	Military	27 November 1940– 30 December 1944
Andō Rikichi	Admiral (Imperial Japanese Navy)	Military	30 December 1944– 25 October 1945

government considered Taiwan's east coast to be an ideal location. This was, however, Indigenous land that had not been settled by the Han Chinese. In response, the colonial government began focusing on the development of Harbor Offices in Hualien and Taitung. Although fifteen areas were designated as fitting destinations for migration, it proved impossible to reach a consensus with the Indigenous people over the purchase of land to accommodate migrating Japanese in the Taitung region. As a result, migration was limited to three villages under the jurisdiction of the Hualien Harbor Office: Chiye/Yoshino Village (Jiye Yimin Cun), Fengtian/Toyota Village (Fengtian Yimin Cun), and Lintian/Hayashida Village (Lintian Yimin Cun) (the latter two still exist today as exhibitions of cultural heritage). In 1917, the government-run immigration project was discontinued. Two explanations were given for this. One was that the Taiwan Governor's Office had already achieved its goal of model immigration, and there was no longer any need to continue with the government-run projects. The other was that the cost of developing areas on the east coast was too high, and the program had not been successful (Lin Cheng-jung 2006).

Policies promoting and subsidizing subsequent private immigration initiatives were primarily developed in response to earlier government-led projects being nonprofit ventures. These projects required large capital investments, prompting the government to shift the focus of their immigration efforts. In 1917, the colonial government introduced a plan called Essentials to Encourage and Reward Immigration (Yizhu Jiangli Yaoling). The Taitung Sugar Manufacturing Company was the first to benefit from this scheme. With financial support from the Taiwan colonial government and the company's own investment, the Taitung Sugar Manufacturing Company and the subsequent Taitung Development Company built eleven immigrant villages in the Taitung region. However, by 1924, difficulties in acquiring land for the Pijun Irrigation Region made it impossible to balance income and expenses. Additionally, the Bank of Taiwan was inflexible in providing loans to the company, making it increasingly challenging to showcase its accomplishments. Many immigrants left, and the company ultimately collapsed (Lin Cheng-jung 2001).

Japanese immigrant villages in Taiwan were established to provide suitable land for settlers. They imitated Japanese villages on the home islands. The main agricultural crops were sugarcane, tobacco, and rice. The government provided three years of free medical care and built clinics, schools, shrines, and other public facilities. Between 1909 and 1918, roughly twenty villages were constructed via such programs, each housing less than 1,700 immigrants. Since Japanese authorities did not consider these villages successful, the bulk of those who migrated, both individuals and families, moved to Taiwan through other means. Most Japanese settlement was urban, as the principal occupation for Japanese men was government and professional work, commerce, and manufacturing (George Barclay 1954, 67). At the close of the Japanese colonial period, an estimated 312,000 Japanese civilians resided in Taiwan (George Barclay 1954, 116). They went from being referred to as "homelanders" (J. *naichijin*) to "overseas Japanese" (J. *nikkyō*). One such overseas Japanese was Shimizu Teruko.

Shimizu Teruko, also known as Shih Chao-tzu, was born in Kyoto, Japan, on 30 March 1909. The oldest of four daughters of a wealthy paper merchant, she graduated from Kyoto Prefectural Second Girls' High School (present-day Suzaku High School). Shimizu was well informed and often read about events in the Japanese Empire. She became infatuated with Shih Chien, a Taiwanese civil engineer who had been tasked with surveying poverty in the market town of Banka. Following the government-led survey, Shih founded a charity, Aiai Ryou (Aiailiao), to help the homeless. Shimizu had learned about Shih's achievements from Japanese writers such as Kikuchi Kan and was deeply moved by his ideas. Her neighbor in Japan, Shih Hsiu-feng, was Shih Chien's cousin. Shih Hsiu-feng introduced Shimizu to Shih Chien, and Shimizu learned about his charity. The two started to write to each other, and in 1934, Shimizu married Shih Chien despite her parents' objections.

After arriving in Taiwan, Shimizu went from the life of a wealthy young girl to caring for the homeless. Shortly before the end of the Second World War, Shih passed away, and Shimizu was suddenly faced with the prospect of being deported along with the other Japanese families. She renounced her Japanese nationality and changed her legal name to continue her husband's legacy. In addition to working with the charity, she raised six children (including two girls from her husband's former marriage). Following the arrival of the Chinese Nationalist government, Shimizu was determined to continue her charity. Fortunately, she received American funding and was able to find work for some of her clients assisting the city government in cleaning the streets. As the charity grew, it took in disabled people, the elderly, and orphans. At its height it had more than two hundred clients under its care (Yuan 2021).

Shimizu witnessed the 228 Incident but was emotionally unable to talk about it. She worked daily from eight in the morning to four in the afternoon until she was in her eighties. An incredibly humble woman, she received numerous awards but never collected them, the only exception being in 2000, when she received an award from Rotary International given to successful women. She told the press that her life over the past fifty years was always the same, so there was nothing worth writing about. Shimizu passed away in 2001 at the age of ninety-one. Her son, Shih Wu-ching, took over the charity.

The Japanese colonial period was not singular, and the colonial nostalgia that exists among some in Taiwan comes from differences in colonial management. The broad powers of the governor-general included filling most of the positions in the colonial government. This meant that during the two periods of military governorship these positions were given to people from similar backgrounds. The high-cultural civilian period was no different. In 1921, during a civilian period, the colonial authorities allowed for greater local input through the establishment of the Advisory Council (J. Hyōgikai; Roy 2003, 37). Although most of its members were Japanese, there was a dominant Taiwanese contingent. In 1935, the authorities expanded this by allowing elections for half the seats in the provincial and town assemblies. This enabled many Taiwanese to have substantial input into local governance. Although this did not shift the balance of power, the electoral procedures would have long-term consequences for Taiwan's political development (Rigger 1999, 36; Roy 2003, 37). It created incentives for politicians to focus on local issues, and it helped foster and cultivate local power bases. The reforms acclimated the Taiwanese to orderly democratic participation.

Economic growth during the Japanese period led to Taiwan being ranked second among East and Southeast Asian colonies in terms of GDP growth between 1913 and 1938. This would prove to be a significant asset for Taiwan's postwar economic development. Agricultural growth, with rice and sugar replacing tea and camphor as the primary exports, enabled Taiwan to move by the late 1930s from a traditional agricultural system to a modern one. Rice yields, for example, were much higher in Taiwan during this period than in other parts of Asia (Booth 2007, 25), although this fact did not translate to any real change in Taiwan's economic structure. By 1938, agricultural output accounted for 35 percent of Taiwan's GDP, whereas mining and manufacturing accounted for only 24 percent (Samuel Ho 1978). By the end of the colonial period, Taiwan was still a predominantly agricultural society and not an example of "Japanese colonial exceptionalism" (Booth 2007, 33).

The Japanese colonization of Taiwan occurred at significant global junctures. Many newly introduced ideas and institutions translated well in Taiwan. Education in the burgeoning physical sciences and mathematics became standard in the Taiwanese education system, and Taiwan achieved significant improvements in sanitation and health care. By the 1930s, many in Taiwan saw significant rises in real wages and a noteworthy growth in living standards and consumer purchasing power. There is every indication, however, that Taiwan could have achieved this level of growth without Japanese input. Indeed, Taiwan—or, specifically, northern Taiwan—had moved significantly in this direction prior to Japanese colonialism.

Assimilating Taiwan into the Japanese Empire was the principal motive behind the colonial administration's effort to develop Taiwan. Encouraging more Japanese immigration would alleviate the overpopulation of Japan's home islands and create a community in Taiwan that would mirror that of home. The education system was designed to teach the Taiwanese how to be Japanese, with a curriculum that would guide these students to be loyal to the emperor and to respect and uphold Japanese values. Administrators sought to weaken displays of Taiwaneseness. The most comprehensive of these policies involved language. Japanese was to be the language of Taiwan. It was the language of instruction; the language of the economy, banking, and the civil service; and most significantly, the language of culture: the language of *being*.

Shimizu Teruko was perhaps an exception. She told her grandchildren that one should not marry a place where you cannot speak the language. Shimizu, or rather Shih Chao-tzu, married Taiwan. She never taught her children or grandchildren to speak Japanese. She *became Taiwanese*.

PATHWAYS TO WAR

1930–1945

5

A Hunter's Tale

RO'ENG

Dakis, when you die, are you entering a Japanese
shrine, or the heavenly home of our ancestors?
Are you Dakis or Hanaoka Ichiro?
MONA RUDAO · 1930

In the pre-Columbian world, Austronesian speakers were the most widely
dispersed ethnolinguistic population (Bellwood 2009, 336). The languages
spread south from Taiwan, through the Philippines, into Indonesia and
Malaysia, across all the Pacific islands, and as far west as Madagascar.
Because Austronesian is for the most part a linguistic term with few pre-
served samples of writing, its history has proved difficult to reconstruct.
Documentation of the spread of Austronesian speakers has been primarily
made through an understanding of the evolution of boatbuilding technology and archaeological findings. The 1,200 Austronesian languages fall into
ten subgroups, nine of which (twenty-six languages in total) are spoken by
the Indigenous peoples of Taiwan (Blust 2014, 314). The tenth subgroup
encompasses all the Austronesian languages found outside Taiwan (Diamond 2000). From this fact, it can be deduced that the early diversification
occurred on Taiwan itself. The linguistic differences between the languages
suggest a long pause between the settlement of the language on Taiwan and
its expansion out of there. Then there is an additional long pause between
the original migratory language and those now spoken throughout the

Pacific. This is confirmed by evidence in archaeological finds. The farming colonization of Taiwan and the subsequent move to the Philippines took about a thousand years, with an additional thousand years for the colonization of Near Oceania and on into Remote Oceania, the latter being the greatest migration in geographical terms.

The ancestors of the Pacific Islanders thus originated in this voyaging corridor. The significance lies in the development of interconnected and intertwined long-distance exchange rather than a migration of peoples from a single waystation, which implies that routes of migration characterized by intermarriage, cultural exchange, trade, and subsequent language borrowing along this corridor were not necessarily linked to the initial dispersal of peoples from Taiwan. They nevertheless would have come into contact with each other to spread linguistic and cultural variations. Maritime gardening and horticulture therefore had local origins during the initial spread into maritime Southeast Asia (Solheim 1996). For much of the history of Indigenous peoples, migration both within and outside Taiwan was a product of specific push and pull factors, which varied among different communities. Population growth, environmental changes, and war and conflict all fostered migration. As communities began to move and interact with other communities, occasionally assimilating, concepts of identity evolved. Yet, for the most part, those born in a particular Indigenous community expected little change over their lifetimes. This was true also of their offspring. Such constancy was, of course, the reality of all premodern peoples. For Taiwan's Indigenous peoples this changed with the beginnings of colonization, first by Europeans and later Chinese, Manchu, and Japanese. From the seventeenth century the colonization of Taiwan is particularly important in understanding contested markers of the *past* as a charter for understanding a Taiwanese *present*.

Taiwan's colonial history began with the arrival of the Dutch on Taiwan proper in 1624. The various periods of colonization had different effects on patterns of migration and subsequent notions of identity among Indigenous communities. This is particularly significant in understanding processes of Indigenous integration and assimilation. The first form of colonization was hybrid: most of the agricultural settlers were Chinese (imported foreign labor), but the administrators and military were Dutch controlled (Andrade 2005). After establishing the Dutch settlement in present-day Anping, the

Dutch began to trade with the Sirayan- and Taivoan-speaking peoples (Shepherd 1995, 52).

In 1629, after a Dutch expeditionary force was killed, the Dutch retaliated by burning the village of Mattau (Madou), the most powerful in the region, and subjugating its people. The Dutch expanded their rule through the construction of schools and mission churches. This initiated an evangelizing project over Taiwan Indigenous peoples (Wills 1999, 92). To expand their influence, the Dutch brought in a romanization system to represent the Sirayan and Taivoan languages. The Dutch trade in deerskin became a lucrative business and a significant source of local employment. Contracts were given on the basis of acculturation. Demand in Japan affected supply, and many who could not compete in the market adopted farming practices that they learned from the Chinese, who had begun to settle on previous grazing lands (Andrade 2005, 303). The competition for land between agricultural Indigenous and Chinese communities was frequently violent. The Dutch used the Chinese as agents to collect taxes and sell hunting licenses. This practice pushed a number of Indigenous communities away from the fertile and game-rich areas while locking in settled and assimilated communities. Allegiance and resistance to the Dutch and their Chinese agents would have enormous consequences for the shaping of Indigenous identity. Taiwan's integration into the Manchu Empire in 1683 influenced how the Indigenous peoples on Taiwan were interpreted and labeled.

As in other settler colonial societies (Australia, the United States, Canada, and New Zealand), the settler colonial period on Taiwan witnessed the replacement of Indigenous populations with an invasive and violent settler society. Over time, these communities would develop distinct identities. The almost complete acculturation of western plains Indigenous peoples would result in the rudimentary classification of all of Taiwan's Indigenous peoples into "raw" and "cooked" categories (Emma Teng 2004, 122). The contemporary classification of mountain and plains Indigenous groups has its roots in this period. Territorialization of land on Taiwan has had consequences for Indigenous recognition. The distinction between the "raw" peoples of the mountains and the assimilated "cooked" peoples of the plains forced a boundary on Indigenous identity. This boundary was not static and not always physical. The shifting patterns of ethnic designation continue to this day, reflecting a complex intersectionality of Indigenous cultures and habitats (Emma Teng 2004, 123).

Toward the end of the nineteenth century, this intersectionality changed with the arrival of the treaty port system and semicolonial conditions throughout the island. The almost complete conversion of Indigenous peoples to Christianity and the demographic changes on the island ushered in the beginnings of a pan identity (Alsford 2021, 23). Christianity is practiced by 70 percent of the Indigenous population. Most adherents attend the Presbyterian Church, which has roots in the nineteenth-century treaty port system (Alsford 2018). Concepts of community in converted villages centered on the church. Adaptation to changing practices would continue throughout the period and into the metropole-settler coloniality of the Japanese in 1895.

One major difference between policies toward Indigenous communities under Japanese rule and those under Manchu rule was the Japanese colonial government's wish to consolidate rule over the entire island. Like other expansionist empires, Japanese colonial authorities placed importance on understanding the cultures of the colonized people. This served two purposes. The first was to assess the degree of resistance. It allowed authorities to understand the military capabilities of different Indigenous groups. The second was to satisfy a growing domestic interest in an "ethnographic other" of peoples in their empire. Imperial expansion costs money. The first Japanese ethnologist tasked with surveying the island was Inō Kanori. His research grouped concepts of indigeneity in eight formalized groups based on linguistic variation. In many ways, this locked Indigenous communities into imagined boundaries that not only prevented some forms of Indigenous cultural unity but also imposed cultural compartmentalization on those who had not previously identified with such labels.

The taxonomy of linguistic boundaries continues to categorize Indigenous peoples today and affects how they are recognized. As Japan began its movement into militarism in the 1930s, many traditional structures were replaced. Ideas of improved status meant many communities sought out education rather than headhunting, a practice that nearly all Indigenous groups on Taiwan had performed, as an important coming of age marker.

To garner support from all ethnic groups in Taiwan, the Japanese, much like the Qing and Dutch before them, crafted a divide-and-rule policy by pitting Indigenous against Chinese. The hardline position toward the Indigenous peoples led to systematic resistance from various groups. Many in Japan, however, wished to know more about their empire, thus fueling a "civilizing project" to document and understand Indigenous cultures. Cooperating with the Japanese earned elite positions for families in villages, and the Japanese in turn encouraged certain traditional customs. During the colonial periods in Taiwan, there was no single narrative—no unified forms of imperialism and, consequently, no common experience of indigeneity. Instead, the systematic acculturation of Indigenous peoples to a non-Indigenous identity continued in the postwar colonization by the Chinese Nationalists in exile.

From the cession of Taiwan to Japan in 1895 to 1906, Japanese colonial authorities refrained from systematically interfering in Indigenous affairs aside from setting up schools and initiating the initial ethnographic surveys of the island. A number of Indigenous leaders visited Japan. Yet in the period after 1906, things began to change. Once local resistance among Chinese settlers had been stabilized, the Japanese shifted their attention to the Indigenous borders in the mountains, and by 1909 the Indigenous peoples were essentially imprisoned.

Indigenous resistance to the Japanese was piecemeal. According to historian Paul Barclay, Japanese ethnographers saw the Indigenous peoples of Taiwan as "invested with a cultural authenticity that marked them as avatars of prelapsarian Taiwan antedating Chinese immigration, based in part on high Japanese appraisals of Austronesian cultural production" (Paul Barclay 2018, 3). Yet the Japanese colonial partitioning of Indigenous homelands into zones of administration created friction. By the early twentieth century, this resistance to colonial authority was both local and part of international movements for self-determination. The Indigenous peoples of Taiwan were not isolated from these global discourses. Their resistance to the Japanese colonial authority mirrored similar Indigenous movements found elsewhere.

Yet the Japanese policy of mere assimilation (*dōka*) of both Indigenous and non-Indigenous Taiwanese changed following Japan's full-scale invasion of China in 1937. Its policy of imperialization (*kōminka*), which started the year before, was delegated to Kobayashi Seizo, the seventeenth governor-general of Taiwan, who with his wealth of experience organized development in Taiwan in three key areas: (1) development of industry, (2) use of Taiwan as a springboard for southbound advancement through southern China and Southeast Asia, and (3) full integration of the population into Japanese language and culture. By 1941, the success of these policies became clear as Japan went to war with the United States and its allies.

———

Ro'eng was born Amis in E'tolan (Dulan) on the east coast of Taiwan in 1921. In March 1943, he and three male companions were part of a youth group (*qingnian tuan*) assigned to patrol the coastline for potential danger (Tsai Cheng-liang 2011, 22). Their three months of work as sentries informed their identity as a Japanese *us* against an external *other* and would subsequently aid the Japanese in recruitment for military service.

The Imperial Japanese Army viewed the Indigenous peoples of Taiwan as potential servicemen in the tropical and subtropical regions. The Takasago Volunteers (J. Takasago Giyūtai), as they were subsequently known, were trained in the Nakano School (J. Rikugun Nakano Gakkō), which specialized in insurgency and guerrilla warfare. At the onset, it was expected that they would be assigned to transport and supply units; however, as the war progressed, the Takasago Volunteers were moved to the front lines. The Indigenous men saw conflict in the Philippines, Netherlands East Indies, Solomon Islands, and New Guinea. Given the secrecy at the time, it is difficult to assess the total number, but estimates range from five thousand to eight thousand men (Huang Chih-huei 2011, 143).

When Ro'eng and his companions volunteered to be part of the youth group, the Japanese police informed them that they had been selected to form a fifth group of soldiers destined for the front line. Four other groups (ten men in total) had already been sent. Men of a similar age set (important markers of masculine identity in Amis Indigenous culture) were recruited together, and Ro'eng recalls how he and his friends were both worried and scared. They did not want to die in a war, and they lacked formal military training. But despite their reticence, Ro'eng and the other men remember feeling pride in being asked (Tsai Cheng-liang 2011, 24).

Not long after receiving orders, Ro'eng got his military uniform. Ro'eng recalls feeling that in uniform he was given more respect by the younger name set groups in the community (name sets refer to a practice of putting Indigenous men into loose generational groups). He noticed that even the police gave him greater deference. Ro'eng was given a military registration that included his Japanese name, Yoshimura Tadashi (Tsai Cheng-liang 2011, 26).

By the start of April 1943, Ro'eng was ready to set off. His father had prepared a sharp knife for him, following an order given by the Japanese police. The police station had arranged a farewell banquet for the four young men. After the meal, a photograph was taken of the group and their families. After some goodbyes, the men left.

Ro'eng boarded a military truck headed down the east coast to Taitung. On the truck in Taitung he met many soldiers from different Indigenous groups. Men from the Bunun, Puyuma and Paiwan—all in southern Taiwan—communicated in Japanese, and Ro'eng was surprised to find that some of them had actually volunteered to go to war. The troop had pictures taken in Taitung, and the following day they headed for Kaohsiung. While they were waiting to board the ship, they were given guns. Ro'eng felt very different from the other soldiers, since he could not easily join in the discussion on the quality of the firearms. He was overwhelmed. The ship was large, carrying more than five hundred soldiers (Tsai Cheng-liang 2011, 29).

Their first call was Manila. They stayed for three days but were not allowed to leave the ship. Instead, they were put through military drills on deck. They learned about battle infrastructure, how to transfer supply, and how to teach local children to speak Japanese, but they learned nothing about using a gun. Ro'eng thought maybe his role would be to deliver supplies. This prospect made him feel slightly better.

After three days in Manila, they continued south for another five days before arriving in Palau. Here everyone disembarked, and they were taken to a military base where they continued their basic training. At the base they learned how to help build houses and grow food. Ro'eng thought the local population looked similar to those from the Paiwan Indigenous group, and some even reminded him of people from his own Amis community (Tsai Cheng-liang 2011, 30).

Ro'eng stayed in Palau for roughly two months before the group started learning to use their rifles. Following another month of training they were deemed ready. Everyone was called to gather around, and they began to sing "The Honorable Soldier." Following this, they all sang "The Song of the Taiwanese Soldiers":

> The southern cross is shining in the sky of the Pacific
> The waves of the Kuroshio Current break through the equator
> The Taiwanese soldiers guarding the south!
> The well-disciplined Taiwanese soldiers. (Tsai Cheng-liang 2011, 33)

Following their training, the men boarded the boat for what is now Papua New Guinea, their final destination. The New Guinea campaign, as it would later be termed, lasted from January 1942 to the end of the war in August 1945. The first phase of the conflict was the Japanese invasion of the Australian-administered Mandated Territory of New Guinea on 23 January 1942 and then the Australian Territory of Papua on 21 July, finally overrunning western New Guinea (then part of the Dutch East Indies) beginning 29 March 1942. In late 1942, the Allies (mainly Australian and US forces) began clearing the Japanese-held territories, beginning first with the city of Rabaul at the northeastern tip of New Britain Island (Papua), then the Mandate, and finally the Dutch colony. The overall campaign was devastating for the Japanese, as disease and starvation claimed more troops than enemy conflict (Huang Chih-huei 2011, 146–47).

The Indigenous men from Taiwan, upon their arrival in Papua New Guinea, traveled for two days before they reached a white sandy beach known locally as Wewak. It reminded Ro'eng of a beach in southern Du-lan. They landed in small groups and, upon hitting the beach, made a run for the jungle, covering about a kilometer ahead. Ro'eng recalled that as the men looked back at the sea, his feeling of being at war began (Tsai Cheng-liang 2011, 34).

The use of Indigenous communities for the Pacific war effort was not limited to the Japanese Empire. Allied forces throughout in the region recruited Indigenous volunteers. On Papua, Loa Daera, a member of the Hanuabada (the name given to a group of villages on the western side of Port Moresby), learned of the war while working at the press office in Port Moresby. His first thoughts were that the war was between Germany and England and would not involve Papua. However, in June 1940, Loa joined the newly established Papuan Infantry Battalion (PIB), a unit of the Australian Army formed in the territory of Papua. The PIB consisted of Papuan soldiers under the leadership of Australian officers and non-commissioned officers. Although it was evident that literate Papuans, such as Loa, could comprehend the developments of the war, information about the war primarily spread through oral communication. Loa recalls engaging in discussions about the war with his neighbors (Robinson 1981, 100). The evacuation of European women and children toward the end of 1941, on instruction by the Australian Government, indicated to local communities that war could soon descend upon them. For Loa, the air attacks on Port Moresby in February 1942 signaled that war had begun. Loa and the PIB served in several Allied campaigns in New Guinea that included the advance to Salamaua in 1943 before battling their way along the Sepik River—a major link to Wewak—as part of the Finisterre Range campaign, which forced the Japanese to withdraw to Wewak. Ro'eng and the other men formed part of the Japanese effort to resupply.

The Japanese controlled the jungles south of Wewak, but they were beset by humidity, insects, and a shortage of supplies. Many soldiers had already died of malaria and hunger. The Japanese referred to the place as hell on earth, as they attempted in vain to move forward to Port Moresby, which was controlled by the Americans and Australians. The subsequent Aitape-Wewak campaign was one of the final campaigns of the Pacific War, as the Australian Sixth Division began to "mop up" (a phrase coined by the Australians) the Japanese Eighteenth Army in northern New Guinea. Although the operation was deemed successful, the significant number of casualties gave rise to controversy, as it became evident that the Japanese were on the brink of defeat.

This was unbeknownst to Ro'eng, who was given different daily tasks. He helped repair the airport in Wewak and delivered supplies to different bases. Some of the Indigenous soldiers that Ro'eng met on the ship were chosen to be in the special forces, and they were sent to the front line immediately upon arrival. Ro'eng's friend from Dulan was appointed to teach local "cook boys" Japanese. Because Ro'eng could not communicate well with the boys, he knew only that many of them and their families were hiding deep in the mountains to escape the war (Tsai Cheng-liang 2011, 37).

In August 1943, just seven days after Ro'eng arrived in Wewak, the US Fifth Air Force began to bomb the town, and Ro'eng experienced his first air raid. People rushed to the jungle nearby. The bombing did not last long, but walking back to the base was the first time Ro'eng had seen so many dead people. Of the four young men from Dulan, one did not survive this bombing. In total, twenty-six died. The captain commanded them to clip off a piece from the nails of each deceased soldier before burial as a means to ensure that the fallen were properly honored. This practice served as a form of remembrance and facilitated identification of the fallen soldiers, providing a tangible connection to them for memorialization. For the Japanese this was "the Black Day," as their air strength in Papua New Guinea had all but been wiped out (Costello 1982, 420). Following the bombing, Ro'eng and the other men began a retreat toward the west. It was incredibly hard to march through the jungle at night. They marched for five days and made it to the base in Polancia. Ro'eng started to hear occasional gunshots in the jungle. Their supplies were low, and they were given only one meal per day. Ro'eng became very thin (Tsai Cheng-liang 2011, 41).

By February 1944, the monsoon season had begun. Shortly afterward, the captain ordered them to march eastward. Near the end of the volunteering period, there was a chance that Ro'eng could soon go home. He remembers being extremely excited. A day after they started the march, they were trapped by the Americans. They had no choice but to change direction and head uphill through the jungle to the mountains toward the south.

While hiding in the mountains, the shortage of food became a serious problem. Many became extremely weak and died of malaria. Some suggested hunting for food, but this, along with picking up coconuts, was forbidden by the Japanese captain, who worried that the soldiers would desert or attract American attention. Ro'eng remembers that it was torturous to look at the coconuts in front of them. Since he was asked to collect water, he had an opportunity to find food along the way. As the situation worsened, five men were sent out to find food. They came across an old Japanese base that had been taken by the Americans. They sneaked into the kitchen and stole as many cans as they could carry, which turned out to be only butter (Tsai Cheng-liang 2011, 47–48).

When they got back with the butter, they started to worry that the Americans would track them. Their concern was justified. Shortly after they arrived back in camp, five American soldiers appeared. Ro'eng fought back and killed his first man. The other four escaped immediately and came back with more soldiers (Tsai Cheng-liang 2011, 49–50).

By the end of the fight, five people had died on Ro'eng's side. There were two dead Americans as well. After burying their own people, Ro'eng recalls that the soldiers, out of hunger, started to cook the Americans (Tsai Cheng-liang 2011, 50–52). Ro'eng was in shock, and he did not know how to react. He would later recall how similar humans are to pigs in both cooking and taste (Tsai Cheng-liang 2011, 52).

Ro'eng soon lost track of time. He thought they were in the mountains for at least a year. The group had set out with fifty men but had dropped to thirty by the end of the year.

Ro'eng remembers the day they encountered other Japanese. After the initial excitement, he noticed something strange. Sitting with the Japanese were Americans. They were not ordered to fight but were instead informed that Japan had lost the war. Ro'eng and his mates did not know how to feel; they were simply too hungry. They dropped their weapons and left the mountains but had to remain at a holding camp before they could return home (Tsai Cheng-liang 2011, 54–55).

Of all the Pacific theaters of the Second World War, hostilities lasted the longest in Papua New Guinea, and the territory saw the most casualties. Of the 300,000 Japanese who landed in New Guinea and the neighboring Solomons, only 127,000 survived (Firth 1997, 296). More died from disease than from bullets. The Japanese general Hatazō Adachi of the Eighteenth Army would commit ritualized suicide at Rabaul, where it had all begun in 1942.

In December 1945, Ro'eng arrived in Kaohsiung on an American ship, which was met not by Japanese soldiers but by Chinese soldiers. For Ro'eng and many others like him, the war changed not only themselves but also the island they had left only a few years earlier.

The history of Taiwan's Indigenous peoples is wrapped in migration, both the early linguistic and cultural migration that forms part of the Austronesian story and the migration of colonial settlers. It is a history that mirrors the nation's narrative of inbound and outbound migration. These histories define senses of tradition, identity, and values across Taiwan's ethnic spectrum. The interaction of Indigenous peoples with colonial authorities is embedded in their myths, stories, and legends. For those who have settled and colonized the land, their relationship to this "native other" will inform policy and action, whether this is through a process of oppression—or, in some cases, genocide—or via inculturation and assimilation, as was the case for Ro'eng and the Takasago Volunteers.

The forms of colonization experienced by the Indigenous peoples of Taiwan are all modern from their beginning: the expansion of European corporations and missionary organizations, the migration of Chinese settlers from Fujian and Guangdong, the incorporation of the islands into the Qing, and the imperial colonization by the Japanese. All of these were backed by government armies and colonial settlers and sojourners with the purpose of expropriating lands and resources. Key to the survival of these Indigenous communities has been the maintenance and the flexibility of their concepts of tradition.

6

A Miner's Tale

JACK EDWARDS

Down the mine bonnie laddie, down the mine you'll go.
Though your feet are lacerated and you dare not answer no;
Though the rice is insufficient, and we treat you all like swine,
Down the mine bonnie laddie, down the mine.
GUNNER J. M. M. SMITH · 1942

On 7 December 1941, the Empire of Japan launched coordinated attacks from Taiwan and Japan on Pearl Harbor in the Hawaiian Islands. Throughout the war, Taiwan was to play a key role for the Japanese Empire, not only as a base for expanding the Greater East Asia Co-Prosperity Sphere but as a site for imprisoning enemy combatants. POW camps existed throughout the Japanese Empire, some more infamous than others. In Taiwan there were fifteen camps in total, seven of which were considered major, with eight considered minor or temporary holdings. The treatment of prisoners varied. Maurice A. Rooney, a prisoner from the Kinkaseki (Jinguashi) camp, wrote from one of the American vessels that liberated the island that although it was difficult to describe his thoughts and feelings as the island of Taiwan disappeared into the horizon as the ship sailed north, he could compare it to an escape from hell (Rooney 2020). Upon his return to Britain, Maurice developed a fascination with Taiwan, a feeling he did not expect to have. He mentions that the "made in Taiwan" label, famous in the 1970s and 1980s, had an impact that he noted was not shared by others. A *making* that perhaps he himself had felt.

The exact number of prisoners held in Taiwan is still largely unknown. Since prisoners were often moved between camps, records could simply be duplicates, but the approximate figures in table 3 indicate the size and scale of each camp.

With over four thousand POWS, the camps in Taiwan were some of the worst in the Pacific theater of the Second World War. It is estimated that more than 10 percent of those imprisoned on the island died from sickness, starvation, overwork, and systematic abuse. The fourteen camps were spread across the island. Jack Edwards, the protagonist of this tale, was, like Maurice, held first at Kinkaseki in the north of the island, which opened on 14 November 1942 and closed on 30 June 1945.

Other notable camps included the Taichū camp in present-day Taichung, where the Pacific typhoon path blows through the center of Taiwan during the monsoon season. The Tatu River, in the center of the island, south of Taichung, was subject to flooding. The POWS at the Taichū prison camp were forced to excavate a huge diversion channel in the riverbed in order to prevent the bridges across the river from being swept away in the floods (Hurst, 1998). The POWS were required to move large boulders embedded in the river. The excavation had to be done by hand and the rocks carried in bamboo baskets. In June 1944, when the channel flooded, the men were relocated temporarily to a nearby school, and then many were transferred to Heito, where in the summer of 1942 a large group of British Commonwealth POWS had arrived from Singapore.

Prisoners at Heito in Pingtung County were tasked with clearing rocks from a former riverbank to prepare the land for sugar production. Former POWS described the camp's commandant, Lieutenant Tamaki, as "vicious and sadistic." One mentioned that in one of the first of the many daily roll calls in the camp Tamaki told the POWS that he would fill the camp cemetery (Hurst 1998). In addition to clearing the riverbank and working the fields, many POWS were compelled to work at a nearby sugar factory. Because of the climate in Heito, disease was rife, especially malaria, dysentery, and beriberi (thiamine deficiency). Though all major POW camps were provided with shelter and water, toward the end of the war in the Kukutsu and Oka camps, near present-day Taipei, prisoners were forced to build

TABLE 3. Taiwan POW camp locations and prisoner figures

CAMP	LOCATION	POPULATION	DATES	CAMP	LOCATION	POPULATION	DATES
Kinkaseki	Jinguashi	1,127	14/11/1942–30/6/1945	Kukutsu	Taipei	350	16/5/1945–24/8/1945
Taichū	Taichung	700	27/9/1942–7/1/1944	Oka	Taipei	150	12/6/1945–21/8/1945
Heitō	Pingtung	>1,100	2/8/1942–15/3/1945	Toroku	Touliu	300	8/11/1944–11/4/1945
Shirakawa	Bai He	1,200	6/6/1943–26/8/1945	Inrin	Yuanlin	300	1/7/1944–5/3/1945
Taihoku/Moksak	Taipei	32	24/6/1943–22/1/1945	Inrin Temporary	Yuanlin	200	8/11/1944–16/1/1945
Taihoku	Taipei	1,250	14/11/1942–6/9/1945	Takao	Kaohsiung	unknown	7/9/1942–15/2/1945
Karenkō	Hualien	400	17/8/1942–6/6/1943	Churon Evacuation Camp	Taipei	348	25/8/1945–5/9/1945
Tamazato	Yuli	117	2/4/1943–24/6/1943				

Note: Approximate maximum numbers in each camp. Source: Hurst 1998.

their own huts from trees and bamboo (Hurst 1998). In both camps, little food was available in the area, and as a result the prisoners were forced to work on the nearby mountainside digging out the tea bushes and planting sweet potatoes and peanuts. Incidentally, the POWs never at the produce they grew, as the camps were liberated before the crops matured.

The story of Kinkaseki and the captured is presented here through the eyes of prisoner 159, Sergeant Jack Edwards. His story, like Ro'eng's, provides a nuanced understanding of the role Taiwan played in the Second World War and is important in understanding concepts of social identity in the period immediately following the war. Kinkaseki also illustrates the role that mining played in Taiwan's industrial development.

MINING IN TAIWAN

On the northeast coast of Taiwan, close to the port city of Keelung, lies a mine, known to the locals as Jinguashi. Jinguashi and the surrounding area contain deposits of coal, gold, and copper. The discovery of gold in Taiwan has a long history (Yu Bingsheng 2011). In the areas in and around Jinguashi and Jiufen, the search for gold intensified during the Qing period. According to Ji Qiguan, a county governor (*zhixian*) between 1684 and 1685, "gold as big as a fist or as long as a ruler" could be found on the mountain situated at the back of the Sanchao River in Keeling (Cheng Hsi-fu 1977, 35–36). Since mining was forbidden during the Qianlong period, no excavation was done then. However, in 1891, during construction of the railway between Taipei and Keelung, a worker found gold in the Keelung River, triggering a gold rush and paving the way for an onrush of prospectors seeking their fortunes. When news reached the Chinese mainland, many who had returned from the gold rushes of California, the Klondike, and Australia began to migrate to Taiwan (Davidson 2005, 464). They brought with them specific methods that included the use of washing cradles. The prospectors then either built temporary housing along the river or lodged on boats. The close quarters resulted in numerous outbreaks of infectious disease. Following a typhoon in 1892, high rivers swept away many and produced significant loss of life (Davidson 2005, 464). Despite an edict in September 1891 that prohibited all "gold washing," since policing the activity proved difficult for the authorities, licenses were issued at convenient stations spread throughout the region. Licensed workers were given a wooden tag with a government seal and were required to pay a fee every five days that was based on their license classification. In 1893, a group of five wealthy families purchased a monopoly on the license issuance process with the intention of profiting from the sale of licenses. As a result, they controlled the distribution of licenses. The same year, a large deposit was found in Jiufen in northeastern Taiwan. Since the industry was now more profitable, the government took over this lease and established gold offices. Control of gold extraction at Jiufen remained in place until the island was ceded to Japan. For the first couple of years of colonial rule, Japanese authorities made no attempt to control gold extraction, and local prospectors continued as they had done prior to Qing controls.

In December 1896, the Fujita Company became the first Japanese company to engage predominately in copper mining. In 1899, a steam plant was put in place and a tramline erected to move the ore from the mines. In Jinguashi, the mine was owned by the Tanaka Company, established in 1885. As with the Fujita mine, the Tanaka mine housed deposits of coal close to gold deposits, allowing both companies to mine more than one mineral. In 1918, Fujita, in cooperation with Mitsui, invested with Yen Yun-nian, a local of Keelung, to establish the Keelung Coal Mining Company and later the Taiyang Gold Mine Office (Taiyang Kuangye Shiwu Suo; Gold 1988, 111). By the 1930s, Jiufen had developed a reputation as a "Little Hong Kong" due to its get-rich-quick town development. In 1971 Taiyang ceased all operations in Jiufen. Hou Hsiao-hsien's 1989 movie *City of Sadness* was shot largely in the town, fostering almost overnight fame, and the town became a tourist location. Hayao Miyazaki, of the famous Japanese Studio Ghibli, who is a fan of the area, used Jiufen as inspiration for the 2001 anime *Spirited Away*.

Throughout the Japanese colonial period, the Japanese maintained direct control over the mines in Jinguashi. In 1905, silver was discovered and became one of the primary mined commodities alongside copper. By 1930, the town was home to roughly eighty thousand people, and the mine honeycombed with six hundred kilometers of tunnels. During the Second World War, Jinguashi was the largest, and the most profitable, copper mine in the Japanese Empire. Following the Japanese surrender in 1945, the Kuomintang (KMT) took control over the company and transferred it to the

Taiwan Gold and Copper Mining Bureau (Taiwan Jintong Kuangwuju). The bureau was subsequently renamed Taiwan Metal Mining Company (Taiwan Jinshu Kuangye Gongsi) but closed in 1987 after the state-run company went into liquidation.

The importance of copper for the Japanese war effort meant that the mines on Jinguashi were strategic. Efforts were thus quickly made for the mines to accommodate POWs following Japanese successes in Hong Kong, Malaya, and Singapore. Jack Edwards, Prisoner 159, was one such POW sent to work the mines of Jinguashi.

Jack Edwards was born in Cardiff, Wales, on 24 May 1918. Prior to the outbreak of the Second World War, Edwards was part of the local Territorial Army. When Singapore fell in February 1942, he was an army sergeant in the Royal Corps of Signals. Following a short stay at the infamous Changi Prison in Singapore, Edwards was put on board the *English Maru* for Taiwan. After brief stops at Saigon and Kaohsiung, he arrived at the port of Keelung on Saturday, 14 November 1942 (Edwards 1988, 43). He and his fellow prisoners were sprayed with disinfectant on their disembarkation and ordered to march, in lines of six, out of the harbor and into the town square, where they were to assemble. Edwards recalls, "Here, it seemed, the whole population had turned out to see the spectacle of the British prisoners which the all-conquering Imperial Japanese Army had taken at Singapore in their conquest of Malaya. There were huge groups of schoolchildren in uniforms, and hordes of what appeared to be police. Even the townspeople seemed to be dressed in the same sort of uniform clothing, including a peaked cap" (Edwards 1988, 43).

Tang Yu, an elementary student from Jinguashi who was present at that time, remembers their teacher announcing that the "Western prisoners" would arrive and that they were permitted to witness it. The teacher sternly reminded them that they were to remain quiet as their behavior reflected on their nation. Shortly after 2 p.m., the children witnessed the prisoners' arrival (Tang Yu 2005). Edwards recalls being greeted not quietly, as their teacher had wished, but "by the noise of children's voices in excitement and derision" (Edwards 1988, 45). As the men, wearing only shorts and military boots, marched, Tang remembers that most of them had green eyes and long red hair on their arms. He also recalls that some were carried on stretchers. Their camp would be referred to locally as "the hut for the tall nose" (Zhuobizailiao / TH. Tok-phīnn-á-liâu; Tang Yu 2005).

The camp's official name was Kinkaseki. There, with 525 other inmates, Edwards would work the mine for copper. On arrival the prisoners were ordered to strip, their boots and shorts removed, and were given threadbare Japanese uniforms and *geta* footwear. Edwards recounts that walking in these wooden platforms with straps was especially difficult. At 2 a.m. the following morning, the men were led into their huts after being given two thin army blankets each.

Prior to the arrival of the POWs, locals had called the camp "the hut for the Wenzhou people" (Wenzhouliao / TH. Un-tsiu-liâu) since the camp was occupied by Chinese laborers from Wenzhou who arrived in 1933. As Japanese-Chinese relations began to deteriorate toward the end of the 1930s, it became more difficult for the Japanese colonial authorities to hire Chinese labor. The camps were modified prior to the arrival of the POWs. The most significant change was the erection of high walls, beyond which locals were not permitted to pass. Yet, from the surrounding hills, the local population could see into the camp and watch the prisoners (Tang Yu 2005, 18).

The Monday following the prisoners' arrival, they began work in the mines. Each prisoner was given a wooden lunch box and a light. Toward the end of the war, this light was shared between three or four people. Each morning, the prisoners walked up the two hundred steps to the cable car (*changrenkeng chedao*) and then down the 1,186 steps into the mine (Titherington 1993, 88–89). The "incline," as it was colloquially known, was 170 meters long, with a train going in each direction. This train was regularly used, for free, by the local population but was forbidden to the prisoners. That walk was known locally as "Tall Nose Road" (Zhuobizailu / TH. Tok-phīnn-á-lōo). According to Arthur Titherington, another prisoner held at Kinkaseki, the camp was not configured like other POW camps. There was no barbed wire and no high watchtowers with searchlights and patrolling dogs (Titherington 1993, 74). They were on an island, and escape was not

A MINER'S TALE   77

possible. Furthermore, they could not easily identify any local sympathizers. Without known resistance movements, it was out of the question for escapees to find safe houses.

Supervision of the prisoners was constant. At the mine, there were four levels of management. The highest levels were purely Japanese, with some Taiwanese in lower-level management. Among the Taiwanese miners, top management was referred to as *sijiaozai* (TH. *Sì-kha-á*), or four-legged management, a reference to animal rather than human behavior. Lower-level positions were known as *sanjiaozai* (TH. *Sann-kha-á*; three-legged)—not-quite animal and not-quite human (Tang Yu 2005, 27). The prisoners called these men "runabouts," summing up "their purpose in the service of their masters" (Titherington 1993, 76; Edwards 1988, 48). One such official, Xuchun, was notorious for his violent behavior. Tang Yu writes that after the war, some former prisoners returned to Taiwan in search of Xu. Upon learning of his death, they destroyed the ancestral tablet in his home and vandalized his gravestone by shooting at it (Tang Yu 2005, 27–29). Afterward, several former guards became terrified. On occasion, prisoners did come into contact with Taiwanese guards who were more sympathetic. Tang mentions two guards who shared cigarettes and pickled plums with the prisoners. Some Taiwanese miners recount that the prisoners were often given bamboo shoots in autumn as part of their daily lunch boxes. According to Tang, since the prisoners did not know how to eat this, they often threw away the core (a local delicacy). Children collected the discarded parts to bring home for dinner (Tang Yu 2005, 30).

Arthur Titherington, a former POW in Taiwan, recalls that work in the mine was not dissimilar to Dante's *Inferno* (Titherington 1993, 125), as it consisted of a web of underground cave pits, tunnels, and crevices. The darkness crept all around, illuminated only by the carbide lamps given to the prisoners. The only respite was that prisoners could sing without consequence there. Daily quotas for the copper mining increased throughout the war. This became difficult to achieve as the prisoners became weaker. Toward the end of 1944, trips to the mine were made slightly easier by a new tunnel entrance that led directly from the camp.

Jack Edwards and Arthur Titherington were among the POWs to be transferred to Kukutsu on 1 June 1945. There they were tasked with constructing a camp on an abandoned tea plantation. On 28 August 1945, the

US Army Air Forces began to drop food supplies, Edwards was liberated on 5 September by the US Marine Corps. He was subsequently transferred back to Britain, where he spent a year. In 1946, he returned to Asia to assist as a witness in the International Military Tribunal for the Far East, giving evidence and testimony to the war crimes investigation team in Hong Kong. When visiting Kinkaseki, Edwards located Document No. 2701, which ordered the Japanese to massacre all prisoners if Allied troops landed on the Japanese home islands—including Taiwan. This sole surviving copy provided important evidence for the tribunal.

Back in Britain, Edwards worked for the local government. At first, he felt unable to discuss the horrors of the war, but after forty-five years of writing, his book *Banzai you Bastards* was published by Corporate Communications in Hong Kong in 1988. In 1963, he moved to Hong Kong, where he took up a post as a housing officer for the Hong Kong administration. He later became housing manager for Hongkong Land, a property investment group. In Hong Kong, Edwards was actively involved in the Ex-Servicemen's Association as well as the British Legion, where he served as chairman.

Following the Tiananmen Massacre in 1989, Edwards assisted the people of Hong Kong with British Dependent Territories Citizenship to fight for recognition as British citizens. In his capacity as chair of the British Legion, Edwards succeeded in 1991 in winning a monthly pension for ethnic Chinese veterans and their widows. In 1996, he won the campaign for widows of these veterans to be granted British citizenship.

At the request of Princess Diana, Edwards was asked to locate the grave of Major-General Merton Beckwith-Smith, the father of Diana's lady-in-waiting, who had died of diphtheria at Karenko Camp in Taiwan. Jack Edwards died on 13 August 2006, at eighty-eight.

The complexity of Taiwan's wartime history underlines a layering of colonization and competing geostrategic interests that has enveloped the island and its past. The history of prisoners-of-war in Taiwan was suppressed in the postwar era by the Chinese Nationalists. Chiang Kai-shek cast himself, Franklin Roosevelt, Winston Churchill, and Josef Stalin as allied leaders. He had participated as one of the "big four" delegates in the Moscow and Tehran conferences in 1943 and the subsequent Dumbarton Oaks Conference held in Washington, DC, in 1944, which set the

United Nations' structure and the composition of the UN Security Council. Chiang's Republic of China was to become a permanent member of the Security Council when the UN came into existence on 24 October 1945. Following Chiang's defeat on the Chinese mainland by the Communists, the Chinese Nationalist government attempted to erase Taiwan's role in the Japanese war effort, including the American bombing of the island as well as the housing of POWs. This historical silence continues to obscure large parts of Taiwan's war history.

7

A Child's Tale

CHEN PI-KUEI

After a few minutes Jim was forced to admit
that he could recognize none of the constellations.
Like everything else since the war, the sky was in a state
of change. For all their movements, the Japanese aircraft
were its only fixed points, a second zodiac
above the broken land.

J. G. BALLARD · 1984

The Second World War had a massive effect on children. In the United Kingdom almost two million were evacuated from major towns and cities, and all had to endure the consequences of rationing, gas masks, and for those who had to move, life passed with strangers. The child death toll in London during the Blitz was one in ten. In the United States, more than sixty thousand Japanese American children were interned. Some estimates state that 1.5 million children, nearly all Jewish, were murdered as a result of the Holocaust. Jack Edwards's tale in the previous chapter reinforces a common understanding that interned POWs were soldiers. Yet in Japanese-occupied areas, thousands of European children spent up to three years as prisoners of war. This history is highlighted in J. G. Ballard's semi-autobiographical novel, *Empire of the Sun* (later made into a film), in which Jamie Graham, a British upper-middle-class schoolboy, is imprisoned at the Suzhou Internment Camp in China. For children, life in internment camps was more than just a matter of surviving. It was also about adjusting to great change and staving off boredom (Wilkinson 2014, 5–6).

A 2005 UNICEF report focuses on this relationship between military conflict and children, starting from the premise that childhood should be "free from fear, safe from violence, [and] protected from abuse and exploitation" (UNICEF 2005, 1). The Second World War challenged the concept of childhood. In many ways, the protagonists of the following tale were children deprived of a proper childhood. Yet, while the impact of war on the relationship between children and childhood appears evident, it can still be challenging to quantify. In many instances, war simply worsened existing issues, such as poverty, discrimination, and unequal resource distribution, all of which robbed children of their rightful childhood.

Children born in Japan in the late nineteenth century were referred to as "new age Japanese children" and were seen as instrumental to the future of the Japanese Empire. Japanese colonial authorities saw a similar role for Taiwanese children. In 1898, the government announced the Taiwan Public School Decree, which made children between eight and fourteen eligible to enroll in public schools, initiating the primary school system in Taiwan. In 1919, the Taiwan Education Decree cemented this as a complete education system. It provided an opportunity for colonial authorities on Taiwan to articulate a vision of social order and the future of Taiwan-Japanese subjects, socializing young people into the service of the nation. Yet, in spite of numerous efforts, primary school education in Taiwan was not compulsory, and by 1940 only around 53 percent of children attended school.

Like elsewhere, education for children needed to be arranged around agricultural calendars, as families required their children's labor in picking fruit and farming the land in the summer months and assisting in the home in the late afternoon and early evening. The 1919 Education Rescript produced by Governor-General Akashi Motojirō stated that "the basic principle of education is to cultivate loyal citizens" (Dawley 2019, 89). Key to this was learning Japanese. Debates over education edicts centered on questions of uniqueness and superiority and whether opening previously Japanese-only primary schools (J. *shōgakkō*) to island children undermined this. Both Japanese officials and settlers supported the common school (J. *kōgakkō*) as a place for island children and underlined the need to learn

Japanese language, history, and manners, but they resisted a shared common education (Dawley 2019, 89).

The year 1919 was pivotal in the education and assimilation movements as a result of the arrival of Governor-General Den Kenjirō. Den was the first civilian to hold that position. As governor-general, Den promoted new policies for fostering social and political assimilation, repealing discriminatory laws in education. His tenure saw significant reforms in various administrative systems, including an expansion of the education system and legalization of Japanese-Taiwanese intermarriage. His stated goals were to eventually give the same rights to Taiwan islanders as the Japanese main islands had. In 1936, Kobayashi Seizō, a former admiral in the Imperial Japanese Navy, became the seventeenth governor-general and the first non-civilian one since Den. Kobayashi's principal policy was "Japanization" of the island. He believed that colonial status should be abolished in favor of removing distinctions between Taiwanese and Japanese, thus incorporating Taiwan as one of the home islands. In 1937, Kobayashi implemented a ban on all Chinese-language media in schools. The policy, termed *kōminka*, sought to transform *conquered people* into *subjects* of empire. The authorities encouraged school attendance, yet many children in Taiwan continued to work to support their families (Liu Yen-Chi 2016, 83–157). Forcing the Taiwanese to become Japanese deprived them of a sense of selfhood. As Taiwan shifted from colonial status to being a more integral part of the "home islands" (though not quite Japanese), Kobayashi oversaw the beginning of the Greater East Asia Co-Prosperity Sphere.

The capacity of future generations to revisit their childhood years and effectively process the anxieties of that time period, which they may have struggled with during adolescence, is a factor of historical transformation deserving further examination. Thus, comprehending the history of childhood in Taiwan during the Japanese colonial era contributes to a better understanding of the postwar distress that greeted the arrival of the Chinese Nationalists.

This tale concerns the complex identity of wartime *shōnenkō*, child laborers, who moved to Japan to assist in manufacturing military aircraft. Following Emperor Hirohito's radio announcement of defeat at the end of the Pacific War, the children in the factory were forced to see themselves no longer as Japanese but as Chinese.

At fifteen, Chen Pi-Kuei, after graduating from Sui-Rin Grade School, close to Beigang in Yunlin County, volunteered to join the *shōnenkō* program. His teacher informed him that he would be given a vocational diploma after interning for five years. He recounts that he found the opportunity too good to miss, and he was keen to leave the small rural village where he had grown up. His father had been clear that only one of the two boys in his family could go on to further education due to financial concerns. Although Chen was a better student than his younger brother, he wanted his brother to have the opportunity to further his education and decided that joining the *shōnenkō* program was an opportunity for both he and his brother to achieve a broader education. Chen recalls stealing his father's stamp and submitting the consent form without the approval of his parents (Chen Pi-Kuei 1998, 58–65).

Chen arrived in Gangshan in Kaohsiung for his initial training in July 1943. Since he had been the class leader at his elementary school, he was assigned to be team leader for the group. Chen recalls that although he felt very independent, this was his first time away from his parents, and he missed them greatly. On the final week of the two-month training, when his father came to see him in Kaohsiung, he realized that his decision greatly concerned his family but he could not turn back. The fact that Chen discusses turning back is quite revealing. This was apparently the moment when he began to have regrets, which grew after his arrival in Japan. He recalls that his first surprise was the condition of the dormitory. Seeing the poor quality of the room and the standardized work clothes instead of formal school uniforms, Chen began to understand that his role in the factory was that of a laborer and that he would have no chance of completing a training program. He felt cheated (Chen Pi-Kuei 1998, 69–72). To increase production, factory management reduced school time and extended working hours.

Between 1942 and 1945, more than 8,400 youths from twelve to nineteen were recruited as *shōnenkō*. Most saw this voluntary action as a patriotic duty (Jonas Chang 2001, 1). For Taiwan, unlike Korea, the basic infrastructure to implement nationalization in elementary schools was established relatively soon despite slow progress in transforming social values and ways of life (Chatani 2018, 129).

Following a series of successes for the Japanese military after the bombing of Pearl Harbor, the Japanese colonial government heightened its fanning of nationalistic sentiment among the "new age children," particularly in rural areas (Chatani 2018, 145). However, the Battle of Midway of 4–7 June 1942 was a decisive defeat for the Japanese, though this was never fully disclosed to the Japanese public. Among its casualties were four Japanese fleet carriers and 3,057 Japanese, among them difficult-to-replace, highly skilled aircraft maintenance personnel.

Hideo Sawai, a captain in the Japanese Navy, proposed creating the Navy's C Aircraft Factory (called Koza after 1 April 1944). An aviation technocrat under General Yamamoto Isoroku, Sawai was appointed the factory's first head. In May 1943, Sawai began asking school principals and teachers in Taiwan to start recruiting boys between thirteen and sixteen to volunteer in the factory (Henry Tsai 2009b, 166). Having laid the groundwork for the single-location manufacturing plant, Sawai, after his retirement, passed on the responsibility of completing the factory complex in Kanagawa (a coastal prefecture just south of Tokyo) to Captain Ikichi Honda. Negotiations between the Naval Ministry and the Government House of Taiwan began almost immediately. They set a three-thousand-person quota for 1943, and five thousand for each year thereafter. In 1942, a quota was established for students: "Two hundred from the graduating classes of high schools, comprised of 100 from *Taihoku* (northern), 25 from *Taichū* (central), 60 from *Tainan* (southern), 15 from *Takao* (southernmost) areas. For grade school graduates, the quota of 2,800 consisted of 600 from northern, 400 from *Shinchiku* (mid-northern), 650 from central, 650 from southern, and 500 from southernmost areas" (Jonas Chang 2001, 8). The letter of recruitment speculated, "In comparison to those living in the Main Islands, more mothers of the Taiwanese are attached to their children and hate to let their child leave. . . . In order to prevent nervous breakdowns from homesickness, it is most important to convince the parents, especially the mother, that there is nothing to worry about" (8).

A total of 8,419 boys, with an average age of fourteen, were brought to

Japan. There they trained for three months. The boys were informed that their work manufacturing aircraft would result in engineering degrees after three years of work. With the assistance of Japanese aeronautical engineers, *shōnenkō* assembled planes such as the infamous Zero and Moonlight fighter planes that were used to attack the American B-29 Superfortress Bombers (Henry Tsai 2009b, 166). Twenty-one percent (128 in total) of the Mitsubishi J2M Raidens, the "Lightning Bolt," were built by Taiwanese children (Chen Po-Tsung n.d.).

Starting in April 1943, the boys left via Kaohsiung and Keelung for Kanagawa. Once at the factory complex, they began their three-month orientation. The youth were instructed in strict martial modes of physical training and spiritual cultivation in *dōjō*-like settings that included intensive skill-based training such as hammer work and metal cutting (Ambaras 2004, 33). In *Confessions of a Mask*, the Japanese novelist Mishima Yukio, who was a librarian at the naval base, recalled interacting with the children: "These young little devils were my best friends. They taught me some Taiwanese and in return I told them stories." He recounts that "they were naughty and always ate a lot" (Mishima 2016, 71). Both the accounts of *shōnenkō* themselves and that of Mishima indicate that there was no visible discrimination. However, this was not necessarily the case for interned Korean teenagers. Yang Nan-chun, a student in the *shōnenkō* program who went to Kanagawa County to build Zero fighters, recalled seeing Korean teenagers at the factory. When the Japanese military ordered the factories to be moved into a cave, the task of digging it out was relegated to Koreans (Hsu Ju Lin 2017, 28–40). As for Japanese youth, the authorities conscripted thousands of elementary and middle-school graduates to replace the conscripted adult workers in munition factories. By 1943, between 50 and 80 percent of these industrial workers (J. *sangyō*) were young people (J. *seishōnen*; Ambaras 2004, 31). As this practice gained prominence, reports emerged of police conducting sweeps in metropolitan centers like Tokyo and Osaka, apprehending youths suspected of engaging in criminal or perceived immoral behavior (Ambaras 2004, 37).

Following the surrender of Japan, all Japanese military personnel were discharged. All official documents were ordered destroyed, and servicemen rushed home before occupying forces arrived on the main islands. The *shōnenkō* were left to their own devices. No effort was made to repatriate them. The dormitories at Koza following the surrender had approximately eight thousand inhabitants. Koza was for all intents and purposes a Goldingian juvenile colony—a true *Lord of the Flies*. According to Jonas Chang (2001, 17), almost immediately, there were around twenty high school graduates and individuals over the age of twenty-one. They quickly organized "the Taiwan Provincial Self-Governing Body of Koza" with the goal of repatriating laborers to their respective places of origin. The efforts of the Japanese elite "to provide young workers with a sense of the significance of their work [and] cultivate their desire for self-improvement" had clearly begun to rub off in spite of the lamentations of some observers in Japan that wartime conditions had made young male industrial workers rough and violent (Ambaras 2004, 32, 37).

Following the arrival of the Allied Occupied Forces, repatriation began in January 1946. However, because mines surrounding the port of Maizuru needed to be removed, this was put on hold, and the children were returned to their dormitories. Finally, on 26 January, the *Hikawa Maru* left Japan bound for Keelung. Following an outbreak of smallpox on board, the ship made a weeklong stop in Kyushu, then arrived at Keelung, where it was held in quarantine for nine days. On 25 February 1946 the former *shōnenkō* were permitted to leave (Ambaras 2004, 24). The youth had arrived home.

The former *shōnenkō* became intricately entwined with the war, and as a result, nation-building efforts encompassing a Taiwanese identity also evolved. The war's impact on the youth shaped their responses to new challenges, as it had armed them for Japan's mobilization machine but had not prepared them for the political upheaval that followed the war (Chatani 2018, 25).

In 1941, the governor-general of Taiwan and the High Command of the Armed Forces in Taiwan issued a joint statement that the Taiwan Army Volunteer System would be implemented the following year. In the first round of recruitment, more than 420,000 people applied, but only one thousand were accepted. It is evident that the volunteer system, like the *shōnenkō*, was not forced. After six months of training, enrollees joined their military units. The second round of recruitment included a naval volunteer system. During the war, Taiwan, like the Japanese home islands, had universal conscription, with all eligible men serving as soldiers. A total of 207,183 Taiwanese "volunteered" for the Japanese Empire, with 80,433 serving as regular soldiers and 126,750 as auxiliaries. The total number of deaths was 30,304 (Tsai Hui-yu 1996, 174).

By late 1944, the US Air Force had begun systematic bombing of Taiwan. The bombing raids over Taipei, in particular, are not regularly taught in schools and have only recently begun to be fully researched (Hung 2015). The wartime period in Taiwan has been overlooked because the Republic of China was an Allied Power in the Second World War, and after losing the Chinese Civil War it was dependent on assistance from the United States.

The shifts in allegiance were necessary in nurturing national identity in the postwar period. The education system needed Taiwan's population to identify as Chinese. Chinese people had fought against the Japanese, so why, they wondered, would the United States bomb Taiwan? Following the Japanese surrender, the Republic of China's need to reeducate and recolonize the island was almost immediate.

On 14 August 1945, Emperor Hirohito accepted the Potsdam Declaration and announced the Japanese surrender via radio. The *shōnenkō* boys listened attentively to the last passage of the speech: "Let the entire nation continue as one family from generation to generation, ever firm in its faith of the imperishableness of its divine land, and mindful of its heavy burden of responsibilities, and the long road before it. Unite your total strength to be devoted to the construction for the future. Cultivate the ways of rectitude, nobility of spirit, and work with resolution so that you may enhance the innate glory of the Imperial State and keep pace with the progress of the world" (Hirohito [1945] n.d.). The boys' most immediate reaction was to wonder how and when they would return home. They did not consider that this return would be no longer as subjects of Japan but instead as citizens of the Republic of China, a nation founded in 1911 when Taiwan was still part of the Japanese colonial project. Within a few days, they began to notice the flag of the Republic of China on the walls of the dormitory and on the copies of Sun Yat-sen's *Three Principles of the People* that were distributed among them. Almost immediately, *shōnenkō* were taught to see themselves as Chinese. Oral histories from the boys suggest that their feelings were neither happy nor unhappy. They simply longed to go home. Yet home, for the moment, belonged to the newly formed United Nations, with their fate yet to be decided.

The effects of colonialism in the sociocultural sense of the word had profound effects on the Taiwanese psyche, especially for those brought up in the colonial education system. The *shōnenkō*'s navigation of identity fits the model proposed by political philosopher Frantz Fanon in *Black Skin, White Masks* in that the boys resisted any objectification of themselves produced by the colonizer (Fanon 1952). The intersection of nationalism and community has meant that no *shōnenkō* account alludes to any Japanese home island children working in the factories, nor do their accounts question why this was not the case. This is despite the evidence that many Japanese youth did work in such industries (Ambaras 2004, 31–61). For the *shōnenkō*, the "uneven and unequal consequences of colonization," in the words of Homi Bhabha, meant that they thought not according to ideas of nation or statehood but rather according to a shared community of young Japanese-speaking boys working in an aircraft factory (Bhabha 1994, 245). For the boys at Koza, the end of the war was a reminder of their own enigma. A Taiwanese nation did not exist. They did not know that Taiwanese consciousness had been awakening both before and during their time at Koza. Their existence was disconnected from this awakening. In the immediate aftermath of the Japanese surrender, the Taiwanese conceptualized a radical consciousness that insisted on a complexity and variety of identity formation that defied a final and complete endorsement of being "Japanese," "Chinese," or "Taiwanese" (Ching 2001, 209). For many in Taiwan, the years that followed the Japanese surrender would usher in a period of start-again nationalism in which a Taiwanese consciousness would begin as a new layer of colonization enveloped the island.

For the Taiwanese "new age Japanese children," this ushered in the "silence." The colonization of Taiwan ceased in 1945, and they would no longer to refer to themselves as Japanese. The period immediately following the Japanese surrender witnessed people, out of necessity and in the transition of nationhood, engage in a time of silence—"the silence of peace, the silence of shame, the silence of victim and the silence of the guilty" (Marchand 2010, 165). As both children and adults started to make sense of their new emerging identities, seeds of discord took root, as animosity toward their new "colonial" layer emerged. This discord would come to a head on 28 February 1947.

WHITE TERROR

1945–1987

8

A Diplomat's Tale

GEORGE H. KERR

The "smallness" of Formosa and the lack of experienced
leadership are sometimes cited to belittle Formosan
appeals for autonomy. Formosans answer that the
American rebellion took place when the colonies
had a population of less than four million.

GEORGE H. KERR · 1966

When Emperor Hirohito announced his surrender, he appealed to his
subjects to bear the unbearable; they must be dutiful and accept defeat, be
loyal and obey and cooperate with the Allied forces. The feelings of those
in Taiwan were mixed. Some Taiwanese met the news with excitement and
joyous anticipation, as a return of some sorts to an imagined "motherland"
(Chen Tsui-lien 2016, 201). The Japanese in Taiwan listened attentively,
filled with both awe and regret. Across the various ethnic groups, the news
was largely met with profound relief. Higher up, however, military officials
responded with anger and bitterness (Kerr 1966, 61). Despite the regular
US bombing of Taiwan, they were in disbelief that they had lost. What is
more, two days later the emperor offered an emendation. Taiwan had not
surrendered to China, but to Chongqing—the wartime capital—where
both Chinese Nationalists and Americans had military headquarters. This
adjustment was significant, particularly because it introduced a sense of
dark ambiguity—a state of unsettled obscurity and uncertainty—that

persists in Taiwan to the present day. Some 5.5 million Taiwanese, at the time, believed that their liberation was a product not of the Chinese Nationalists but of the Western Allies (Henry Tsai 2009b, 174).

In Taipei, the news of surrender was followed by intense debate, as the Taipei government considered its options. Some Japanese felt that the emperor's speech could not have been genuine; it must have been given under some form of duress. The emperor would expect his subjects to continue fighting. Others, such as General Andō Rikichi, the commander-in-chief of military forces and head of civil administration, insisted that they capitulate. Andō Rikichi was put under the command of General Okumura Yasuji, the supreme commander of Japanese forces in China. According to George H. Kerr, a US diplomat during the Second World War, this was the "first formal indication that Formosa must look thereafter toward mainland China for authority" (Kerr 1966, 62).

As the feeling of profound insecurity spread, the phrase *guangfu,* or "retrocession," began to be widely used to describe the postwar state of affairs, referring to the end of Japanese rule and the so-called return to China. This concept started to take shape on 5 October 1945, with the formation of the American Liaison Group, and was formally recognized as a public holiday on October 25. The American Liaison Group, which included more than one hundred staffers from Lieutenant-General Albert C. Wedemeyer's headquarters, utilized American ships and airplanes to begin transporting thousands of Nationalist soldiers and KMT officials, along with their families, to Taiwan (Henry Tsai 2009b, 174). As representatives of the Japanese military and the Chinese representing the Allies met on 25 October, the concept of retrocession would take form and solidify how Taiwan was to be governed. After half a century of Japanese colonial rule, Taiwan would now be governed by the Chinese Nationalists.

Although Taiwanese families began to study Mandarin, the new national language of the KMT, and become acquainted with specifically "Chinese" customs—enthusiasm for learning Mandarin was widespread after October 1945 (see Phillips 2003, 43; Hsiau 2000, 55). However, the lack of knowledge among Taiwanese regarding their new governing authority revealed a distinct cognitive divide. This was further exacerbated by the *kōminka* movement over the previous eight years, which had been instrumental in the Japanese war effort. It was hard for many to understand terms such War of Resistance against Japanese Aggression (Zhongguo Kangri Zhanzheng). This began the period of "silence" as many Taiwanese experienced the feeling of enmity that Chinese people—in particular, the arriving soldiers and their new government—bore toward the Japanese. This identity crisis ensured that the people of Taiwan would struggle in how they saw themselves. In spite of their colonial education, the language they had learned, and the governance they had experienced, they were not Japanese. The Japanese were leaving the island without them. Many experienced difficulty in recognizing a similarity with the arriving Chinese, whose national consciousness had been born in revolution in 1911 with the overthrow of the Manchu dynasty. Although neither Japanese nor Chinese, many turned out at Songshan Airport to welcome the newly appointed chief executive of Taiwan Province, Chen Yi, on his arrival on 24 October 1945, not unlike how many had greeted the arriving troops at Keelung and Kaohsiung. Retrocession was raising Taiwanese expectations that this would be an opportunity to obtain political influence (Phillips 2003, 10). On 25 November 1945, when the Sixty-Second Army arrived in Kaohsiung, the Taiwanese had prepared food, firecrackers, flags, and signs to welcome the soldiers. They observed the orderly and smartly dressed Japanese lining up to board another vessel. When the Chinese soldiers began to disembark, many Taiwanese felt that they were not in fact soldiers. There was no order. Some soldiers were carrying shoulder poles, umbrellas, and kitchen utensils. Some wore shoes, and some went without, each man climbing over the next to quickly exit the ship. Observing this, Peng Ching-kao, Peng Ming-min's father, later told his family, "If there were a hole on the ground, I would have buried myself with shame" (Lung 2009, 186). By 1946 an increasingly restive elite openly criticized the Chinese Nationalist state as inept and corrupt (Phillips 2003, 10).

The oddness of the arriving troops and contrasting tales of the gallantry of the Nationalist Army began to sow the seeds of doubt among many Taiwanese. For some, it was evident that the "victors" were arriving only because the American military had intervened and stood between them and the Japanese (Kerr 1966, 74). Taiwanese distaste for the arriving soldiers began to interfere with acceptance of their supposed shared heritage. One of the informants for Lung Ying-tai's *Big River, Big Sea* (Dajiang dahai), a collection of stories about the Nationalist retreat to Taiwan, was Lin

Ching-wu, a veteran of the Seventieth Army who spoke of his experience crossing the Taiwan Strait. For him there was a clear divide between the Chinese and American troops. He recalls the Americans being friendly, frequently offering him coffee. Upon his arrival the Chinese soldiers were in poor shape, with many still dizzy from the crossing. He saw piles of snow-white salt, or at least that is what he and his fellow soldiers thought it was. Some people reached out their hands to have a taste and found that it was sugar. The group leader subsequently took a large bowl of the sugar for everyone to have "a taste of Taiwan" (Lung 2009, 181). Meanwhile, Lin saw many Japanese at the harbor as they prepared for their departure. This infuriated him and his fellow soldiers as they remembered the past eight years of war. He recalled hearing two of his fellow soldiers raping a Japanese woman that night on the pier. Stories such as this were not limited to the Chinese troops and quickly spread among the Taiwanese. For them, the Seventieth Army looked like beggars. They wore grass shoes and carried paper umbrellas on their backs. Lin Ching-wu did not disagree: "We indeed looked like beggars. I had so many lice in my hair and clothes when I landed in Keelung! Of course we looked like beggars. You need to remember, the eight years before we reached Keelung, we were in constant battle. We traveled for hundreds of kilometers in grass shoes before we got on that American ship" (Lung 2009, 182–83).

For many Taiwanese, the soldiers lacked decorum and discipline. However, their biggest disdain was directed at the corruption of the new provincial government. As prices of local goods began to skyrocket as the exchange rate between Taiwan and mainland China was manipulated, the local economy started to collapse. The Taiwanese would look upon the departing Japanese with a sense of loss. All fixed assets belonging to the Japanese were confiscated, and each person was only allowed to take luggage weighing less than thirty kilograms. All military documents, gold and jewelry, and cash over one thousand yen were contraband (Ou 2010). Many of the departing were Taiwan-born Japanese. The sense of attachment was mutual between the Japanese and Taiwanese.

On 1 April 1946 the last Japanese soldier left Taiwan. On 25 December 1945 the repatriation of 310,000 Japanese, including children, began in earnest. By the beginning of May 1946, the American Liaison Group had gone, but a small consulate headed by Ralph Blake had opened in Taipei.

Blake, who was largely indifferent to the happenings on the island, left most of the correspondence to his vice-consul, George H. Kerr. Kerr would be key in documenting events leading up to and following the 228 Incident and how Taiwan had been betrayed.

George H. Kerr, born on 7 November 1911 in Pennsylvania, served as an American diplomat throughout the Second World War. From 1935 to 1937, he pursued studies in Japan. Upon finishing his studies, he relocated to Taipei to teach English and stayed there until 1940, when all foreigners were expelled from the island. During the war, Kerr worked as a Taiwan expert for the US Navy and a lieutenant in the US Naval Reserve. From 1942 to 1943, he was appointed an analyst and consultant on Taiwan for the US Department of War, and from 1944 to 1946 he was director of the Formosa Research Unit at Columbia University. Kerr returned to Taiwan in October 1945 as a naval attaché, arriving at Songshan Airport with Chen Yi as part of the American Liaison Group.

The concept of a joint Sino-American occupation of Taiwan did not sit well with many in the upper echelons of the KMT. Kerr was of the opinion that the Chinese Nationalists were purposely trying to undermine the American presence to save face as they confronted the now clear discontent of the Taiwanese. To many in Taiwan, it seemed that the Chinese Nationalists were dependent on the United States. They arrived on American ships and aircraft, and American weapons ultimately enabled them to stay (Kerr 1966, 76). In many ways, Japan's colonization of Taiwan did not end in 1945, as Taiwanese people relied on the collective memory of Japanese rule to shape an understanding of the Chinese Nationalist takeover of the island (Phillips 2003). The KMT imposed stricter controls over the island as a result of observing the dependence of the central government on the United States. The perceived Taiwanese association with Japan, coupled with the KMT's growing understanding of the United States and its involvement in defeating Japan in the Pacific, led the KMT to harbor suspicions, particularly toward the Taiwanese elite. This attitude would sharpen hostility and stigmatization of the people of Taiwan.

The loss of face in the presence of the Americans was clear. Kerr argues that few Taiwanese accepted the KMT's style of nationalism. Those who did were persuaded by the presentations given by Soong May-ling, Generalissimo Chiang Kai-shek, and the public relations agents of the KMT. The same was true for much of the American public, which heard similar narratives (Phillips 2003, 64). Yet swathes of the Taiwanese population believed in Wilsonian ideals of self-determination (Kerr 1974, 219). They reflected on how these ideals were transforming the Philippines and Korea, and many wanted something similar. George H. Kerr was of a similar mind and advocated that Taiwan should have autonomy—but under American or United Nations guidance.

Kerr was frank with his views. His thoughts on Taiwan are clearest in his two published monographs, *Formosa Betrayed* (1966) and *Formosa: Licensed Revolution and the Home Rule Movement, 1895–1945* (1974), in which he highlights the growing non-Chinese national consciousness among the Taiwanese population. Moreover, he argues that the seeds of self-governance were sown in the colonial period but blossomed upon the arrival of the Chinese Nationalists. *Formosa Betrayed* emphasizes the events from 1945 to 1947. Although championing the Taiwanese cause by stressing how people on the island were treated by the Chinese Nationalists, his main aim is to condemn US secretary of state John Foster Dulles's policy of tying the United States to the Chinese Nationalists.

For the Taiwanese, the American presence aided in the othering they felt toward the arriving Chinese. Perhaps born of years of anti-American propaganda used by the Japanese during the war, this dislike was further exacerbated by linguistic problems. Many Taiwanese were keen to learn Mandarin, but the early enthusiasm dampened as many suffered from stigmatization and accusations of collaboration with the Japanese (Hsiau 2000, 55). The turning point in defining boundaries of identity is to be found in the events of February 1947. The events before and after February 1947 contributed to a consolidation of identity that separated those who had experienced the Japanese colonial period (*benshengren*, original Taiwanese, or those who had settled on the island prior to the Japanese colonization) from those who came to Taiwan in the postwar period (*waishengren*, mainlanders, literally "people from outside"). The pursuit of self-determination garnered an act of definition: a nativization of identity and the writing of a national history. Key to this was the process of filling the gaps. Writers such as Kerr began to prescribe an identity for the Taiwanese—or Formosans, as he described them—that was presented as something that is normal, self-evident, and most importantly, simple common sense: the people of Taiwan have a Taiwanese identity. Yet the homogenizing of identity on the island became reductive. The backdrop of the 228 Incident is a testament to their differences. People's relationship to Taiwan and thus to themselves was anything but homogenous. These differences can be traced to linguistic problems, indices of the divides within Taiwan (Hsiau 2000, 55). Although Kerr was prescribing a collective identity in the *benshengren* group as something not *waishengren*, he carelessly footnoted only specific ethnic groups, most notably Indigenous peoples, in this emerging national imagination. How, with such complexity and so many competing identities, anthropologist Stevan Harrell asked in 1990, does one go about studying culture in a place like Taiwan? (Harrell and Huang 2018, 19). In the postwar period, one could not easily fit Taiwan into existing theoretical models. The question of identity was simply too multifaceted. It was a square peg being forcibly fitted into round holes.

Many Taiwanese, writing in exile, would also find difficulty in shaking Han-centric narratives of authenticity in what constituted being from Taiwan.

9

A Preacher's Tale

SHOKI COE

> Unborn generations will think it strange that
> the vastness, the completeness, the pervasive force
> of missionary enterprise, made so small an
> impression on the public mind.
> CAMPBELL MOODY · 1912

The early twentieth century witnessed radical changes as Christianity propagated itself and diversified to the extent of becoming more a religion of peoples of non-European descent (Stanley 2003, 1). The word *mission* is often associated only with Western colonialism rather than understood as a complex and multicultural historical process. Furthermore, the term *missionary* is too often "caricatured as representing a white Anglo-Saxon man in a pith helmet, preaching to unwilling 'natives' in a steamy jungle" (Robert 2009, 1). Corrections of such prejudice require a reconceptualization of missionary experiences outside the postcolonial framework but in a way that does not necessarily exonerate missionaries "from all charges levelled against them" (Stanley 1990, 12). Even the history of imperialism has demonstrated limitations in mission representation, and any reference to religious expression—whether revivalism, material commitment, or expansion—suggests a wider oversight of empire historiography that has tended to lie "in the constitutional, political, and economic aspects" of imperial expansion (Porter 2004, 2). Indeed, by the mid-twentieth century, missionaries were increasingly perceived as unsympathetic, self-serving, and narrow-minded imperialist agents (Porter 2002, 556; Kaplan 1986, 166). Yet, alongside the role of missionaries in imperial expansion, their contributions to both education and medicine have not gone unnoticed (Alsford 2015, 4). In areas of Taiwan, such as among Indigenous communities, this contribution is reinforced in historiography (Tsai 2009b, 6).

The mission in Taiwan has been part of the history of Protestantism in China from the beginning of the nineteenth century. Its story arguably begins on 7 September 1807, when Robert Morrison, the first Protestant missionary to China, arrived in Canton (Guangzhou). Although Morrison accompanied the London Missionary Society, he was a Presbyterian of the High Bridge Presbyterian Church in Newcastle. Morrison cooperated with other missionaries, including Walter Medhurst, William Milne, Samuel Dyer, Karl Gutzlaff, and Peter Parker (the first medical missionary), and after spending twenty-five years in China he translated the entire Bible into Chinese.

Following the First Opium War (1839–42), the Presbyterian Church of England (PCE) published a pamphlet by an unknown author urging the synod to consider establishing a mission in China. The PCE appointed William Chalmers Burns to lead the mission. Burns arrived in China via Hong Kong in November 1847. In 1855, in Shantou, he met James Hudson Taylor, a British Protestant missionary and founder of the China Inland Mission, and thereafter the two men worked together until Taylor relocated to Ningbo in 1857. Key to this relationship was their desire to conform the activities of the mission as closely as possible with local customs and traditions (Standaert and Tiedemann 2010, 185–86; Burns 1870). This conformity would prove crucial in the development of a native church. The fact that Burns had befriended James Young, a medical doctor, who had agreed to join the mission, would provide the knowledge needed to underpin the success and legitimacy of the mission. Young was deeply committed to combining his medical knowledge with the missionary's work.

Translating the Bible motivated a number of missionaries to study both Chinese language and culture. In May 1855 Burns arrived in Amoy with Carstairs Douglas, who was known chiefly for his writings on the Southern Min language of Fujian (Alsford and Fuehrer 2017). It was Douglas, alongside H. L. Mackenzie, also a missionary, who first traveled to Tamsui, in northern Taiwan, in 1860 with the intention of opening a mission station on the island as part of a wider extension of the treaty ports on the island (Otness 1990, 45; Alsford 2010a, 330).

In Amoy several missionaries shared Douglas's vision of establishing a mission on Taiwan. During his short stay in Tamsui, Douglas had noted that the local community shared the same language as those in Amoy, and in the absence of any linguistic barrier the Foreign Missions Committee began training missionaries for Taiwan. The first permanent Presbyterian to settle in Taiwan was Dr. James Laidlaw Maxwell, a medical missionary. After a year and a half of language training, on 26 May 1865, Maxwell and Douglas boarded a steamer for Tai-wan fu (present-day Tainan), the prefectural capital of the island.

Maxwell recalls that despite having at first been greeted in what seemed to be a friendly manner, he and his Christian companions subsequently faced hostility and on 9 July 1865 were assaulted (Matheson 1886, 58). The local authorities dispersed the crowd, and the missionaries were asked to leave the area within three days because authorities were unable to guarantee their safety. The mission subsequently moved to Takao (present-day Kaohsiung), where they had closer contact with other members of the foreign community. By 12 August the following year, Maxwell had successfully established a ministry in Takao and had baptized eight converts (Matheson 1886, 256). Despite the difficulties, by the end of 1871 the mission had grown, and with two medical missionaries in Taiwan, medical work on the island improved and brought the missionary enterprise closer to the local population. By the end of 1873, the mission stations in the south were supervised by Hugh Ritchie and William Campbell. The total membership of the fourteen stations had risen to 931, with an average attendance at Sunday services of around two thousand. Against the background of expanding church activities in the south, the Foreign Mission Committee of the Presbyterian Church in Canada sanctioned the appointment of George Leslie Mackay, from Ontario, Canada, to begin work in northern Taiwan. The dividing line separating jurisdiction of the two missions was the River Dajia, close to present-day Taichung (Christine Lin 1999, 9).

Mackay is arguably the most documented of all nineteenth-century Presbyterians. The missionary pioneers actively sought to establish a native church—one that could identify with the local community and deliver social services as well as preach the gospel (Gardella 1999, 169). The Presbyterian missions in Taiwan thus began to favor an "independent, self-supporting congregation," whereby "Presbyterians laid great stress upon translating the Bible and evangelical tracts into the Southern Min language and training indigenous clergy" (Rubinstein 1991a, 70–72).

The work of the mission in Taiwan provides valuable insights into the subaltern history of native Christian workers. George Mackay, a strong advocate, believed that that the work and success of the mission in Formosa should reflect the "idea of a native ministry" and argued that the "mission lay not in foreign workers" (Mackay [1896] 2002, 285–86) but in the training of "evangelists, teachers, preachers, and pastors" (Campbell 1910, 52). Mackay also made it clear that there were practical and financial reasons for training a native ministry: "One reason for a native ministry . . . is that [it] is by far the most economical, both as to men and money. Natives can live in a climate and under conditions where any foreigner would die, and they can be hale and happy where I would tremble with chills and fever. And the cost of a native preacher and his family is so much less, that the contributions of the churches can be made to support a very much larger staff than if foreigners alone were employed" (Mackay [1896] 2002, 286).

The outcome in Taiwan was that missionaries typically collaborated with Chinese Christians rather than exercising authority over them (Bickers 1996, 236). The best-documented local practitioner in the early history of the mission is perhaps Gaw Bun-sui (Wu Wenshui), who died in 1879. Often known to the mission as simply "Elder Bun," he worked tirelessly with James Maxwell in the church's establishment and was seen as an almost fatherlike figure to the native congregation (Band 1947, 107). Among those who converted during the early years, such as Bun, there seems to have been no immediate benefit aside from raw belief. Access to education and health care may account for the decision to convert in later years, but the earliest became outcasts, pariahs in the local community. This has resulted in questions that may not have answers beyond faith. William Campbell, who spent three years with Elder Bun, wrote that while Bun officiated as a chapel keeper, he very quickly became a vital part of the missionary effort (Campbell 1910, 366). Furthermore, "he became the constant referee in all matters of difficulty which arose amongst native brethren" and "was ever ready to speak of Christ—in the chapel, on the streets, in the Hospital, but most of all to individuals" (Campbell 1910, 366).

This chapter, using the tale of one preacher, highlights how following the 228 Incident, the Presbyterian Church began to define itself as a self-anointed moral compass for Taiwanese in the Republic of China (Rubinstein 1991a, 88). Broadly speaking, the church's position was largely due to the absence of a foreign mission during the war. In addition, it was a reaction to a new political, cultural, and spiritual climate that followed the Chinese Nationalists' loss of the mainland to the Communists. Collectively these two important moments would coalesce in the decision by church elders and pastors to "bind themselves to the cause of Taiwanese selfhood," and more specifically to the people's "sense of ethnic and provincial identity" (Rubinstein 1991a, 88). This is particularly noteworthy given the Christian faith of two Soong sisters—Soong Ai-ling and Soong May-ling, the wives of H. H. Kung and Chiang Kai-shek, respectively—who were key to the Nationalist effort (Jung Chang 2019). However, this collective binding by the Presbyterian Church perhaps first appeared in the effort to "rescue" Peng Ming-min, a noted democracy activist and advocate of Taiwan independence (Amae 2008, 176; Peng 1972; Christine Lin 1999, 35–44).

The "exiled church leaders" carried the beacon of self-determination. Known as Formosan Christians for Self Determination (FCSD; Taiwan Renmin Zijue Yundong), this band, which included Shoki Coe, Dr. Ng Bú-tong (Huang Wudong), Lim Chông-gī (Lin Zongyi), and the Rev. Dr. Sòng Chôan Sēng (Song Quansheng), advocated for Taiwan in the international arena (Zhang 1991, 447).

Shoki Coe (Huang Zhanghui) was born 20 August 1914 in Changhua, central Taiwan, called Shōka in Japanese. His grandfather Ng Leng-kiat (Huang Nengjie), born in 1852, was the first in the family to convert to Christianity. Before his conversion, Ng (romanized in Japanese as *Ko*) had been an active Taoist priest. However, following his conversion, he frequently discussed his vow to commit his firstborn to the ministry. When his first son died in a shipwreck, that promise was transferred to his second son, Shoki's father (Wheeler 2002, 77). Shoki was thus born into a Christian family. Between 1931 and 1934, he studied at Taiwan High School, later renamed National Taiwan Normal University. He subsequently moved to Tokyo to pursue a degree in philosophy at the University of Tokyo, finishing in 1937. He then obtained a scholarship to study theology at the University of Cambridge, Westminster College, and lived with David Landsborough, a missionary to Taiwan. In Britain Shoki, with Rev. W. E. Montgomery (then principal of Tainan Theological College), was invited to attend a meeting of the Overseas Mission Committee on 14 April 1940. The atmosphere was tense as they prepared for the evacuation of all foreign missionaries from Taiwan, who had been ordered to repatriate by the end of 1940 (Crouch et al. 1989, 197; Thomas 1995, 290). The committee unanimously agreed to keep Shoki in England.

Shoki Coe had just completed an assignment at the Presbytery in Newcastle and was at a speaking engagement in Edinburgh when, following a Japanese assault on Hong Kong just eight hours after its attack on Pearl Harbor, he became an enemy alien and lost all freedom of movement as Britain declared war on Japan. Church leaders in Edinburgh urged him to travel south to London. Shortly before leaving Scotland, Shoki was questioned by the transport police, but Mr. MacDonald, whose houseguest Shoki was while in Edinburgh, graciously used his own name to book a berth for Shoki on the night train. Finding a place to stay was not difficult for Shoki. Since he had stayed with the Landsboroughs during his study at Cambridge, they acted as his guarantors, and in London Shoki found full-time employment teaching Japanese at the School of Oriental and African Studies (SOAS) at the University of London and occasionally worked with the BBC World Service.

In early 1947, Shoki left for Taiwan. Having been away for eleven years, he was apprehensive, since his "native land [had] at last been liberated from 50 years of Japanese imperial rule" (Coe 1991, 107). His optimism and excitement suffered a setback when the ship landed in Hong Kong and Shoki met with a former classmate from Tainan who had traveled from Shanghai "to warn him not to return to Taiwan" (Coe 1991, 108). Shoki's classmate had returned to Taiwan in 1946 and witnessed firsthand the horrors of the

228 Incident. Shoki was not dissuaded, and on 27 September 1947, he and his family arrived in Keelung and were greeted by his sister A-Siok (TH. Ng Siok-eng).

Shoki's transnationality becomes clear in his account of leaving Hong Kong for Taiwan in 1947. He discusses the impact that the end of the Second World War and the ensuing civil war had on the colony. Shoki recalls an endless stream of refugees crossing the border. According to him, had it not been for David Landsborough, who "shielded" him from the crowds that were trying to board the ship but were held back by "the whistling sound of police whips," he would never have made it (Coe 1991, 108). At that moment, Shoki felt both familiarity and difference. He anticipated a problem with the police because he looked like the refugees, though he felt different. At that moment he identified more with Landsborough, a feeling that persisted after his arrival in Taiwan.

Shoki, like other notable activists, such as Peng Ming-min, questioned his identity in the wake of martial law, and in particular his position as a "Chinese Christian": "I began by saying that I knew I was 'a Chinese'—or thought I did—and that was one of the reasons why, six years previously, I had gone back from England to Taiwan; but after having been back there all those years and lived under the Chiang regime's martial law, I had begun to wonder whether I was really a Chinese or just a Taiwanese" (Coe 1991, 172; Christine Lin 1999, 42). Infiltration of the PCT was not uncommon, and in the early 1950s a number of pastors who had expressed opposition to the KMT were forced to sign "a confession of guilt" (Christine Lin 1999, 45). As a result, Shoki's concept of the role of the church changed. With new considerations in mind, Shoki coined the term *contextualization* (Wheeler 2002, 78), which for him was an interplay of scripture and the changing context in which it must be interpreted.

In *Recollections and Reflections* Shoki discusses having publicly asked a critical question: "I am amazed that there is so much talk about Nationalist China and Communist China but nothing about what the people in Taiwan hope for their future and the future of Formosa, their homeland. My question is: 'Is a two-China policy a real option? I know the Nationalists in Taiwan wouldn't accept it, though I don't know what the Communist reaction would be.' Why not one China and one Formosa, like one India and one Ceylon?" (Coe 1991, 173).

The inclusion of his "One China, One Formosa" policy in the work of D. T. Niles, a Ceylonese pastor, along with his pro-Taiwan-independence stance, led to him being banned from Taiwan following his return to England in 1965. Yet this exile enabled Shoki to organize ecumenical and political movements from abroad (Jonas Chang 2012, 121–34). Shoki chose a church in Bromley, Kent, for his Theological Education Fund office, as it was close to Seaford, where his family had settled. There Shoki and his wife, Winifred, sought to "indigenize" the church. Yoshihisa Amae argues that the "torch of Taiwanese self-determination lit by the PCT was carried on by the exiled church leaders." In March 1976, Shoki Coe, C. S. Song, Y. Chao (Zhao Youyuan), Daniel Beeby, and Boris Anderson were invited to testify on the "Taiwan situation" before the British parliament (Amae 2008, 190). Moreover, Amae contends that the 1970s were a period in which exiled leaders and missionaries "felt that the Taiwanese church needed to speak on behalf of the 'voiceless' native Taiwanese who have been deprived of their political rights and basic freedom" (180).

The arrest of Kao Chun-ming, general-secretary of the PCT, following the Kaohsiung Incident on 10 December 1979 brought the Presbyterian Church in Taiwan into the maelstrom of democratization and crystallized the KMT's view that the church was a political entity (Jonas Chang 2012, 133; Lu and Esarey 2014, 137; Hu Huiling 2001). In addition, the rallying of "exiled church leaders" and the initiation of the Formosan Christians for Self Determination on 20 March 1973 by Shoki Coe, Dr Ng Bú-tong, Lim Chông-gī, and the Rev. Dr. Sòng Chôan Sēng strengthened the Taiwan cause internationally (Jonas Chang 2012, 126).

On 28 July 1987, thirteen days after ROC president Chiang Ching-kuo ordered the lifting of martial law, Shoki Coe arrived back in Taiwan (Tsai 2005, 183). While in Taipei, Shoki stayed with his former student Kao Chun-ming, who had served four of his seven years' imprisonment for hiding Shih Ing-teh and his then-wife Linda Arrigo (Henry Tsai 2005, 244). Having heard that Shoki was staying with Kao, leaders of the newly formed opposition party, the Democratic Progressive Party (DPP), "made a special trip to see this forerunner of the Taiwan democratic movement" (Jonas Chang 2012, 142; Rigger 2001, 23).

In 1988, Shoki passed away. For him, the hermeneutics of the political situation of Taiwan were contextualized in biblical texts. His interpretation of theology aimed to present the gospel in culturally relevant ways by acknowledging the differences that exist between various interpretations. In so doing he observed "native" expressions of the gospel that met their goals and worshipping patterns. Shoki's devotion to contextual ministry was informed by his own experiences. Outside of Taiwan missiology for scholars of Taiwan's democracy and identity, Shoki Coe is given but a passing mention among those who championed the cause of independence. Lim Iong-iong's documentary *Is Time Still on Our Side?* (Shijian haizhanzai women zhebian ma?) reflects on Shoki Coe's "great disappointment" that self-determination had not been realized in his lifetime and that the Taiwanese are forced to continue their battle with identification (Lim 2012).

10

An Exile's Tale

SU BENG

Everywhere the word "exile" which once had an
undertone of almost sacred awe, now provokes the idea
of something simultaneously suspicious and unfortunate.

HANNAH ARENDT · 1943

The achievements of exile are permanently undermined
by the loss of something left behind.

EDWARD SAID · 2000

In 1964, Peng Ming-min, an advocate for Taiwan independence, created a manifesto calling for the overthrow of the Chiang Kai-shek regime and establishment of a democratic government in Taiwan. On 20 September in the same year, Peng, along with two students, Hsieh Tsung-min and Wei Ting-chao, was arrested and later tried for sedition by a military court. Peng was sentenced to eight years but, following international pressure, was moved from a military prison to house arrest. In 1970, with the support of the Swedish chapter of Amnesty International, Peng escaped Taiwan to Sweden on a forged passport. There he was granted political asylum. On leaving Taiwan, Peng wrote, "The last dim light of the island gradually faded behind me. I was almost to the high sea and beyond the reach of the Nationalist Chinese agents. In my whole life I had never felt such a sense of *real* freedom" (Peng 1972, 1).

His words convey an emotion that many Taiwanese intellectuals would feel as they began their lives in exile. They were not stateless, as many would claim political asylum, but a feeling of placelessness overshadowed them. For Peng Ming-min, this placelessness provoked an identity crisis. His existence blended Chinese heritage, the Japanese world of his youth, and a Western world with which he was "ideologically and intellectually linked" (Peng 1972, 2). His faith was inherited from his great-grandfather, reputedly one of the first to convert under the mission of James Laidlaw Maxwell in present-day Kaohsiung (Peng 1972, 5).

The placeless Taiwanese were not a large enough group to warrant much attention globally. Their displacement was arguably an acceptable price for Chiang Kai-shek's consolidation of power in Taiwan in the wake of the Nationalist loss of the Chinese mainland. The exiled intellectuals understood their reality as a crisis of political and moral authority. However, they did not write as refugees or frame themselves as stateless. Instead, they became known as *haiwai yiyi fenzi* (overseas dissidents). Political philosopher and Holocaust survivor Hannah Arendt, writing on her experience in an essay titled "We Refugees," opens with

> We don't like to be called "refugees." We ourselves call each other "newcomers" or "immigrants." . . . A refugee used to be a person driven to seek refuge because of some act committed or some political opinion held. Well, it is true we have had to seek refuge; but we committed no acts and most of us never dreamt of having any radical opinion. With us the meaning of the term "refugee" has changed. Now "refugees" are those of us who have been so unfortunate as to arrive in a new country without means and have to be helped by Refugee Committees. (Arendt 1943, 66)

Those Taiwanese living in exile were, unlike Arendt, placeless as a result of their political thinking. Like Arendt, they suffered endless anxiety and intense despair. The word they used was *liuwang* (to drift away and die). They wandered in search of dignity and an identity that was truly their own: not Chinese, not Japanese, but one wholly Taiwanese. In the diaspora of exile, a great revision took place, a cultural discussion that contributed to the nationalization of Taiwan. Their writings would "lend dignity to a condition legislated to deny dignity—to deny an identity to people" (Said 2000, 175).

The exodus of political activists and intellectuals from Taiwan can be traced back to the 228 Incident, which confirmed the dictatorial nature of the KMT. Following the execution and imprisonment of several Taiwanese intellectuals, dissatisfaction with the regime began to crystallize in overseas Taiwanese communities. In 1956, Liao Wen-I established the Provisional Government of the Republic of Formosa (Taiwan Gongheguo Linshi Zhengfu) in Japan. This became the foremost center for political activism and anti-KMT intellectual activity in Japan throughout the late 1950s and 1960s. Student movements in Japan followed, with the Formosa Association (Taiwan Qingnianhui) forming in 1963. In 1965, the association changed its name for the third time in three years, this time to United Young Formosans for Independence (Taiwan Qingnian Duli Lianmeng). In the United States, the early 1960s witnessed no unified organization until the creation of the United Formosans in America for Independence (Quanmei Taiwan Duli Lianmeng) in 1966 (World United Formosans for Independence n.d.).

Yet a notable number of groups were actively engaged at the state level in places such as Kansas, New York, Wisconsin, California, Pennsylvania, and Oklahoma (Shu 2002, 53). In Canada, the League for Self-Determination of Formosans (Taiwan Zhumin Zijue Lianmeng) was established in 1964, then renamed the Taiwan Human Rights Commission (Taiwan Renquan Weiyuanhui) in 1965, as it turned its focus to rescuing Peng Ming-min from prison. In Europe, the Union for Formosa's Independence in Europe was founded in 1965.

In 1968, the associations in Japan, the United States, Canada, and Europe published a joint declaration announcing that the magazines *Taiwan qing-nian* and *The Independent Formosa* would join forces, thus forming the first collective overseas movement advocating for Taiwan's independence from KMT rule. This effort came to fruition in 1970 with the establishment of the World United Formosans for Independence (WUFI; Taiwan Duli Jianguo Lianmeng). The organization, which still exists, advocates for peaceful establishment of the Republic of Taiwan. Its manifesto states that "all citizens of Taiwan shall be considered equal [and those] wishing to maintain their 'Chinese' citizenship will be given assistance, if they choose to return to China" (World United Formosans for Independence n.d.). Although the principal objective of their mission was shared among many advocating for independence, some of those championing self-determination did not share their ideology. Complicating opposition in Taiwan during the period of martial law was the fact that those opposing the KMT, and the CCP, came from different parts of the political spectrum. WUFI was considered to represent an elite nationalism that would suppress the working class upon the movement's success. When political activists Liao Wen-I and Koo [Ku] Kwang-ming negotiated return of their family wealth from the KMT government, many saw this as evidence of elitism (Arrigo 2019). Among those who respected the activism of associations but did not get directly involved was Su Beng.

═══

Born Lin Chao-hui and later using his maternal surname, Shih, Su Beng (his adopted pen name, meaning "to clearly understand history") was more than a Taiwanese political activist. He was born in the modern-day Shilin District of Taipei on 9 November 1918, during the period of Japanese colonization. The son of an elite family, he graduated from Waseda University in Tokyo with a degree in political science and economics. In 1942, he left Japan for China, where he worked for the Chinese Communists. Disillusioned, he fled China in 1949, via Qingdao, as the Nationalists were consolidating their final retreat. By the beginning of the 1950s, Su Beng had established the Taiwan Independence Armed Corps, which plotted to assassinate Chiang Kai-shek. When the Armed Corps catchment of weapons was discovered in 1951, Su Beng went into hiding (Su Beng Interviewing Group 2013, 168). In May 1952, he escaped on board a ship exporting bananas. He was imprisoned for falsely entering Japan but later granted political asylum. In the Ikebukuro district of Tokyo, Su Beng was reunited with his girlfriend, Hiraga Kyoko, whom he had met in China, and opened a noodle restaurant named New Gourmet (J. Shinchinmi). Like the Wisteria Tea House (Zitenglu) in Taipei's Daan District, New Gourmet served as a venue for political discussion. There he began to pen *Taiwan's 400-Year History*, published first in Japanese in 1962, then in Chinese in 1980, and finally in an abridged English version in 1986. Su Beng felt that although many advocated for the independence of Taiwan, few truly understood its history. Using an economic historical perspective, Su Beng elucidated the process of social class formation in Taiwan and emphasized the interconnection between periods of social development and international trends.

For Su Beng, nationalism is born of historical consciousness. It has a beginning. There is an evolution to its development. For him, Taiwanese consciousness began in a "start-again nationalism" that many in Taiwan had advocated for in the postwar period. Writing from the diaspora, Su Beng argued for creole nationalism: a homeland based on the independence of settler peoples. His book, *Taiwan's 400-Year History*, served to awaken a modern consciousness in Taiwan, as it "othered" the Republic of China as the new colonial figurehead.

This colonial othering would have consequences. Attitudes toward the other colonial layers that made up the four-hundred-year period improved. The planned building of a Zealandia theme park by Taiwanese film director Wei Te-sheng and the remembrance of the Dutch colonial period are examples of this. Few places in the world would have gone so far in remembrance of European colonization. Yet in Taiwan, few objected. The Taiwanese attitude toward the Japanese colonial period serves as another example, contrasting sharply with postwar literature in Korea that discusses the same colonial period (Shin and Robinson 1999, 3–5).

Su Beng focused his idea of nationalism on self-determination and social equality, and this established *Taiwan's 400-Year History* as one of the first liberal histories of Taiwan. It is important that even with his focus on economics, Su Beng did not adopt a Marxist perspective, despite his own ideological beliefs. This stance situates Su Beng in the wider discourse of Taiwan intellectual history and the complexities that surrounded the concept of nationhood.

Other activists and intellectuals after the formation of the Taiwanese Communist Party in 1928, such as Hsieh Hsueh-hung, argued for a Marxist outlook on the formation of a Taiwanese nation. Hsieh, a leader in the Taiwanese People's Party and the Taiwanese Cultural Association, advocated for a distinct Taiwanese identity. In 1931 she was imprisoned for promoting communism but was released in 1939. Following the arrival of the Chinese nationalists in 1949, Hsieh returned to political activism, stating that "Taiwan must be ruled by the Taiwanese" (Lin Chiung-hua 2013, 36–45). Following the 228 Incident, Hsieh reputedly formed part of the 27 Brigade (*budui*; a guerrilla force) from her home in Taichung, along with the local scholar Chung Yi-ren, with whom she had grown up (Huang Hsiu-cheng 1997, 289–90). Chung, however, claimed that Hsieh did not "convene" the brigade but rather had approached him for its protection. Further, he denied that the brigade had anything to do with the Communist Party (Chung 1993, 499–500). Ku Jui-yun, Hsieh's godson, in contrast, claimed that Chung had only the title of "leader," with no authority within the organization (Ku 1990, 56–57).

Nevertheless, the 27 Brigade was established on 6 March 1947 and was made up of guerrilla fighters (estimates vary from two hundred to four thousand), including members of the Atayal Indigenous group, young students, and discharged soldiers who had fought for Japan (Huang Hsiu-cheng 1997, 290). As the KMT forces closed in on Taichung, a detachment of the 27 Brigade engaged them but was forced to retreat. On 16 March 1947, the brigade disbanded, and Hsieh later fled to Hong Kong (Lin Chiung-hua 2013, 42).

In Hong Kong she formed the Taiwan Democratic Self-Governing League. Not long afterward, she moved to Xiamen and became active in the China Youth League, serving in the Chinese People's Political Consultative Conference. Despite her ideological support for communism in China, Hsieh maintained her views on Taiwan's self-determination and was subsequently targeted for this during the Anti-Rightist Movement of the late 1950s. In 1958 she was sent to the countryside to feed pigs. She was accused of being a regionalist and died a victim of the Cultural Revolution in Beijing in 1970 (Lin Chiung-hua 2013, 43–45).

Communism in Taiwan during the period of martial law was complicated, not least because of possible links to the CCP in China. The Tangwai (Dangwai; "Outside the Party") movement primarily focused on issue-based advocacy and strongly emphasized self-determination and independence. The authenticity of the movement did not rest solely on left/right political ideologies. Some believed that the materialist interpretation of social construction was an essential aspect of social consciousness or collective awareness of the goals of the movement. Marxism in Taiwan became complicated when the issue of Taiwaneseness became distinct from Chineseness at a time when the KMT defined communist ideology as pro-CCP.

Thus, the quandary for many in the Tangwai and the exiled intellectuals was what it meant to be a Taiwanese nation. Su Beng struggled with this.

His entanglement in the conceptual framework of Han ethnicity prevented him from incorporating multiethnic nationalism into his vision. In *Taiwan's 400-Year History*, he excludes Taiwanese Indigenous peoples from his category of Taiwanese. The very title of the book assumes that the island's history began with colonizers. In addition, that *Taiwan's 400-Year History* was written in Japanese raises a number of questions. Who was Su Beng writing for? Language is an important consideration in studies of postcolonial nationalism, as it provokes the reader into an awareness of the experience of the colonized (Said 2000, xv). The imposition of colonial language on the colonized is well documented. Some critics advocate for a return to the use of Indigenous languages, while others see the imposed language as a practical alternative in that it can enhance international communication (e.g., people in Morocco, Cambodia, Vietnam, Haiti, and Algeria can communicate with the French-speaking world). Su Beng's advocacy did not entail promoting a postcolonial Japanese period that could also be interpreted by Koreans, nor did it involve advocating for the overthrow of the Communist Party in China. He was concerned only with Taiwan. Su Beng experienced an acute sense of exile far from the communal group for whom his start-again nationalism advocated. Japanese was his preferred written language. As a creole nationalist, he found the native language in Taiwan less important than political identity. Culture, for Su Beng, was not transmitted through language in its universality, nor was it anchored and bound by ethnicity; rather it was grounded in its own peculiarities, encompassing all forms of social behavior, norms, and values. For Su Beng, culture is a society-centered narrative that belongs to all people of Taiwan. The practical aim of his nationalism was to decenter China and build a national boundary by breaking away from mother-country narratives. On the basis of this concept, Su Beng advocated for creole nationalism, a form of nationalism that emerged among descendants of colonial settlers who developed a unique cultural and national identity distinct from their ancestral origins.

Like many other postcolonial elites, Su Beng believed in a socialist utopia that followed historical materialism and a prophesied classless society. The dislocations caused by the Chinese Nationalist colonization of Taiwan and the subsequent period of martial law led to new kinds of colonial spaces and discipline. Under Chinese Nationalist rule, the people of Taiwan experienced new forms of colonial authority and were forced to restart postcolonial imaginings. For Su Beng, this could only be understood within the global fight for the political left. In many ways, he did not face the dilemma encountered by others in the postcolonial left. His model was Western in origin: progress (wealth and power) is achieved through development (economic, technoscience). Yet Su Beng and like-minded activists had an idea that spawned a movement radical enough to make change. Taiwan became a democracy—a mature democracy grounded in civic patriotism. The island's progressive campaigning has made its democracy more than just an issue-based divide. Taiwan, as a result, has left-right consolidated political parties.

Taiwan's 400-Year History is a heroic conception of decolonization that rejects postimperial attachment. Su Beng's ideas were powerful. They were arguably nonaligned in the Cold War framework, and this has played a significant role in the fluidity of Taiwan's nationalism today. For Taiwan, identity is multilayered. There are local, national, and ethnic differences, yet with a consensus that they are part of an island community—a citizenship of difference.

In 1992, President Lee Teng-hui promulgated a revision to Article 100 of the Criminal Code that granted amnesty to political prisoners and ended the overseas blacklist. Su Beng returned to Taiwan the following year. Others on the blacklist, such as Peng Ming-min, Huang Chiau-tong, and Chang Liang-Tse, returned in 1992. Foreigners on the blacklist, such as Linda Arrigo, were permitted back as early as 1990, while others, such as J. Bruce Jacobs, returned in 1993. Chiang Kai-shek's Chinese Nationalist Party had governed Taiwan as a colonial power in exile throughout the White Terror (Baise Kongbu) period. Taiwan's push to consolidate its democracy followed the ending of martial law in 1987, and this would usher in a new hope for Taiwan and its people.

Su Beng was a political exile who wrote a dense history of settler colonialism in Taiwan. Few Taiwanese had read his book prior to the 1990s. Yet its pages spoke of liberation and self-determination. The book became gospel-like in its multiple interpretations. The writer became a lionized figure for independence and a hero for a new generation of Taiwanese, many of whom had never experienced martial law. These young Taiwanese, rather than searching for an identity, are instead confirming one in a world that is wholly theirs.

A NEW HOPE

1987–Present

11

A Writer's Tale

SANMAO

Don't ask from where I have come,
My home is far, far away.
SANMAO · 1979

Notions of identity, particularly those related to ethnicity and nationality, are often depicted as having rigid boundaries. These notions are shaped by deeply ingrained social habits and tendencies that impact individuals' perceptions of the surrounding social world and influence their responses to it. This process of socialization is what French sociologist Pierre Bourdieu referred to as habitus. Within this framework, habitus shapes group behavior and forms the social actions of an individual. In the case of Taiwan, martial law aimed to promote the idea of a shared ancestry, as the government attempted to mold a common culture through language to foster a collective experience and group identity: a Free China habitus.

In some ways, the KMT's social engineering projects during the periods of White Terror and martial law achieved success. They conditioned the Taiwanese people to perceive themselves as part of a distinct China, the Republic of China (ROC), which they believed represented a free China that temporarily existed solely on Taiwan, separate from the People's Republic of China (PRC), which they viewed as illegitimately occupying the historical lands of the Chinese mainland. This fluidity of identity allowed many in Taiwan to navigate between different identities. The geopolitics of the postwar period would further cement the Chinese Nationalist argument that despite its loss of territory on the mainland, it continued to be the legitimate government of China proper. This narrative was backed by the United Nations and a significant number of UN member states. In 1959, the US State Department's official position on Taiwan was the following:

> That the provisional capital of the Republic of China has been at Taipei, Taiwan (Formosa) since December 1949; that the Government of the Republic of China exercises authority over the island; that the sovereignty of Formosa has not been transferred to China; and that Formosa is not a part of China as a country, at least not as yet, and not until and unless appropriate treaties are hereafter entered into. Formosa may be said to be a territory or an area occupied and administered by the Government of the Republic of China, but is not officially recognized as being a part of the Republic of China. (Frank Chiang 2017, 229)

The expulsion of the ROC from the UN Security Council in 1971, as the China seat was transferred to the PRC, and the subsequent loss of its UN member seat and membership in all the intergovernmental organizations attached to the United Nations began the course of the removal of China from Taiwan. Among the countries that switched recognition in light of the UN change, the decision made by the United States to recognize the PRC would have the most significant impact. Not least, the period that followed would usher in a new era in how Taiwan was documented, especially in the English language. As the "Taiwan as China" label began to be discarded, American academics were able to study China in China as opposed to using Taiwan as a surrogate. The field of research on Taiwan changed radically as a result (Alsford 2020). Yet the multiple identities that continued to exist in Taiwan in this new period would appear in the expressions of their members. These expressions would bring attention to the underlying conflicts within individuals.

This was particularly evident in Taiwan literary circles, where regional differences, localized history, and culture strongly influenced discussions surrounding Taiwanese literature after the 228 Incident. It was conceptualized as a literature of borders (*bianjiang wenxue*; Dluhosova 2010, 183–84), originating on the periphery of Chinese literature rather than the center.

Although this implied an unequal relationship, the marginality within enabled a possible decoupling in the 1980s. Debates surrounding what constitutes a Taiwanese literature still exist today. The KMT's social engineering effort to impose a Chinese habitus on Taiwan resulted in writers, such as Lin Shuguang, discussing Taiwanese literature as a response to the May Fourth Movement in China. It was thought that if the literary legacies of the May Fourth Movement were acknowledged on both sides of the Taiwan Strait, the two cultures would merge to form a common identity. Oppositional voices in Taiwan naturally arose who denied that such a legacy existed due to the island's colonization by Japan. The notion of not quite belonging, of being situated at the margins, characterized literary tradition in Taiwan as authors sought to carve out an authentic literary tradition that exemplified their identity.

Much more has been written, and can be penned, on the historical development of Taiwanese literature. Our focus here is on an author known to many by her pen name, Sanmao, or as Echo Chen. It is worth noting for those not familiar with Taiwan literary traditions and to perhaps settle those who are, that Sanmao is not an exemplar of a Taiwanese literary canon. Instead, her writings demonstrate a boundary, a life lived on the margins. Sanmao was an influential writer who inspired a generation of young people and who existed in multiple habitus.

Chen Mao-ping was born in Chongqing, Sichuan, on 26 March 1943. She adopted the pen name Sanmao at the age of thirty-one. The Chen family came from Dinghai, Zhejiang. Her father, Chen Suching, was a lawyer who had been born into wealthy business family. At home, Chen and her three siblings—an older sister, Chen Tienshin, and two younger brothers, Chen Sheng and Chen Chieh—were raised principally by their mother, Liao Chinlin. In 1948, after the Second World War, the family relocated to Nanjing. As the civil war intensified, the Chen family, along with the other notable families, migrated to Taiwan, finally settling with other elite families in Taipei (Sanmao 1991). In 1954, Chen passed the entrance examination to the junior department of Taipei First Girls' School. In spite of this good start in her education, Chen struggled with mathematics, and in her second year of junior school a teacher accused her of cheating. The humiliation she felt triggered periods of depression. Following this incident, she began to dislike school and dropped out completely in 1955. Her parents tried a number of methods to help Chen back into school. She went to the American School in Taipei for a while and was encouraged to take up music and art. Although she regularly saw a counselor, nothing seemed to work. Upon reading magazines and contemporary literature, however, Chen began to develop an interest in creative writing.

At the beginning of the 1960s, Chen encountered the writing of Ku Fu-sheng, a local artist, who introduced her to literary works and also sent a piece of Chen's writing to Pai Hsien-yung, editor of the popular journal *Contemporary Literature* (Xiandai wenxue). Pai greeted her work favorably and "Confusion" (Huo) was published in December 1962. Two years later, Chen was permitted to take classes in the Department of Philosophy at Chinese Culture University, though she did not possess a high school degree. Most of her published work during this period features characters who are confused, almost surreal, and this appealed to a new generation of mainly female readers searching for an identity.

At university a failed relationship resulted in her moving to Spain to study in 1967. After her arrival in Madrid, she started to use the Western name Echo, after the Greek nymph. She spent the first six months studying Spanish, after which she entered Universidad Complutense de Madrid. There she met her future husband, José María Quero y Ruíz, who was a high school student at the time and eight years her junior. After graduation, she went to Berlin to study German and also stayed in the United States for a while. Over this period, she had multiple relationships, and her freedom of movement and expression appealed to readers as more opportunities became open to women. However, her freedom to live such a life was a result of her elite background. She inspired a generation of young people, yet her lifestyle was for many firmly out of reach. Today she would likely be known as an "influencer" and possibly would have a much larger following beyond the Chinese-speaking world.

In 1970, Chen returned to Taiwan and was invited to teach German at the Department of Philosophy at Chinese Culture University. She started a relationship with an artist and planned to marry him but discovered he was already married. The following year, she met a German man playing tennis. They dated for a year and were about to get married, but he died from a heart attack. Heartbroken, Chen left Taiwan again for Spain in 1972. There she became reacquainted with José. By this time, he had graduated from university and was about to join a group of friends to travel around the Mediterranean. He invited Chen to join them. Chen declined as she had already planned to travel to the Spanish-controlled Sahara. José went to the desert prior to her departure and found a job. The two married in El Aaiún (Laayoune), Western Sahara, in 1974 and settled there.

Chen was bored during José's working hours, prompting her to write about her life in the desert. In 1974, she published a piece titled "The Chinese Restaurant" (Zhongguo fandian) in the *United Daily News,* a significant departure from her previous works. At this time she adopted the pen name Sanmao. Sanmao continued to publish articles recounting her life and experiences, eventually releasing her first collection of stories, *Stories of the Sahara* (Sahala de gushi), in 1976 (Sanmao 2019, viii).

In February of that year, Sanmao embarked on a journey away from the desert, leaving José behind to continue his work. Following the transfer of the Spanish Saharan territory to Morocco, José joined her, and the couple eventually relocated to the Canary Islands, residing on Tenerife and Gran Canaria. Tragically, on 30 September 1979, José died in a diving accident. Sanmao's parents were visiting them at the time, and they took her back to Taiwan following the funeral. In 1981, she officially moved back to Taiwan, but in November the *United Daily News* underwrote six months of travel around Central and South America to produce a travelogue. Following this contract, she returned to Taiwan in May 1982 to tour the island giving talks about her journey. All of her writings during this trip were later published.

The same year she was offered a position as an associate professor in the Department of Chinese at Chinese Culture University. She also started teaching at National Taiwan University, but two years later, in 1984, she left teaching due to a troubling health condition. She continued to focus on her writing, and in 1990 she completed her first movie script, *Red Dust* (Gungun Hongchen). The film received twelve nominations from the Golden Horse Awards and won in eight categories. Sanmao, although nominated for best script, did not win the award.

In 1989, Sanmao was able to return to China for the first time since leaving as a child. Her visit to her family's hometown in Zhejiang was covered by the Chinese media and a wave of Sanmao craze (Sanmaore) soon started. She visited China twice in 1990, traveling around multiple provinces and meeting various Chinese writers and artists. During one visit, she met up with the artist Zhang Leping, author of the comic *The Adventures of Sanmao* (Sanmao liulangji), which she had read as a child. The Sanmao of the comics may have been the inspiration for her pen name. Zhang and Sanmao became very close, referring to each other as "father and daughter.'

In January 1991, Sanmao was admitted to Taipei Veterans General Hospital with endometrial hyperplasia. On 4 January, she was found dead on the ward, having hung herself. According to her family, she had been suffering from depression and was extremely fragile (Nengliang Media Official Channel 2016). They refused to accept suicide as the cause of death, however, believing that that it was an accident resulting from the amount of medicine she had been given. She died at the age of forty-seven.

Sanmao was not properly a Taiwanese writer, and her writings are often not included in the Taiwanese literary canon. In many ways, she is both like and unlike many of the tales presented in this book. She was not born in Taiwan and spent her formative years outside of the island. Like Shimizu Teruko, she came to the island through the agency of a colonizing government, but unlike Shimizu, Sanmao did not become Taiwanese. Throughout her life, she considered herself Chinese, yet she typified a period. Taiwan in the 1980s was in transition, and she influenced a generation of young Taiwanese to express themselves openly. This, coupled with developments in the start-again nationalism of the Taiwanese consciousness and the further shredding of Chineseness, began to loosen the grips that decades of (re)sinicization projects were having across the island. This sparked a national outlook as many young people in Taiwan sought to follow in her footsteps. They were inspired to dig farther, to search beyond their borders, their habitus, and their self-determined boundaries. They too wanted to travel and study abroad, and what they brought back was a newfound self: a Taiwanese self.

12

An Activist's Tale

FAN YUN

We shall unite under our belief. If we carry on,
changes can happen.

(*Tuanjie zai linian zhixia, zhiyao chixu,
jiuneng chansheng gaibian*).

FAN YUN · 2015

The 1980s were a decade of inspiration for many young people across the globe. It was the era of antiestablishment subcultures on one side of the political spectrum and social conservatism on the other. This conservatism in Britain began with the election of Margaret Thatcher and the Conservative Party in 1979, and this was matched in the United States with Ronald Reagan and the Republicans in 1980. These elections signaled a turning point. No longer were a good education, a sound job, and a loving family enough to establish success. It was all about how much you earned, the design of your home, membership in exclusive clubs, and what you ate, wore, and used. Films such as *The Goonies* (1985) reflected this in the foreclosure of the protagonists' homes in the Goon Docks to make way for an expanding country club. In both the United States and Britain, this expression of wealth became known as yuppieism. People dressed to impress. The decade, with its advances in technology and a global shift away from planned economies to laissez-faire capitalism, witnessed the beginning of a manufacturing relocation. Although this movement would result in the loss of jobs for many in the working class, this transfer translated into a boom decade for export-oriented countries such as Taiwan and South Korea.

A prime factor in the growth of the so-called Asian miracles, the interconnectivity of economies spilled over into the spread of culture and political ideals. In both Taiwan and South Korea this process culminated in a desire for political change. For South Korea this desire was exemplified in May 1980, when an estimated two thousand people were killed in what became known as the Gwangju massacre, in which demonstrators against martial law were fired upon by government troops. For Taiwan, it arguably began a year earlier, on 10 December 1979—Human Rights Day—when the authoritarian KMT government suppressed political opposition. As their people demanded greater political freedom, the governments in both countries were forced to abandon political authoritarianism and move toward liberalism. For Taiwan, the process began in late 1986 and fed into what political scientist Samuel Huntington refers to as the "third wave of global democratization" and the decrease in legitimacy of authoritarian regimes (Huntington 1991). Expansion of the sphere of liberal democracy throughout East Asia "hammered the final nail in the coffin of the hoary belief that Confucian political culture of paternalistic authoritarianism was incompatible with modern democracy" (Garver 2011, 4).

From 1987 to 1996 Taiwan experienced a period of political vibrancy. The people enjoyed a system that guaranteed freedom of speech, public assembly, the right to protest, the rule of law, a multiparty electoral system, and an opportunity to vote for their leader. In short, in less than ten years, Taiwan successfully established a liberal democracy, with the credit going firmly to those who challenged the system to reform. Fan Yun's tale begins on 16 March 1990, at the Memorial Hall Plaza in Taipei, when students from National Taiwan University (NTU) began a six-day sit-in that quickly grew to twenty-two thousand demonstrators, all seeking the right to vote in direct elections for the president and vice president and representatives in the National Assembly. The movement became known as the Wild Lily student movement (Ye Baihe Xue Yun), named for the Formosan lily that protesters wore as a symbol of Taiwan's fledgling democracy. The protests were to coincide with the "election" and appointment of Lee Teng-hui as president for a six-year term that would begin 21 March, in which only 671 members of the National Assembly could vote: one party, one candidate.

On his first day in office, Lee welcomed fifty students into the presidential office and expressed his support for their goals. He promised full democracy, and reforms were initiated in the summer of that year. Six years later, Lee became the first popularly elected president, taking 54 percent of a vote in which 95 percent of eligible voters had participated. Less than a year after the eventful and traumatic day in Tiananmen Square in Beijing, on 4 June 1989, Taiwan firmly shifted onto a completely different political trajectory from that in China. Relying on notions of civic nationalism, it began to dilute the ethnic nationalistic divide that had plagued the island since the arrival of the Chinese Nationalists in 1945.

All organized attempts to change society in Taiwan since its transition in the 1980s were products of the societal environment that made up the island. In 2010, sociologist Ho Ming-sho categorized Taiwan's social movements into five core categories (Ming-sho Ho 2010). His more recent work adds to these the 2014 Sunflower Movement. The first category, "fermentation," extends from 1980 to 1986. This was an era of discontent, during which social conditions for many became dire as the island went through rapid industrialization. Environmental degradation, exploitation, and rural impoverishment disenchanted many with the political system. The disconnect between the classes stimulated social agitation for change. Among the advocates for change were members of the emerging middle class who had adopted a more direct approach in expressing their grievances. For example, in 1986, community-led activism to oppose a project by the American corporation DuPont in Lukang gained international attention and arguably kickstarted Taiwan's environmental movement (Grano 2015, 44).

For Ho, the second period began in 1987 with the lifting of martial law and ended with the Democratic Progressive Party's (DPP) victory in the legislative election in 1992. This period, "popular upsurge," saw the growth of social movements spurred on by the liberalization of the political system. The right to public assembly that was partially allowed in 1988 would pave the way for antinuclear activism in the same year, as well as the Wild Lily movement two years later.

The third phase, "institutionalization," emerged in 1993 with the removal of the preventive and politicized policing of popular protests (Ming-sho Ho 2010, 10). For Ho, it ended in 1999 with a series of social movements that focused on marginalized groups in Taiwan, most notably, LBGTQ demands for civil rights, which would result in the first gay pride parade in September 2000.

The fourth period, "incorporation," starts with the election campaign of DPP candidate Chen Shui-bian in 2000 and ends with the party's loss to the KMT in 2008 and the election of Taipei mayor Ma Ying-jeou. The social movements of this period also led to the establishment of the Council of Indigenous Peoples and the Council of Hakka Affairs as part of the Executive Yuan (Xingzhengyuan). Following Chen's second electoral success in 2004, the presidency would be mired by financial scandal, and in October 2006, large-scale mass demonstrations by Pan-Blue supporters took place across the island. Ho refers to the period between 2008 and 2010 as a resurgence. With a KMT landslide victory and possession of nearly three-quarters of the seats in the Legislative Yuan, social movements struggled to mobilize mass constituencies as they started to lose their ability to liaise with the government.

Two years into the Ma presidency, a resurgence in student-led movements took hold as protesters took to the streets against police brutality following the visit of Chen Yunlin of China's Association for Relations across the Taiwan Straits. Calling itself Wild Strawberries (Ye Caomei), based on the "strawberry generation" moniker—widely used by older generations in Taiwan to suggest that the youth were pretty to look at but too soft and lacking strength of character and political conviction—the movement spread from an initial gathering of four hundred students for a sit-in in front of the Executive Yuan on 7 November 2008 to extend across the island's west coast. The movement signaled a shift in student-led activism, as politically engaged young people began to define their identity in terms of civil liberties.

Taiwan since the early 2000s has seen a remarkable transformation among civic and social movements (Fan 2010, 65–105). It has, as Ming-sho Ho argues, "been an integral dimension of democratization in Taiwan" (2005a, 401). Social protest, particularly from the "disadvantaged sectors"—farmers, labor, and marginalized ethnic minorities—has been a powerful force in changing the political landscape of Taiwan-based social movements. Work, of course, still remains to be done to assess the impact that democratization has had on social movements in Taiwan (Phillon 2010, 150).

It is not in the ambit of this chapter to contribute to this particular debate. Suffice it to say that many areas addressed by specific social movements do have a direct link to democratization. The labor, environment, and education reform movements, despite different tenets, all used mass demonstration to pressure the government (Ming-sho Ho 2005a, 403, 339–40). In the context of Fan Yun's tale, social movements in Taiwan appear as a type of group action, namely a grouping of individuals whose focus is on specific social or political issues, the intention being to resist, execute, or work against social change. Various academic disciplines highlight diverse empirical research and employ different theoretical analyses. Political science, for example, places significant emphasis on the relationship between popular movements and political parties (Fell 2012, 177–78). In contrast, scholars of anthropology and sociology focus on the dynamics and origin of such movements, and their economic, class, gender, or ethnic characteristics (Tseng et al. 2014, 205–66).

Civic movements, on the other hand, tend to be more transnational, involving equality before the law. These include, though are not limited to, the rights of minorities, women's rights, and LGBTQ rights (Damm 2005; Doris Chang 2009). The present drive to understand social and civic movements in Taiwan comes largely from the energetic behavior of the Sunflower Student Movement. This movement, a coalition of student and civic groups, protested the ruling party's black-box approach, without clause-by-clause review, to passing the Cross-Strait Service Trade Agreement. From 18 March to 10 April 2014, they occupied the Legislative Yuan, and later the Executive Yuan (Lin Nansen 2014. In this instance a politically oriented movement in Taiwan took on a civic rather than an ethnic hue.

This civic hue was previously most notable in the demonstrations in Dapu (2010) and Huaguang (2013), both of which involved many of the same student members who occupied the Legislative Yuan. On 28 June 2010, Liu Cheng-hung, the Miaoli County commissioner, gave an evacuation order for farmland in Dapu village without notifying the resident farmers (Lin Nansen 2013). Despite the efforts of the Dapu Self-Help Organization (Dabu Zijiuhui), the county government continued its land appropriations to make way for the Jhunan Science Park (Zhunan Kexue Yuanqu). On 3 August, a seventy-three-year-old farmer, Mrs. Chu Feng-min, committed suicide by drinking herbicide. Then-premier Wu Den-yih issued a statement demonstrating a complete lack of sympathy: "I understand this woman suffers from chronic disease, maybe even depression, so I don't know the reason for her suicide. . . . Regardless, I am very sorry." Residents and their supporters, including students and academics, were outraged by his callousness and demonstrated in front of the Presidential Office (Ketty Chen 2013).

Grassroots and student protests against land takeovers took place again in 2013 following forced evictions and demolition of houses in the Huaguang Community (Huaguang Shequ) in Taipei. One notable feature of the Huaguang community protests is that the evicted residents were part of one of the last remaining mainlander refugee communities in Taipei (Ho Yi 2013, 12). The students involved in rallying support for them thus in many ways crossed traditional party lines to align more on civic issues of equality than on the traditional ethnic divisions of *waishengren* and *benshengren* that had previously dominated Taiwan's political and social movements (Ming-sho Ho 2014b).

In addition, since 1989 and enactment of the Wildlife Conservation Law, Taiwan has witnessed a massive increase in conservation advocacy. For example, 2011 saw pro-dolphin and antipollution campaigns, the latter championing calls for Ma Ying-jeou to condemn plans for a $30 billion offshore petrochemical refinery (Jennings 2013). Comparing Taiwan and China, political scientist Yanqi Tong sees environmentalism as a social movement dependent on the interaction of three factors: (1) the movement being shaped by the broader political constraints and their opportunities, unique to the national context; (2) organizational resources (such as informal networks, religious groups, and voluntary associations) that are made available to mobilize people into collective action; and (3) the social construction of the collective process, which gives meaning and value to collective action by bringing shared meaning and definition to the situation (Tong 2005, 169).

In March 2011, the interaction of these three factors with reference to environmentalism came to a head following the Fukushima Daiichi nuclear disaster in Japan, when two thousand people in Taiwan demanded an immediate end to the island's construction of a fourth nuclear power plant. The event was repeated the following year with similar numbers, and was also attended by scores of Indigenous protesters demanding immediate removal of nuclear waste stored on Orchid Island (Jackson Hu 2012). Then in March 2013, sixty-eight thousand protesters from across the island converged against continued construction of the fourth plant and the integrity of the existing three (Ming-sho Ho 2014a; Yu-Huay Sun 2013; Ming-sho Ho 2003). Less than a month after the Legislative Yuan was occupied by the Sunflower Movement, social movements supported by Lin Yi-hsiung, a political prisoner during martial law who had begun an indefinite hunger strike, mobilized to force the government to cease construction of the plant (Cole 2014).

With most political parties in Taiwan favoring economic development over environmental safety, environmentalists are frequently sidelined by business lobbying, despite gaining access to policy decision-making (Ming-sho Ho 2005b, 341). An excellent example of this is the National Alliance for the Rescue of the Tamsui River (Quanmin Qiangjiu Danshuihe Xingdong Lianmeng) whose members campaigned against Executive Yuan approval for a highway along the river's north shore. In 2000 the Environmental Protection Administration (Huanjing Baohu Shu; EPA) managed to halt the highway's construction on the grounds that it would damage the local ecosystem (Grano and Tu 2012).

The protagonist of the following activist's tale is Fan Yun, a twenty-one-year-old sociology student at National Taiwan University (NTU) who, along with other students, began a six-day sit-in in March 1990 at the Memorial Hall Plaza in Taipei.

======

Fan Yun was born in Tamsui on 9 July 1968. Like many others, she was the child of a *waishengren* father and a *benshengren* mother. Her father came to Taiwan as a soldier and then opened a grocery shop. He was loyal to the KMT but would eventually support the New Party (Xindang) and the People First Party (Qinmindang). Despite their political differences, Fan Yun contended that her father was open-minded. During the initial sit-in in 1990, her mother, originally from Yunlin, tried to stop her and bring her home. Her father simply retorted, "Just let her be. You can't force her back" (Cheng Chin-yao 2019). As a family, they opted to avoid discussing politics or attempting to change each other's opinions.

Fan Yun is the youngest of three girls. Her parents admit that their relatively larger family was a result of their attempts to produce a son. Fan Yun has said that her parents were disappointed in her for being a girl and that they even considered giving her up for adoption (Cheng Chin-yao 2019). However, since she did well at school, Fan Yun realized she could easily outcompete the boys.

During the Wild Lily movement, Fan Yun attempted to raise the topic of feminism with her male university friends. She recalls, "During the student movement, people began to refer to me as the student leader. Shortly after, I became known more as the beauty of the student movement [*xueyun meinü*]" (Cheng Chin-yao 2019). This displeased her, as she wished people would concentrate more on her cause than on her gender.

It was during her time at university that Fan Yun first became Involved in politics. She ran for leader of the NTU Student Association and recalls that she had to compete against three other candidates, one an active KMT supporter. Over 14,000 students voted, and Fan won with over 5,100 votes. During her term, she oversaw the finalizing of the NTU Student Association Autonomous Regulations (Guoli Taiwan Daxue Xuesheng Zizhi Guizhang). Her vice president at the time was Ma Yung-cheng, who later became chief of staff to the Taiwan president Chen Shui-bian. Although Fan knew many people in the DPP, she didn't join the party until 2019.

Fan was a leader of the Wild Lily movement, although she did not participate in the hunger strike. After the success of the movement and the completion of her bachelor's degree, she moved to the United States. After finishing a PhD in the Department of Sociology at Yale University, she moved back to Taiwan and became a lecturer at her alma mater. Throughout her career, she has been active in advancing civil rights, particularly women's rights, in Taiwan. In 2006, when President Chen Shui-bian was accused of bribery, Fan, along with a number of academics, signed the 715 Announcement (Qiyiwu Shengming), which urged the president to step down, as he had lost the confidence of the Taiwanese people.

Between 2006 and 2014, Fan Yun was known for promoting women's rights as well as LGBTQ rights. Prior to the presidential elections in 2012, when Ma Ying-jeou won a second term, Fan Yun openly called for the voice of "rainbow citizens" to be heard and urged them to vote. In 2014, she participated in and supported the student-led Sunflower Movement

(Taiyanghua Xueyun). That year, she joined like-minded individuals in establishing the Taiwan Citizen Union (Gongmin Zuhe) as a precursor to forming a new political party. The union's objective was to challenge the prevailing two-party conflict between blue and green coalitions, which represent different ideological and policy positions regarding China (see Fell 2012). On 29 March 2015, the Social Democratic Party (Shehui Minzhu Dang; SDP) was officially founded. The party aimed to break the political knot of the KMT and DPP. In March, Fan represented the SDP and entered the legislative election for the Daan District, in Taipei City, but lost that race.

In May 2018, Fan declared that she would run for election as Taipei mayor. However, she withdrew when she was unable to raise the NT$2 million registration fee. In November 2019, she joined the DPP and was nominated to run for election in the Legislative Yuan (Lifayuan), winning a seat in the 2020 national elections.

Fan Yun's story is emblematic of the relationship between the forces of democratization and the social and civil movements that enabled Taiwan to follow that pathway. In Taiwan today, the head of state is popularly elected, and multiple political parties exist. The National Assembly of the Republic of China was dissolved by a popular vote in 2005. Activism by people like Fan has translated into real change. Taiwan today is a vibrant democracy because of their efforts and sacrifices.

13

A Pop Star's Tale

TZUYU

The ultimate orientation of Korean Wave (Hallyu),
we can safely conclude, is not a hegemonic cultural
imperialism, but a "World wave" which harmoniously
embraces all kinds of cultures in a global village.

ELSA SEBASTIAN · 2022

On 16 January 2016, the people of Taiwan voted for president in the sixth direct popular election, electing DPP candidate Tsai Ing-wen—the fourth president chosen by direct election and first female president. Her landslide victory was spurred on by another female: a then sixteen-year-old Taiwanese K-pop idol from the girl band twice. Tzuyu, a Taiwanese national, waved the flag of Taiwan along with a Korean flag on the *My Little Television* (K. Mai liteul telebijeon) variety show. When first aired on 22 November 2015, there was no controversy over her flag waving (Ahn and Lin 2019, 159), but the incident caught the attention of Chinese netizens when Huang An, a Taiwanese singer who had migrated to China years earlier, posted a message on his Weibo social media account decrying Tzuyu as a separatist supporter. The Chinese media caved to collective demand and canceled a scheduled performance by twice on its widely viewed Lunar New Year programming. JYP Entertainment, one of the three biggest South Korean entertainment management companies and the group's manager, was also on targeted for boycott. JYP immediately canceled Tzuyu's appearances in

China. For JYP Entertainment, the Chinese market was just too large to overlook.

On 15 January, JYP Entertainment posted a video online. In it, Tzuyu bowed and apologized for the "mistake in her image." She was forced to say the following:

> Hi everyone, I am Chou Tzuyu. Sorry, I should have come out and apologized earlier. Because I didn't know how to face the current situation, I have been afraid to face everyone directly, so I'm only speaking out now. There is only one China. The two shores are one. I feel proud being a Chinese. I, as a Chinese, have hurt the company and netizens' emotions due to my words and actions during overseas promotions. I feel very, very sorry and guilty. I have decided to halt all current activities in China in order to reflect seriously. Again, I apologize to everyone. Sorry. (Koreaboo n.d.)

Taiwanese began to respond the following morning, which was election day. For many there was no better motivation. Democracy, the most clearly defining separation between the people on Taiwan and those in China, became the weapon of choice.

Although some have argued that the reaction fostered a 10 percent increase in the vote for the DPP, Tsai Ing-wen would still have won even if the incident had not occurred (Cheng Chung-lan 2016). However, the incident proved that such tactics do not help the Chinese government in altering its perception by the Taiwanese. The video clearly targeted a Chinese audience and aimed to safeguard profitable markets for the South Korean entertainment industry. It was a demonstration of Chinese sharp power. The effort to censor and use manipulation to sap the integrity of the South Korean music industry could not have been clearer. But the Chinese media did not expect the collective reaction of not just Taiwanese netizens but rather wider K-pop fandom.

Not long after the apology was released, the video went viral throughout Taiwanese social media and the fan websites of TWICE followers. The transnational discursive space captured the complex dynamics between K-pop idols and a wide range of social actors, including agents and their corporations. The support offered to Tzuyu expressed dissatisfaction with both the Chinese government and JYP Entertainment. Waving Taiwan's national flag as a display of support for independence led many in the pan-green political parties to claim that former President Ma Ying-jeou's 1992 Consensus was a false notion—one that current president Tsai Ing-wen has since refused to endorse.

Immediately following release of the video, all major political figures in Taiwan, including Ma Ying-jeou, condemned Huang An. As the election results started to come in on the evening of 16 January, An's articles on Weibo regarding Tzuyu had all disappeared (Horwitz 2016). All comments had been deleted. An admitted shortly afterward that this one post had transformed him from a "national hero" to someone who was "hated by all" (SET News 2016). What An experienced was the same power of collective action that he had called for in his initial Weibo post. One significant factor in this transformation was the mobilization of K-pop fans who stood behind their idol.

Korean Wave (Hallyu) fandom has built its support base by championing a paradoxical message of individuality and tribal identity. Stans, who are dedicated fans that closely follow their preferred K-pop "biases," exhibit a fervent level of devotion comparable to other types of media influencers. They must walk their own paths, find their own voice and taste, but demonstrate a far-reaching cultural phenomenon that exceeds the scope of traditional fan clubs through collective action. Cultural theorists Park Shin-Eui and Chang Woongjo have identified four oxymorons that describe Hallyu fandom: (1) digital intimacy, (2) nonsocial sociality, (3) transnational localism, and (4) organizing without organization (Chang and Park 2016).

For the most part, Hallyu fandom is not disseminated to promote social goals. Instead, it is like a viral meme that spreads undirected. Its disseminated issues trend, then disappear, only to resurface and be reborn, transforming themselves once again, and reproducing and self-propagating in this circle of life in the depths of cyberspace (Chang and Park 2016, 263). K-pop fans are, therefore, both human and algorithmic. They are created through likes, posts, retweets, gifs, memes, and hashtags. They are a collective of young, mainly female, global fans of Korean popular music. Their social activism as stans, however, is the opposite of the physical and digital worlds. K-pop is a cultural complex. It encompasses more than simply the music industry. It is a trendsetting phenomenon that influences not just fashion and cuisine but also politics.

A Twitter thread started by AllKpop highlighted wide support for Tzuyu (Tzuyu Support Union 2016). This was quickly followed by a Tumblr post seeking to mobilize online collective action that included attempts to remove the apology video (Chewytzuyu n.d.). Other stan communities, including Army (the tribal name of supporters of BTS, a K-pop band also known as the Bangtan Boys, which is one of the largest with more than 50 million stans), came out in support of Tzuyu via Twitter posts. The hashtag #StandByYu quickly went viral, and numerous stan communities began posting images of their tribe, reaching to support Tzuyu.

The digital identities encoded in these likes, tweets, memes, gifs, and hashtags are a structural template that enables the user to create layers of meaning. Gifs and memes are easily reproduced, decoded, and transnationally understood in specific cultural contexts (Wagener 2020, 833). The collective response, with English as the language of disseminated support, highlights the complexities of language use, signs, symbols, and communication that are embedded with each animated gif or carefully selected meme. Each like and retweet enforces a hypernarrative that has the power to shape discourses beyond music. K-pop celebrity culture is profoundly based on transnational fandom (Ahn and Lin 2019, 162).

K-pop fandom thus has the potential to serve a utopian view of cultural participation. Fans can act as gatekeepers of accountability, herding digital activism toward important social issues and encouraging sociocultural change. Their numbers ensure that they are both heard and listened to. Yet there is also a dark side. They have the potential to assist in a dystopic reality of algorithmic cyber-vigilantism, where the personal details of perceived wrongdoers are published and shared, and the openness of voice that some have championed is unwittingly silencing people fearful of collective retribution—a "canceling" of their own digital identities. The collective action of Chinese netizens following Huang An's Weibo post sought to cancel Tzuyu through collective pressure on Chinese media and JYP Entertainment. For the non-K-pop-following Taiwanese netizens, they sought collective action over Tzuyu's forced denial of common heritage.

The principal social media outlet for communal interaction in Taiwan is a bulletin-board system known as PTT. The behavior of many young and politically active Taiwanese on PTT constitutes a community of practice (CoP), as it consists of a shared domain, a common passion, and a community. Online activists are able to sustain a CoP by maintaining a common marker: *Taiwanese Nationalism*. To achieve this, they engage in regular interaction and contribute to a community in their own capacity. Their synergy forms a symbolic and symbiotic whole—an imagined community. They become the intricate matrices of sociality with Taiwan.

Chou Tzu-yu was born in the East District of Tainan in southern Taiwan on 14 June 1999. In 2012, Tzuyu, as she is known in Korea, was discovered by talent scouts at the MUSE Performing Arts Workshop in the city of her birth. In November of the same year, she moved to South Korea to begin her training. She completed her studies at Tainan Municipal Fusing Junior High School in 2016 and went on to study at Hanlim Multi Art School in South Korea, graduating in February 2019. In 2015, Tzuyu participated in a reality TV show created by JYP Entertainment and MNET, a South Korean music channel. The show, known as *Sixteen* (K. Sikseutin), had nine successful participants, including Tzuyu—although she was the only one selected by audience vote. She went on to form the girl band TWICE. In October 2015, they debuted their first extended play, *The Story Begins*, and their lead single, *Like Ooh-Ahh*, was the first K-pop debut song to reach 100 million views on YouTube. According to Gallup, in 2016, Tzuyu was the third most popular idol among South Korean fans. The following year, she slipped to ninth, then twelfth in 2018. In 2019, Tzuyu was ranked the second most popular female artist among Korean male soldiers doing their mandatory military service (Sun I-Hsuan 2019).

Tzuyu's apology video garnered global attention. Three days following its upload on YouTube, it had been viewed 5.7 million times. With more than 300,000 dislikes to 22,000 likes, it became clear from the more than 140,000 comments that global support was for Tzuyu. For Ji-Hyun Ahn and Tien-wen Lin, Tzuyu, dressed in a black turtleneck without makeup on a plain gray background, recalled a hostage video. Tzuyu came across as a victim. The video was a desexualized mirror image of a female K-pop idol. The video portrayed her as "a vulnerable teenage girl . . . a naïve girl who does not know much about politics but who worked so hard to make her dream . . . come true" (Ahn and Lin 2019, 164). This image translated across media channels. JYP had intended the narrative of innocence to evoke compassion, but Taiwanese netizens saw cruelty behind the video. They rallied behind the narrative that Tzuyu was childlike and in need of rescuing. Her image shifted from a popular cultural icon to a national one, and the video was seen as a denial of a Taiwanese identity. The slogan "Today it is Tzuyu, tomorrow it is all Taiwanese people" crossed multiple platforms in Taiwan in expressing the political implications of Tzuyu's canceling in China.

The early 2000s marked the beginning of active utilization of the internet as a prominent platform for political discourse. Specifically, between 2005 and 2009, widespread adoption of social medial platforms and online forums opened new avenues for individuals to express political views. Taiwanese social activists embraced these online platforms as powerful tools to mobilize support for prevalent social issues during that period. More often than not these were nonpartisan issues. For example, in 2007, people rallied behind the closure of the Lo-Sheng (Lesheng) Sanatorium and Hospital, and in 2008 the internet served as a vehicle for the Wild Strawberry movement and again in 2010 for the Anti Guo-Kuang (Guoguang) Petroleum Plant protest. In 2013 it provided the necessary communication for activists of the White Shirt Army (Baishanjun). Then in 2014, it played a vital role in the successful occupation of the Legislative Yuan during the Sunflower Movement (Ming-sho Ho 2019, 71–72).

The internet plays a profound role in all aspects of everyday life. Particularly during a global pandemic, it has provided the tools to build alternative networks, both personal and professional. It aids in strengthening preexisting relationships—and has ended relationships by identifying previously unknown social and political divisions. It provides an alternative political dimension. Where a voice is often ignored in the traditional public sphere, it is amplified online. This has influenced how politicians and the media reach the voting public. No longer are television, radio, and print media enough. The internet has also challenged traditional types of political participation. Since the internet provides a global platform for local issues, it has created a new entry into political processes The Occupy Movement of 2011 demonstrated how a social movement can grow out of personal social networks to dominate social movements online (Graeber 2013, 41). Occupy engaged in both the digital and real worlds. It existed between the public space and virtual social networking sites.

A social movement's ability to transcend that which is rooted in ascribed characteristics to channel a cause through cyberspace makes possible an alternative platform where the barriers of entry are lowered. The movement offers a user-friendly infrastructure that contributes to the popularity of active participation. This popularity stems from the fact that users feel fully capable and competent in navigating and utilizing the platform effectively. The global reach of cyberspace addresses a number of core challenges in collective action, most notably access to resources and increased participation. Thus it alters the scope and scale of a Habermasian public sphere by shifting the discursive space. Participatory forums create communities, and these communities effect social change. Online forums thus serve as a platform for expressions of protest that help establish solidarity among participants. By pushing for support of a social issue, the internet reinforces an ideology. It can create cohesion and solidarity, but it can also create or exacerbate inherent divides. The arrival of the smartphone in the first two decades of the 2000s would dramatically alter how social issues are communicated.

The innocuous waving of flags by global pop stars promoting their homelands has become a political action. The consumption of popular culture has shifted the transnational imagery of space to reterritorialize national boundaries into new cultural maps. The revision of Tzuyu's allegiance (three times) on JYP Entertainment's web page blurs the boundaries of nations in the region. The global reaction to this change brings it back into focus. However, this may come at a cost for Tzuyu. For her, the sharp power of China and the profit-seeking actions of South Korean entertainment companies relegated Taiwan from her nationality (K. *gukjeok*) to simply her birthplace (K. *chulsaengji*).

When the video of Tzuyu's forced apology went viral in Taiwan the day before the 2016 presidential elections, it became a point of public discussion, with all presidential candidates compelled to express their disapproval of her treatment. Although the incident probably did not change the election result, it displayed a new politically engaged youth profile that had evolved following the Sunflower Movement in 2014. The incident demonstrated the power of digital activism and the role the internet plays as a major platform for political discourse.

PART TWO

Pivotal Events

ESTABLISHMENT OF THE TAIWAN CULTURAL ASSOCIATION

1921

14

A Doctor's Tale

CHIANG WEI-SHUI

The road to creativity passes so close to the madhouse
and often detours or ends there.

ERNEST BECKER · 1997

It was the winter of 1919, and Paris was the center of discussion, as the place where the world's most powerful decision-makers had congregated to confabulate the creation of new countries and new organizations. Their purpose was to fashion peace on a continent that had been shaken to its very foundations by an adopted discourse of global supremacy. After four years of war Europe had been ripped apart, and although its major cities remained and its railway and harbor infrastructure were more or less intact, the loss was most keenly felt in the very fabric of its vision of a world order (MacMillan 2001, xxvi). The mechanized slaughter of millions removed any notion of the "civilizing missions of empire" that European powers believed they had. Europe was humbled. The revolutions of 1917 and the overthrow of the tsar pushed Russia outside the imagined boundaries of Europe. The Austro-Hungarian Empire had ceased to exist. The Ottoman Empire—the very "other" to the European "self"—had also vanished. Imperial Germany was now a republic. Old nations reemerged—Lithuania, Poland, Latvia, and Estonia—and new nations formed: Czechoslovakia and Yugoslavia. Lines were drawn in the sand, and new boundaries emerged as the Treaty of

Versailles and the Paris Peace Conference were discussed, debated, agreed, and eventually conceded.

The winter of 1919 spoke many languages. It made many demands and complaints—and these were emphatically not just European.

However, amid the support for the right to independence or self-government, people from different parts of the world shared a common language of uncertainty. The way these issues were debated raised questions about whether this new world order would be an improvement. One method employed by a number of public intellectuals was to frame the past order as embedded in sickness. New nations would thus provide a cure.

The significance of these events did not go unnoticed in Taiwan. Economically, Taiwan benefited greatly when Japan filled the void left in the region by European powers preoccupied with European battlefields. Intellectuals like Chiang Wei-shui joined the writers utilizing analogies of sickness, madness, and disease as a means to express their demands for political change. Chiang translated incisive analyses of social issues into a transcultural context, offering a perspective on existentialism that sheds light on personal reflections amid the significant societal changes taking place. The beginnings of a nation were disruptive, and this period of the twentieth-century *interbellum* is especially illuminating, not just for Taiwan. Chiang's 1921 "Clinical Notes: A Patient Named Taiwan" (Linchuang jiangyi: Guanyu Taiwan zhege huanzhe), familiarly known as "A Patient Named Taiwan," in which the protagonist—a doctor—prescribes a maximum dose of education for slow but full recovery of the nation, contrasts with the Chinese writer Lu Xun's *Diary of a Madman* (Kuangren riji; 1918), where cannibalism serves as a metaphor for the oppressive feudalistic society of China. The sickness of insanity is particularly visible in the breakdown of the human spirit as a result of this oppression. European intellectuals similarly wrote about the consequent frustration and lack of individuality, which caused the descent into madness. Franz Kafka's protagonist in *A Country Doctor* (1917) is at an impasse, a conflict without clear resolution. The doctor—symbolic of the nation—is confronted with a choice between professional responsibility and desire. The experience of spatial and temporal disorder is intensified by the presence of shame and embarrassment: "It is a shame. And yet I am a doctor. What am I to do?" The internal conflict leads to self-exculpation, with the expression of difficulties being faced by saying: "Believe me, it is not too easy for me either" (Kafka 1995, 224).

The doctor thus fights ignorance, selfishness, and superstition. He describes the condition of society as "the frost of this most unhappy of ages." For Kafka, this is mirrored in the beginning of the end. This sense of doom and superstition is repeated in the work of Abdullah Cevdet, an Ottoman Kurdish intellectual and medical doctor. In "Mezheb-i Bahaullah-Din-i Umem," published in *Ictihad* on 1 March 1922, Cevdet puts forth the argument that the challenges faced by Ottoman society can remedied only by addressing the "illnesses" present in the broader Muslim world. According to Cevdet, the nation's "sickness" is a result of the presence of institutionalized religion (Hanioğlu 1997, 140). His personal angst reflects the major societal change that came with the end of the Ottoman Empire and the beginnings of the modern Turkish state. In "A Patient Named Taiwan" Chiang Wei-shui depicted the country as afflicted by moral decay. According to Chiang, Taiwan was the victim of a corrupted human nature, as its people were focused solely on material possessions. The absence of spiritual guidance and the prevalence of polluted customs led them to immerse themselves in superstitions that were deemed detrimental. Chiang identified the sickness as a consequence of the absence of long-term planning, where the focus was solely on short-term profit and rampant corruption. For Chiang, the country was a "mentally retarded child of world culture" (Chiang 1921). Chiang's prescription was a heavy dose of education and wider readership, with a full recovery expected within twenty years. Much like Su Beng after him, Chiang's narrative of Taiwan history was strongly Han-centric, invoking an ancient lineage, much like other writers seeking to birth a modern nation-state. Chiang accentuated Taiwan's complicated history and called attention to a perceived lack of cultural wealth in Taiwan under the Qing and Japanese rule. Yet for Chiang and other like-minded Taiwan intellectuals, such as Lien Wen-ching and Tsai Pei-huo, this calling was anticolonial and, more importantly, Taiwanese. They sought greater voice for Taiwan in the Japanese Diet (Chou Wan-yao 2015, 236–37).

During a period of significant transformation, Chiang Wei-shui emerged as a prominent public intellectual in Taiwan. He diagnosed the nation as afflicted by moral decay and corrupt humanity, expressing the horrors and existential angst of the early twentieth century. It is crucial to consider the transnational and historical dimensions of the nation-body metaphor in order to comprehend the global significance of the emergence of the modern Taiwanese nation-state and the existentialism inherent in its contemporary state. The tale revolves around a public intellectual—a doctor—during the transition of the long nineteenth century.

Albert Camus once wrote that "an intellectual is someone whose mind watches itself," who both watches and is watched. Intellectuals reflect on the reality of society and engage critically in a quest for solutions to its ailments. The connections among intellectual histories of the world are most evident in the lives of notable people who figure in national history. One pervasive influence on national historiography has been nationalism.

The existential attitude, or *authenticity* according to Camus, begins with a sense of disorientation, confusion, and dread in an apparently *absurd* or meaningless world. For many the First World War reflected a darkness in which the appalling capabilities of humankind became real. This modern world, a world of industry, migration, and citizenship, also featured militarism, class conflict, gender hierarchy, and imperialism. The mechanized killing of millions during the First World War led many intellectuals to question notions of the self and the limits of human capabilities. Mankind had demonstrated that it had the ability to act on specific notions of consciousness, including radical freedom. The very idea of radical freedom spooked people. The ability to realize the extent of one's freedom became what Jean-Paul Sartre and Martin Heidegger called angst (Bakewell 2016, 154). Intellectuals used this notion of angst to philosophize their existence within contemporary society.

This absence of being—or of having—proved important in how intellectuals made sense of the global realities born out of the fractures of the First World War. There was a clear and direct link to the idea of an existential crisis. The existentialism of Søren Kierkegaard, Martin Heidegger, and the three young philosophers—Sartre, Simone de Beauvoir, and Raymond Aron—who frequently sat in the Bec-de-Gaz bar on the rue du Montparnasse in Paris drinking apricot cocktails at the turn of 1933, was not limited to European philosophy. In fact, much of the philosophy written during this period had radical existential undertones. In Taiwan, Chiang Wei-shui contextualized the international situation through the lens of existentialism and applied this to early thoughts of Taiwan as a nation in and of itself. Events in China, although disconnected from Taiwan, would influence intellectual thought leading to what Chou Wen-yao refers to as a "cultural enlightenment movement" that would see Chiang Wei-shui, Lin Hsien-tang, and others establish the Taiwan Cultural Association (Taiwan Wenhua Xiehui; Chou Wan-yao 2015, 231).

On 4 May 1919, students from thirteen colleges in Beijing listened attentively to speeches being made in protest as China shamefully accepted the Paris Peace Conference settlement. The former German colonies in Shandong, rather than being returned to China, would instead be handed over to Japan (Mitter 2004, 3). Shortly after two o'clock the students congregated in the diplomatic quarter demanding justice. Lasting no more than a couple of hours, the sequence of events would become an important marker in modern Chinese history (Harper 2020, 352). The upsurge of nationalism that followed shifted toward a populist base and away from intellectual-led cultural activities. The May Fourth Movement encompasses the period from 1915 to 1921 and is also known as the New Cultural Movement (Xinwenhua Yundong). However, it's important to note that the artistic movements of that time had little connection to the nationalistic demonstration that the name suggests.

The two main centers of activity were Beijing, home to Peking and Tsinghua Universities, and Shanghai, where much of the publishing sector was located. The intellectual circles of the movement centered on Peking University, where Cai Yuanpei became chancellor and Chen Duxiu was dean. In 1915 Chen founded *La Jeunesse* journal (*New Youth;* Xin qinqnian) in Shanghai. The journal would later draw inspiration from the 1917 October Revolution in Russia and become an important mouthpiece for Marxism. Its editorial pieces emphasized the new vernacular literature (*baihua*) and social rebellion against established society and Confucian values. The explosive output of literature, due in part to the substantial literary establishment, including literary societies and publishing houses, saw many of its writers become famous. Among them was Lu Xun.

The intellectual circles in Beijing and Shanghai, and the literary societies that accompanied them during this period, were not unique. The power of coffee shops and teahouses as sites of intellectual exchange transcended cultural boundaries. These spaces fostered exchange, communication, sociality, and perhaps most importantly, creativity. They became the main arena where news was created and consumed (Cowan 2005, 172) These political spaces brought together like-minded people and divided others in a regularized manner. They were, as described by the philosopher Jürgen Habermas, a public sphere, a space for an imaginary community, a "theatre in modern societies in which political participation is enacted through the medium of talk" (Fraser 1990, 57). The site of exchange, or the bourgeois public sphere (*Öffentlichkeit*), took form as a result of specific historical circumstances as a new form of civic society emerged, driven by growing rates of literacy and new forms of critical journalism. Habermas identified the discursive arena as an important institutional criterion in the emergence of a new public sphere. This new public sphere includes coffee houses in Britain, salons in France, *Tischgesellschaften* in Germany, and teahouses and restaurants in East Asia. Although differing in size, discussion, and composition, all brought together people who shared common concerns (Habermas 1989, 36). Following the end of the First World War, those concerns transcended boundaries.

At two o'clock on 1 March 1919 at the Taehwagwan Restaurant in Seoul, Korea, this aspect of Japanese colonialism was called into question. There twenty-two activists—the core of the March First (Sam-il) movement—read out the Korean Declaration of Independence. Inspired by Wilsonian ideals of self-determination, crowds assembled in Pagoda Park to hear student activist Chung Jae-yong read out the declaration that had been drawn up by historian Choe Nam-seon earlier that day in a restaurant in Insa-dong, Seoul (Hwang 2017, 140). As the crowd grew, Japanese residents of Seoul panicked. Violence ensued, resulting in the massacre of several Korean civilians. Subsequent events provided the catalyst for the Korean Independence Movement and would inspire other movements of resistance in the Japanese Empire.

In Taiwan, during the twenty-odd years since the start of the Japanese colonial period, armed resistance to the Japanese, such as that following the Beipu Incident of 1907 and the Tapani Incident of 1915, had, for the most part, been replaced in urban centers by more peaceful forms of political and cultural activism. The fallout of the Sam-il Movement (K. Samil Undong) would reverberate beyond the borders of the Korean Peninsula and would kindle thoughts of independence for the Taiwanese, especially those studying in Japan. As a result, Japan would prove to be not only a hub of advanced learning for the Taiwanese elite but a place to study revolutionary ideas that were born out of that fateful day in Paris in 1919. Taiwanese intellectuals in Japan petitioned the Japanese government to permit representation for Taiwanese people modeled on the Irish Home Rule Movement. The Petition for the Establishment of a Taiwanese Parliament committee was formed in 1921 and led by Lin Hsien-tang (Huang Deshi 1965). In Taiwan, on 17 October 1921 in Dadaocheng—a hub of social and political reform in northern Taiwan during the nineteenth century—the Taiwanese Cultural Association was founded by Chiang Wei-shui and Lin Hsien-tang.

Born in Yilan on 6 August 1890, Chiang Wei-shui had an older brother and a sister who was given away as a *sim-pū-á* (*tongyangxi*; a preadolescent girl adopted for future marriage). His younger brother, Chiang Wei-chuan, would, like Wei-shui, become a public intellectual. His daughter was killed in the 228 Incident, and his son was badly injured (Kao 2016). Chiang Wei-chuan had joined the KMT shortly after the Nationalists arrived in 1945, and after the events of February 1947, he was put in charge of the February 28th Incident Handling Committee. Chen Yi gave him responsibility for broadcasting to the Taiwanese on behalf of the government.

The Chiang family was poor. The father, Chiang Hong-zhang, was a fortune teller who worked outside the Chenghuang Temple (Chenghuang Miao) in Yilan. Most of his income went to feeding his opium addiction, leaving very little to feed the family. When Chiang Wei-shui was four years old, the family adopted their own *sim-pū-á*, Shih You, as a future wife for him. At ten, he began studying under the tutelage of Zhang Jingguang, a Confucian scholar. In 1915, Chiang Wei-shui graduated from the Taiwan Medical College (present-day National Taiwan University College of Medicine), and in 1919 he took Chen Tian (Chen Jingwen), a Taiwanese geisha and later political activist, as his concubine. The political center of their activism was Dadaocheng.

Dadaocheng's history is linked to a Quanzhou immigrant who moved to the area in 1851. After arriving from Keelung, Lin Lantian constructed three properties and converted them into the earliest known retail establishments in Dadaocheng (Alsford 2019a, 123). Two years later, conflict broke out between members of the Quanzhou Sanyi clan and the Quanzhou Tongan clan in Banka. The Tongan clan lost and was forced to leave the area. In Dadaocheng, they built new houses and temples along the riverside, and soon a new market was formed. As clan-based violence plagued settler communities in northern Taiwan, the losers were banished from their districts and settled in Dadaocheng. Dadaocheng became particularly tolerant of people of different clans and ethnic groups. It was more resilient in accommodating the arrival of foreign merchants, following the opening of Tamsui harbor as a treaty port in 1862, than its neighbor and competitor, Banka. This is particularly evident in the census of 1898, in which the population of Dadaocheng (31,533) overshadowed Banka (23,767; Alsford 2019a, 123).

The initial survey carried out by the Japanese in 1897 clearly demonstrates that the streets of Dadaocheng were highly diverse. Houses along Jianchang Street, Qianqiu Street, Liuguan Street, and Jianchang Back Street all had a mix of foreign and local residents. In 1885, the district was given special administrative status, and one of the four tax offices on the island was located there. The establishment of the tax office followed the arrival of several foreign companies partnered with international commercial banks. The British trading company Cass and Company, for example, represented Hong Kong Shanghai Banking Cooperation, Tait and Company, the Bank of England, Jardine Matheson and Company, and the Japanese Yokohama Specie Bank (Alsford 2018, 144). This interconnectivity between Taiwanese local spaces and the international market made Dadaocheng a prime location for the Taiwan gentry to engage in trade.

The cosmopolitanism of the district and the mixing of cultures became a canvas for the first group of Taiwanese Western-style artists, including Ni Jianghui, who was recognized as the first, Yang Sanlang, and Lan Yinding, a famous watercolorist. To train the next generation of artists, they established the Research Institute of Painting (Huihua Yanjiusuo), funded by Ni Jianghui, as an ersatz art school in Dadaocheng. Under the reforms initiated by Liu Mingchuan, the first provincial governor, success in business led to increased social mobility, and in Dadaocheng, the city's diversity allowed for the emergence of a new urban elite.

Dadaocheng was globally situated in the period of uncertainty that followed the day of discontent in 1919. Through a network of connections, numerous Taiwanese individuals were able to transmit influence and patronage. This networking played a crucial role in the development of a Taiwanese identity. Interurban links among Taiwan, Japan, Korea, and Shanghai facilitated a flow of ideas and people, leading to the formation of new networks.

Chiang Wei-shui established Taian Hospital (Daan Yiyuan) in Dadaocheng, which served as a gathering place for Taiwanese intellectuals to engage in discussions, debates, and political planning. In 1920, this assembly of intellectuals aimed to establish a Taiwan Assembly, and the subsequent year, Chiang played a significant role in the formation of the Taiwanese Cultural Association (TCA). His activism led to imprisonment in 1923 and again in 1925. In 1927, the TCA split along ideological lines. Chiang advocated for unity by founding the Taiwanese People's Party, the first legal political party established in Taiwan. The party's political philosophy was rooted in Sun Yat-sen's *Three Principles of the People*. As a result, Chiang's legacy has been subject to dualistic interpretations within present-day political divides in Taiwan.

Public intellectuals such as Chiang were not always in agreement on what constituted a Taiwanese national consciousness. What is more, they differed on the correct pathway for Taiwan. Li Ye-Isi, the grandson of Li Chungsheng, the protagonist of the following tale, was among those who opposed damaging the relationship between Taiwan and colonial Japan and instead advocated for closer integration.

ered by some ...

15

A Philanthropist's Tale

LI CHUNSHENG

Are we Chinese Christians uniquely denied of the joyful
choice of building our own Church?
LI CHUNSHENG · 1875

Following the First World War, a global period of intellectual uncertainty
had an impact on Taiwan, leading it to be described as the "marginal man,"
a term used by sociological theorists Robert Ezra Park (1950) and Everett
Stonequist (1937). This concept highlights the state of being suspended
between two cultural realities. Taiwan grappled with the challenge of establishing its identity during this period. Drawing inspiration from civil
rights activist W. E. B. Du Bois and his semi-autoethnographic work on
the African American experience, *The Souls of Black Folk* (1994), Taiwanese
intellectuals framed their identity with a sense of double consciousness,
constantly viewing themselves through the perspectives of others. In return, they drew on a sense of plurality that permeated their writings, their
paintings, and their poetry. Chiang Wei-shui encapsulated this in his desire
to place Taiwan within an ancient lineage that many felt it simply no longer belonged to. Taiwan's marginality consisted of not just two refractory

cultures, but many, some of which were melted in while others were either partially or fully fused. One united aspect in the intellectual thought of this period was Sartre's notion of that which "blares out loud and clear: the Absence"—the "not being." The tale of marginality continues here, and Dadaocheng once again provides the backdrop.

As noted in Chiang Wei-shui's story, the history of Dadaocheng is one of migration and partial exile. The people who would build its markets, construct its temples and churches, fund the paving of its streets, and design its buildings had mostly been banished from neighboring towns and farmsteads. Dadaocheng featured both economic and political centrality and social and cultural marginality. It provided a canvas onto which newcomers painted their existence. Nonetheless, what was written, painted, and spoken was not always conciliatory. Some wished to merge their double self with their colonial overlords; some sought to readdress an ancient, imagined lineage; others hoped that there would be no loss to their older selves while having no wish to become colonial subjects; and some wished to emulate the West. This might take the form of architectural inspiration (as seen in the shophouses) or in theology, namely Christian thought. The fusion of peoples and cultures led to new and hybrid intellectual forms. In Taiwan, Li Chunsheng encapsulates this in his intellectual struggle with multiple systems of thought.

Born in poverty in Xiamen on the Fujian coast on 12 January 1838, Li Chunsheng grew up to be an influential comprador, a trading middleman, and a successful trader in his own right after migrating to Taiwan at the age of twenty-six (Alsford 2010a, 309). His father, Li Desheng, was a boatman. In 1851, Li Chunsheng, like his father, converted to Christianity. He learned to speak and read English, and at twenty he joined the British trading company Boyd and Company. In 1864, under the direction of another British company, Elles and Company, he would join John Dodd as a comprador, helping him establish Dodd and Company, which he would inherit on Dodd's departure from Taiwan in 1890, though by that time it was worthless (Tu 1963). Li was instrumental in helping Dodd develop the tea industry in Taiwan. The trade of various goods, such as camphor, coal, rice, and tea, by Dodd and Company led to notable changes in population patterns. As economic demographics shifted with this trade, a significant number of merchants relocated north from the previous capital of Tainan to seize the emerging opportunities for profitability. In 1887, Taiwan became a province of the Manchu Empire. Its first governor, Liu Mingchuan, oversaw construction projects that were both public and private. This included the development of Dadaocheng beyond the North Gate of the walled city. Liu asked Li and Lin Weiyuan to combine their efforts and develop Qianjiu and Jiangchang Streets with Western-style shophouses for foreign trading companies. Li proposed to Liu that a railway be built between Dadaocheng and Keelung, and work began in 1887. In 1890, Li was made director of the Taiwan Silk Industry Bureau.

As a result of his contribution to the development of industry in Taiwan, in particular the construction of the walled city, he was awarded the title *tongzhi* (subprefect). *The History of Taiwan* (Taiwan tongshi) by Lien Heng (1878–1936) places Li Chunsheng alongside Ku Hsien-jung, Chen Fuqian, and Huang Nanqiu as the most successful businessmen in Taiwan (Huang Fu-san 2004). In 1895, prior to the Japanese attack on Taipei, he joined Bai Longfa and other leading figures to greet the Japanese as they entered the city in an effort to avoid conflict and destruction of property (Alsford 2018, 175).

Li was not just astute in business; he was also an intellectual, particularly versed in Christian theology. During his lifetime, he authored twelve books, including a collection of essays (1894), a travelogue (1896), two books on religious conflict in China (1903, 1906), three theological tracts (1907, 1908, 1911), and a bible commentary (1914). Li wrote broadly, crossing various subject areas. It was, however, in theology that he made his most significant contribution to public intellectual thought in Taiwan at the turn of the twentieth century. Li wrote some of the earliest Chinese Christian commentary in Taiwan in the period following the arrival of the Presbyterian Church in the 1860s. He was respectfully critical of how missionaries had misrepresented Christianity in China. Specifically, he criticized the rendering of biblical vocabulary into written Chinese, and thus unknowingly prepared the foundations for the eventual nativization of the church in Taiwan. Although Li and his family had a positive relationship with

Japanese colonial authorities, he never learned Japanese. His vision for a native church thus was framed in sinocentric terms.

Central to his thought was the idea that Christianity was a lost religion of China. His grafting of Christianity onto Chinese cultural elements toned down its foreignness (Ya-pei Kuo 2017, 44). He followed the Italian Jesuit missionary Matteo Ricci (1552–1610) in presenting Christian doctrine that reinforced the teachings of Confucianism. Li utilized the cultural capital of Confucianism in his apologetics for Christian theology, arguing that the spread of Christianity in China had been slowed by Western missionaries' poor translation of Christian scriptures, compounded by discrepancies between versions made by different Christian denominations, which raised suspicion. Li proposed that all churches and chapels should be declared "the sacred palace of the High God who created the world" (*zhuzai zaohua Shangdi sheng dian*) and that all places of teaching should have the following over the entrance: Tandao Yimen (Entry Door to the Heavenly Way; Ya-pei Kuo 2017, 47).

Li moved away from the foreign mission enterprise (but not from Christianity) as he refined and published his thought. His growing awareness of his own suspension between two cultural realities came to the fore in a conversation about the implementation of a "self-supporting church" (*zili jiaohui*). Li's frugality, a result of his faith, caused him to be marginalized by other successful merchants, such as Lin Hsiung-cheng, who were known to display wealth. This left Li outside certain elite circles. Yet despite this "absence," the first Japanese governor, Kabayama Sukenori, invited Li, then fifty-seven, to assist the colonial government. Li subsequently transferred his businesses to his sons to focus on political and social affairs.

Prior to the arrival of the Japanese, there were numerous institutions for social care in Taiwan. During the Japanese colonial period, many of these were reformed and regulated. Among those under Japanese control were institutions for the care of the disabled, the homeless, the elderly, and orphans. Taipei Renjiyuan, for example, was funded by the Banqiao Lin family in 1866, but was taken over by the colonial authorities in 1899. Over the course of the colonial period, the Japanese established seven care homes, twelve government-led organizations offering free medical treatment, and forty-three private organizations also offering free care (Lai 2008, 84).

The most prominent recipient of Li's philanthropy, beyond the church and associated organizations, was the Taipei Natural Foot Association (Taibei Tianranzu Hui), formed in 1900 by Dr. Huang Yujie in Dadaocheng. Huang was a traditional herbalist who frequently treated patients without charge and made a significant contribution during several epidemics, including the plague of 1896. He received his license as a herbal doctor—the first to receive one—from the Japanese government in 1897. Li joined Huang and forty-eight other elites to fund the association. This mutual aid association was largely a response to a much larger movement, the Foot Emancipation Society (Buchanzuhui), in China. The formation of such associations would inspire others, such as Lin Qingyue, who in 1919 established Hongji Hospital (Hongji Yiyuan) in Dadaocheng to treat social issues such as opium addiction (Alsford 2019a, 129).

An additional form of cooperative philanthropy occurred during the annual ritualized practice of Pudu (Universal Salvation Festival) to appease ghosts and the "restless" dead during the seventh month of the lunar year. These "ghosts" for the most part functioned as metaphors for the socially marginalized, paupers, beggars, and prostitutes—the *jianmin* (lit. "filthy people"; Weller 1985, 46). As part of the ceremony, ritualistic food was first offered to hungry ghosts but subsequently consumed by the poor (Wu Yingtao 1980, 24). The ceremony is colorfully described by George Leslie Mackay:

> The seventh month [of the lunar calendar] was the time for making offerings to all departed spirits. It was a time of great festivity and excitement.... Immense quantities of food [were] offered to the spirits.... When night came on and the time summoning the spirits approached [a] very unspiritual mob—thousands and thousands of hungry beggars, tramps, blacklegs, desperadoes of all sorts, from the country towns, the city slums . . . swelled in every part of the open space, impatiently waiting their turn. [When] the spirits were satisfied, and the gong was sounded, [this] was the signal for the mob. (Mackay 1896, 130)

Although violent cases of "food robbery" led Governor Liu Mingchuan to ban the festival in 1889, descriptions of the event elsewhere in China allude to the hunger and alms basis of the ceremony (Weller 1985, 50).

Widespread income disparity, resulting from commercialization and the rise of the urban middle class, brought systematic attempts to alleviate poverty and associated social issues. One example involved the *yutingtang*, or orphanages. Most children admitted were girls, and the largest institution in northern Taiwan was the Taipei Jen-Chi Relief Institution (Renjiyuan), established in 1870 by Li Chunsheng and Lien Chen-tung, the father of Lien Chan, a Taiwanese politician, on land donated by the Banqiao Lin family.

Among other notable philanthropists was the husband of Shimizu Teruko, Shih Chien, often referred to as the Father of Homeless People, who was born in Tamsui in 1899. After graduating from Taihoku Industrial School (J. Taihoku Kōgyō Gakkō) in 1923, he funded Aiailiao, a hostel for homeless people, in Banka. Shih wrote on the plight of homelessness (Shih Chien 1925). In 1926, he established the Association for the Care of Homeless People (Qigai Pumie Xiehui). He invited thirty-six social elites of Taiwan to join the committee, among them wealthy merchants, such as Lin Hsiung-cheng and Ku Hsien-jung. Li Chunsheng had died two years earlier so was not part of that committee. His earlier philanthropy provided important foundations for the establishment of the later charitable organizations in the region.

Li financed the construction of two churches, Jinan Presbyterian Church in 1897 and Dadaocheng Presbyterian Church in 1915, when he was seventy-eight years old. Li was an evangelist dedicated to the spread of Chinese Christianity throughout Taiwan and China, as is clear in his published writing in Fuzhou.

Li did much to improve the lives of people in Taiwan, but he was unsuccessful in mobilizing large-scale conversion. For most Taiwanese, Christianity remained alien but not incompatible with their own culture. He was successful in partially fusing it with the identity of the district, but it would be another belief system born out of the West that would ultimately take hold: self-determining nationalism and democracy. These ideas continue to fuel Taiwanese sociopolitical thought.

Li Chunsheng was a marginal man. He features little in mission history of Taiwan. George Leslie Mackay and other foreign missionaries in northern Taiwan seldom refer to him in their diaries and correspondence. The history of philanthropy and charity equally marginalizes him. Fate condemned him to live in the shadows of contrasting societies that were not merely different but culturally antagonistic. He was an ally of the "barbarians" or "the man empowered by the foreigners" (*fanshi lizaichun*). This providence of pluralness shaped all Taiwanese starting with the earlier layers of colonization, the departure of the Japanese at the end of the Second World War, and the events of February 1947, which in turn fractured this dialectal subjectivity and forced many to choose a side.

THE 228 INCIDENT

1947

16

A Hawker's Tale

LIN CHIANG-MAI

The lights on the street were coming up,
and people—artists, writers, actors—the types who
would drink, smoke, and laugh their way through
the end of the world—drifted out of the teahouse.
Often, they stopped at the widow's stand. She even
sold American cigarettes. They tore open the pack right
there, lighting up with a match she gave them.
SHAWNA YANG RYAN · 2016

As Emperor Hirohito read out the declaration of surrender on 15 August 1945, his words would trigger one of the most significant movements of people in the Asia Pacific: "After pondering deeply the general trends of the world and the actual conditions obtaining in our Empire today, we have decided to effect a settlement of the present situation by resorting to an extraordinary measure. We have ordered our Government to communicate to the Governments of the United States, Great Britain, China, and the Soviet Union that our Empire accepts the provisions of their joint declaration."

Chen Yi, the Chinese Nationalist–appointed chief executive, arrived on 24 October 1945 at the port of Keelung in the north of Taiwan, to govern the island as provincial head for the Republic of China. It was the first time Taiwan would be governed as a part of a modern Chinese republic.

As for the Japanese, many who had settled and made Taiwan their home were now forced to leave as a condition of that surrender. In turn, many others began arriving from China. These exoduses would mark Taiwan. The harbors of Keelung and Kaohsiung became crammed, and ferries started to move people and their belongings to and from the island. This movement ushered in an era of placelessness in which the sense of belonging became liminal and uncertain.

At the start, many of Taiwan's inhabitants were enthusiastic about, or at least interested in, this idea of a returning to a motherland. The expectation of the end of the empire triggered expectations of greater equality and participation in society and politics. Within a very short period, these expectations were met with disappointment. Taiwan under Chinese sovereignty was not what many had expected. Incompetence and corruption were rife, and many were dismayed by the physical state of the arriving troops. Soldiers disembarked at ports without full uniform, some without shoes. Many carried nonmilitary equipment: kitchen utensils and other sundry goods. The local inhabitants keen to see "the army that had defeated the Japanese," as propaganda leaflets claimed, were shocked. They were unable to stop comparing these arrivals with the smartly dressed Japanese departures. Some Taiwanese rationalized that these soldiers had been fighting for several years. Yet as more Chinese soldiers arrived and began filtering into urban areas, the behavior of many would sour the opinions of their supporters.

As tensions heightened, the situation gave rise to the expression "Out with the dogs and in with the pigs" (*Gouqu zhulai*), solidifying a new layer of coloniality on Taiwan as a colonization in exile. The signifier of this was the creation of two distinct groups of "ethnicities": the *benshengren* and the *waishengren*. These distinctions have defined Taiwanese nation-building processes.

For the *benshengren*, during the fifty years of Japanese colonization, Taiwan had experienced significant economic development and an increased standard of living. By swiftly confiscating five hundred Japanese-owned factories, mines, and former homes of Japanese residents, Chen Yi quickly consolidated his governance over Taiwan. Hopes of greater equality among the Taiwanese were dashed, and Chen Yi earned the moniker *jieshou* (robber). With the confiscation of property, the Chinese government, like the Japanese before them, now had a monopoly over key industries and began handing their management to the business tycoons and technocrats arriving from China. Taiwanese discontent grew rapidly, and economic mismanagement led to a large black market, heightened inflation, and food shortages. Many of those arriving from China made punitive demands on local Taiwanese businesses, asking for either a significant discount on products or, in some cases, free items. For many in Taiwan, the incoming Chinese nationalists were erasing successes they had achieved during the colonial period, especially in self-government.

Between the end of 1945 and early 1947, Taiwan was a whistling kettle. The boiling point occurred on the evening of the 27 February 1947, when a Tobacco Monopoly Bureau enforcement team in Taipei went to the district of Dadaocheng and confiscated "contraband" cigarettes from Lin Chiang-mai, a forty-year-old widow, outside the Tianma Tea House (Tianma Chafang).

<hr>

Taiwan's political reality and the historiographic divisions in the postwar period have left us with a fractured view of the background of Lin Chiang-mai, the "silent mother of the 228 Incident." Piecing together her biography has not been easy. Lin is thought to have been born in 1907 in Hsinchu County. At the time of the incident she resided at 9 Erdingmu, Rixinding, in Dadaocheng. Her two older sons had been left in Taoyuan with her father-in-law while she lived in Taipei with her other two children. At the time of the incident, Lin's youngest son, Lin Wen-shan, was twelve, and her only daughter, Lin Ming-chu, was ten. She had been widowed since before the birth of her last child.

According to the official report filed by the Ministry of Justice Investigation Bureau in 1947, Lin claimed that when she pleaded with the enforcement team to return her stock, a man hit her on the head with the butt of his gun. As observers descended onto the scene, in the chaos, she could not remember the attacker's appearance. However, she was certain that the Tobacco Monopoly Bureau enforcement team was responsible, as the agents had taken all her cigarettes (National Archives Administration 1947). She claimed that she had begged but they simply ignored her. She stated in her record that she would like the bureau to return her cigarettes. When the investigator asked her what language was spoken during the incident, Lin said that it was all done in the "local language," giving no indication that there had been any language barrier (National Archives Administration 1947).

In 2006, the writer Yang Du produced a documentary, *Looking for the Silent Mother of the 228 Incident* (Xunzhao ererba de chenmo muqin). In the documentary, Yang interviewed Lin's daughter, Lin Ming-chu. Yang pointed out that Lin Ming-chu had later married a *waishengren* and that the daughter was a witness to the incident, arguing that Lin Chiang-mai's "misfortune" was simply a misunderstanding caused by a language barrier as opposed to *waishengren* mistreatment of *benshengren*. The documentary was funded by Taipei City's Department of Cultural Affairs, whose mayor at the time was Ma Ying-jeou, the later KMT president. Moreover, Yang had declared himself a KMT supporter (Chen Hsiao-I et al. 2007).

Yang presents Lin Chiang-mai as a neatly dressed widow who never wore "Taiwanese outfits" but rather an eloquent *qipao* (cheongsam). He asserts that Lin often told her daughter, "We are not trying to look glamorous, only to be neat and presentable. It doesn't matter if we are poor. People would respect you as long as you look presentable" (Yang Tu 2015). He explains that Lin made her living by selling cigarettes, that she was highly noticeable when working the streets, and that bodyguards from restaurants and clubs felt sorry for her and often purchased cigarettes from her. He claims that Lin Ming-chu did not attend school but rather helped her mother on the streets. She was thus present and witnessed the whole incident.

Lin Ming-chu states in the interview:

On the evening of 27 February 1947, Mum was selling cigarettes as usual. I was holding a tray of cigarettes close by. A soldier-looking man came over, picked up a cigarette and lit it. He didn't pay at first, so people started to stare at him. He then put his hand into his pocket. I thought he was going to get his money, but a bodyguard next to me thought he was taking out a gun, so he started to shout, "What's the man doing?" in Hokkien. Since everyone was speaking in Hokkien, the soldier couldn't understand and got nervous. He thought people were going to hurt him. He left the money and escaped. Shortly after, a car came with six or seven police and things got out of hand. Many other cigarette sellers ran away. Mum was unable to run because she was wearing a *qipao*, and I was too young to escape. Soon mum was attacked and people around me got furious. (Yang Tu 2015)

Yang's documentary caused a controversy in the reactions from victims of the 228 Incident and the White Terror that followed. One of those involved was Juan Mei-shu. Juan was nineteen at the time of the incident and had lost her father, a Taiwanese elite who fell victim to the White Terror. Juan started to investigate the 228 Incident in the 1960s and was viewed as one of the leading figures for revealing the truth behind the story (Juan 1994).

Juan's reaction to Yang Du's documentary was published in the *Liberty Times* on 9 February 2007 as an opinion piece titled "The Truths and Lies of Lin Chiang-mai" (Lin Jiangmai de zhenzhen jiajia; Juan 2007). Juan argues that the documentary seriously twisted the truth and that many of Lin Ming-chu's statements were misleading. Juan claims that Ming-chu told a very different story when she discussed the incident with her in the past. Her own investigation concluded that Lin Ming-chu was not out with her mother that evening, as she was not even in Taipei. According to Juan, it was Lin Chiang-mai's third and fourth sons who were out helping her that night. Various witnesses, including Li Hsien-wen, Huang Shou-li and Wang Kuei-jung, were all present that night and all told Juan that they had not seen a little girl with Lin. Wang Kuei-jung's account is particularly important, as he was selling cigarettes next to Lin Chiang-mai.

Juan writes:

I first approached Lin Ming-chu back in 2001. She told me that she wasn't at the scene as she was too young. As a result, she had very few details. Later in the interview she told me to go and speak to her older brother, Lin Pao-lo. However, she stressed that I must not tell her brother that she gave me his contact details. I didn't think much about it then. It wasn't until later that I found out that Lin Pao-lo has a deep hatred toward the *waishengren* and since Lin Ming-chu had married a *waishengren* there was resentment. Later, I became a good friend with Lin Pao-lo and he agreed to be interviewed for the documentaries that I produced. He was in his seventies when he was interviewed, and he was in good health. Some people from Taoyuan had told me that the Department of Cultural Affairs intend to build a road that leads to Lin Chiang-mai's grave, and her grave will become a cultural monument. Many local people objected to this idea. Lin doesn't need to be apotheosized! Lin was one of the victims during the 228 Incident, but what about the other mothers, wives, and of the many other victims? Who is using Lin to make up a new story? How can the Department of Cultural Affairs make it up to the other victims?

The premise of Juan's argument is that Lin Chiang-mai was not the trigger for the 228 Incident. She was a symptom, the affront that lit the powder barrel. For Juan, the causes of the incident were social and economic. However, authors such as Tsai Hui-ping (2006 argue that the 228 Incident was caused by a language barrier. For Tsai, this claim comes from repeated interviews in which Ming-chu emphasized the difficulty of her mother's life. She says her father had died before she was born, and her mother had to live with her husband's large family. According to Ming-chu, Lin Chiang-mai was bullied by her sisters-in-law, and as a result, she left Taoyuan. She first lived with her parents-in-law, who ran a tea shop in Taipei. After the tea shop closed, she started to sell cigarettes around Dadaocheng. On the night that Lin Ming-chu claimed she was helping her mother, the soldier who tried to ask the price of the cigarette spoke in Mandarin. She did not understand him as she spoke only Japanese and Hokkien. Before she could react, some local gangsters started to shout, "Someone's not paying for the cigarette!" Soon people went up to the soldier, and the situation deteriorated because people could not communicate.

United Daily, which published Tsai's article, is a pan-blue paper, generally supporting the KMT, whereas the *Liberty Times*, which published Juan's opinion piece, is a pan-green paper, affiliated with the DPP. The political cleavages in Taiwan make understanding the history of Lin Chiang-mai's cigarette incident difficult. Tsai's argument is that although the 228 Incident is often associated with the conflict between *waishengren* and *benshengren*, Lin Chiang-mai allowed her only daughter to marry a *laoyuzai* (literally, "old taro," indicating a *waishengren* male)—moreover, a *waishengren* police officer. For Tsai, this is a touching account of how the two ethnic groups integrated: "Lin Ming-chu feels that Taiwan should allow this sixty-year-old wound to heal" (Tsai Hui-ping 2006). This stands in stark contrast to other victim and onlooker stories, which portray the history not as healing but rather as a continuation of the *waishengren* silencing of the *benshengren*.

Shawna Ryan, in her novel *Green Island*, highlights the confusion and panic that accompanied the incident:

> The cigarette vendor clutched her head. Her fingers were greasy with blood. Pain rippled through her skull in slow waves. She imagined she heard her children screaming in the chaos. The Monopoly Bureau agents, pressed to the widow's fallen body by the crowd rolling angrily toward them in a fog of cursing, kicked her. Eyes wild, the agents waved their guns and threatened to shoot, but the crowd's cries swallowed their words. The people would not retreat; some fought to get the bleeding cigarette vendor while others surged forward in rage. The agents began firing and the crowd collapsed, fleeing, breaking into hundred splinters. (Ryan 2016, 7)

George Kerr, who was in Taipei at the time of the incident, relates that the bureau agents, firing into the crowd, killed one person and left Lin Chiang-mai bleeding on the side of the street, close to death. The agents ran and hid in a nearby police box to wait for police to arrive. The crowd allowed the police to remove the agents but set fire to the bureau truck and its contents. The following morning, a crowd of at least two thousand marched, according to Kerr, carrying banners and placards that had been made overnight, to the office of the bureau chief, demanding the death sentence for the agents who had committed manslaughter the night before (Kerr 1966, 254). Finding the chief absent, they marched to the governor's office to present the petition directly to Chen Yi. According to Kerr, during the march, more agents were discovered abusing two children selling cigarettes. Kerr writes, "This was too much; an angry crowd beat the Chinese agents to death within a few feet of the Bureau Branch Office" (Kerr 1966, 255). Kerr, who was having lunch close to the scene, recalled hearing machine gun fire. Leaving the restaurant, he proceeded toward the Monopoly

Bureau, knowing that the protest was centered there. Finding it empty, he proceeded to the governor's office. There he saw the line of heavily armed Nationalist soldiers facing an unarmed crowd. On the roadway between them lay the bodies of civilians who had been shot down. This was now a massacre, not simply an incident.

Understanding the partisan divides behind the biography of Lin Chiang-mai does not change what is known about the events on 28 February. Lin Chiang-mai was given a permit to sell cigarettes, and thus she was not illegally hawking. Language would have been an issue. Many Taiwanese did not speak Mandarin. Hokkien and Japanese were the principal languages spoken, reinforcing the divide in nation-building processes. For the Taiwanese, the 228 Incident triggered their start-again nationalism. Their perception of the Japanese did not parallel that of people in postcolonial Korea and China. Lin did not die on the streets of Dadaocheng, but her health did decline following that evening. She died in 1969 at the age of sixty-four due to liver problems. Her legacy is a salient reminder of the complexities of identity in Taiwan.

17

A Refugee's Tale

JIN SU-QIN

Our optimism, indeed, is admirable,
even if we say so ourselves. The story of our struggle
has finally become known. We lost our home, which
means the familiarity of daily life. We lost our occupation,
which means the confidence that we are of some use in
this world. We lost our language, which means the
naturalness of reactions, the simplicity of gestures,
the unaffected expression of feelings.

HANNAH ARENDT · 1943

"There have always been refugees," writes Lyndsey Stonebridge in *Placeless People,* yet the mass movement of displacement is very much a product of the twentieth century (Stonebridge 2018, 3). Taiwan's identity is in many ways pockmarked by displacement. The scars of its twentieth-century definition are rooted in three significant mass displacements: (1) the displacement of Indigenous, Hakka, and Hokkien-speaking communities throughout the Japanese colonial period, (2) the displacement of many Japanese following their surrender at the end of the Second World War and the cession of Taiwan to the protectorate of the newly formed United Nations, and (3) the Chinese Nationalists who fled—along with their government-in-exile—to Taiwan after losing the civil war. Unlike many other twentieth-century mass displacements, these resulted not in a stateless people but rather in a stateless nation. Many of those who came to Taiwan in the postwar period did not do so of their own volition but rather were forced there by the government that was becoming exiled (Dominic Yang 2021, 42).

The four years between 1945 and 1949 witnessed two significant displacements: the Japanese *from* Taiwan and the Chinese Nationalists *to* Taiwan. The crises of this period affected not simply the displaced people but also the political and moral authority of the Taiwanese nation-state—in particular, its historical claim. Taiwan's placelessness during this period was felt by all. Among the Japanese who had come to see Taiwan as home, some had put down roots on the island for almost five decades and had no knowledge of the Japanese metropolitan centers where they would have to reimagine their everyday lives (Dawley 2015, 115).

For the Taiwanese, this period ushered in the "silence"; for the arriving refugees, living in Taiwan was akin to homelessness (Joshua Fan 2011, 17). For all involved, the experience was both existential and political. The history of "China's homeless generation" begins with the perceived ineffectiveness of the Manchu Empire.

The Manchus' seeming lack of will to modernize in the face of continued foreign encroachment, coupled with rising modern Chinese nationalism, precipitated the overthrow of the last imperial dynasty in China. The 1911 Xinhai Revolution, named for the year in which it occurred, was followed by establishment of the Republic of China. Although there had been numerous anti-Qing rebellions and attempts to overthrow the dynasty, it was popular unrest over a railway crisis in Wuchang, Hubei, that directly led to the downfall of the Qing dynasty. On 10 October 1911, the New Army stationed at Wuchang launched an assault on the residence of the viceroy of Huguang. Ruicheng, the viceroy, abandoned the residence, and the revolutionaries shortly controlled the entire city. The Wuchang Uprising, as it would later be known, was not necessarily the catalyst that many of the revolutionary leaders had planned or hoped for. It took many of them by surprise. Sun Yat-sen, for example, was in the United States on a fundraising mission. Huang Xing and Song Jiaoren were hundreds of miles from Wuchang at the time of the incident. Following the successes in Hubei, the revolutionary leaders telegrammed the other provinces to secede from the Qing government. Eighteen provinces in Southern and Central China agreed. Sun returned to China in December 1911 and was elected provisional president of the new republic. On 12 February 1912, Empress Dowager Longyu, on behalf of Emperor Puyi, abdicated the Qing throne, marking a new chapter in modern Chinese history.

In Taiwan, the period between October 1911 and January 1912 was unremarkable. Taiwan was a growing part of the Japanese empire, and although some in the literary elite were following events in China, the spirit of Chinese nationalism was markedly absent. Liang Qichao, a Chinese reformist, had visited the island earlier that year, but his meetings were always held privately in specific literary circles. The seismic events unfolding in China were not part of the daily lives of ordinary citizens. This was undoubtedly true for vast swaths of the population in China also. The elites' ability to spawn a movement that could begin consolidating notions of identity in China arguably grew out of the student protests in Beijing on 4 May 1919. The growing anger among the students centered largely on the government's weak response to the Treaty of Versailles, which allowed Japan to retain territories in Shandong that Germany had surrendered following the siege of Tsingtao in 1914. The demonstrations ignited protests across major urban areas in China and an upsurge in Chinese nationalism that revealed a mass base far from traditional intellectual and political elites. Thus began the New Cultural Movement in 1915–21, which criticized classical Chinese ideals in an attempt to attract a new Chinese cultural base that would see China as a nation among other nations, a society that was forward facing and not past dependent.

The New Cultural Movement was wholly Chinese, and although it registered in some overseas Chinese communities and among certain literary elites in Taiwan, the significant developments took place among literary circles and student organizations in Beijing and Shanghai. Key members, such as Chen Duxiu and Li Dazhao, became frustrated by the slowness of change and urged more radical social action. The political left would become a natural home as theories of anti-imperialism were discussed, translated, and shared. Chen and Li used their positions as faculty members at Peking University to actively assist in organizing Marxist study groups, which eventually evolved into the initial gatherings of the Chinese Communist Party. One of the participants in the inaugural meeting was a young and ambitious individual who had worked as one of Chen's library assistants. That man was Mao Zedong (Harper 2020, 353).

The rupture in political thought of the early revolutionary leaders led to decades-long uncertainties in the country as the republic fought for control of the country against militaristic warlord factions and communist insurgencies. Japan used this instability to expand its influence and secure direct access to raw materials. An explosion on the railway in Shenyang (Mukden in Manchu) on 18 September 1931 would change China under the leadership of Chiang Kai-shek, who had become the leader of the republic following Sun's death in 1925. The explosion triggered a Japanese military response to protect Japanese lives and property. The Mukden Incident sparked the Japanese invasion of Manchuria. Japan was successful in supporting and creating Manchukuo, a puppet state led by the last Qing emperor, Puyi. Between 1931 and 1937, Japan and China clashed in a series of incidents. On the night of 7 July 1937, in Wanping, a village fifteen kilometers southwest of Beijing, Japanese and Chinese troops exchanged fire close to the Marco Polo Bridge—named after the Venetian explorer but known in Chinese as Lugouqiao. The unfortunate bridge later gave its name to the incident, which not only triggered Japan's full-scale invasion of China but would define the destinies of multiple nations.

Early twentieth-century China was a period of mixed relations with Japan. The year 1937, although a watershed moment in the clash between the two, was not a starting point. Revolutionary leaders keen to escape the clutches of the Qing empire used Japan not only as a model but also as a refuge. Whether positive or negative, a significant part of twentieth-century China was shaped by Japan (Mitter 2014, 27). Japan's growing strength led many Chinese intellectuals to look toward the West as an answer to the crisis that enveloped China at the turn of the century.

In 1924, in a speech in Kobe, Japan, Sun Yat-sen declared that the peoples of Asia had "shaken off the yoke of European oppression," and Japan had shown what could be done by its victory over Russia in 1905. Sun emphasized his understanding of the meaning of pan-Asianism. In Japan, this was interpreted not as cooperation but as competition.

Sun's political philosophy, the Three Principles of the People—democracy, nationalism, and livelihood—shaped the discourse of competing nationalisms in China. The fight for the heart of the nation between the Kuomintang-led government of the Republic of China and the Communist Party of China flared intermittently between 1927 and 1949. Typically understood as a conflict in two acts, the first act ended with the outbreak of war with Japan, and the second act opened following the Japanese defeat in the War of the Pacific. In 1949, the Communists were successful in gaining control over the Chinese mainland, establishing the People's Republic of China in 1949. The Republic of China fled, setting up a government-in-exile on Taiwan.

The great divide between the Nationalists and the Communists is not a straightforward story of losers and winners. The divide was fractured, uneven. Many people were caught up in the struggle, accidents of history; others made their decisions of their own free will. Some families were forever divided. The "Great Exodus," to use a term coined by Dominic Yang, was traumatic and identity-forming (Dominic Yang 2021, 1). This exodus informs Taiwan. What Taiwan is and what it is not trace their history to this juncture. Taiwan is defined by the stories of its displacements; it is an island of migration. Most who fled China were neither military or bureaucratic elites nor influential business elites. They were common folk and petty civil servants (Dominic Yang 2021, 7). They came, not always willingly, from a multitude of provinces with distinct environments, identities, customs, and languages. In Taiwan, they would be labeled collectively outsiders and confronted by others coming from different environments, with divergent identities, customs, and languages, now referred to as insiders. This cultural blending made for a uniquely Taiwan experience.

The following tale is of a woman who was both a colonist and a refugee: a placeless person who, despite making Taiwan her home, had a secret that continued to tie her to her memory of her birthplace.

<hr>

Jin Su-qin was born in 1925, she thinks. The date is based on her own estimation. She was born in Xiatang village, Lingjing Township, Linhai County, Zhejiang, China. It is hard to locate her hometown precisely, since Lingjing Township was abolished in 2001 and now forms part of the current Hetou Town. It is in a mountainous area approximately 140 kilometers south of Ningbo (Alsford 2010b).

Jin's family was not poor, but neither could it claim to be rich. They owned enough land to maintain a comfortable living, and following Jin's father's passing, her mother hired tenant farmers to work the land. The distribution of tenured farming varied depending on the type of farming, soil condition, and general economic environment. Given that 95 percent of farming communities in the areas surrounding Shanghai (including Zhejiang) were said to be tenanted, any land ownership would have been historical and have remained within families for multiple generations (Tawney 1932, 34). In nineteenth- and early twentieth-century China, landowning, although less profitable than trading and moneylending, was much more reliable, dignified, and considered more honest. As an investment, land was more durable and carried lower risk. Moreover, it did not carry the same stigma as other profit-making enterprises, and if landlords did not make unnecessary demands, the relationship between tenant and landlord was respectful (Zhou 2013). Landownership provided a solid foundation for the financial well-being of families. It secured household income and granted the necessary propriety for family ritual practice.

In early twentieth-century China, one such ritual practice was wrapping the feet of young girls to modify their shape and size. Although the Republic of China had banned the practice of foot binding in 1912, the ban was not enforced. Jin's mother attempted to bind her feet at a young age. Jin resisted, untying the bandages at night after her mother had gone to bed (Alsford 2010b). This continued for a while until her mother threatened that Jin would have to help on the farm if she continued to refuse. Jin happily accepted this proposal and began to learn the trades that would become important to her later in life.

Changes to everyday life in China began piecemeal following the beginnings of the republic. In many locations, especially rural areas, this took decades. One practice the republic considered important was elections. According to the Chinese-British writer Jung Chang, people in China did not seem to find the idea of voting alien. Competition as a route to high office was deeply ingrained in Chinese culture. After all, the political elites were selected via nationwide examination (Jung Chang 2019, 65). Men who had either a middle-school education or large property holdings were eligible to vote (Harrison 2005, 98–99). A county representative tasked with appointing a voter-registration committee visited Jin's family home to inform her father that he was eligible (Alsford 2010b). At some point in either the late 1920s or early 1930s, during a village election likely held at the city god temple, a fight broke out between villages, and Jin's father was killed. Her elder brother took over most of the family business. Jin recalls that she was never allowed to eat at the dining table with her brother and could only eat in the kitchen, though she had prepared all the food (Alsford 2010b).

Until she was seventeen, Jin's only journey away from her hometown was a trip to a temple that took six or seven hours by foot and involved staying at the temple overnight and returning the following day. Jin was able to recount the details of that visit vividly.

Jin had a cousin, Chen Meixiang, who lived in Ningbo. Chen's family was financially better off than Jin's, and she was trained as a nurse (her feet were bound). Chen's husband, Zhang Zhaoze, was an American-trained pilot serving as part of the Flying Tigers in the ROC Air Force. He, too, was from a well-to-do background. Chen and Zhang had four children and were based in Nanjing (Alsford 2010b). Chen knew that her family might soon move with the air force and asked Jin if she would consider moving to Nanjing to help her. Jin excitedly agreed. For Jin, there was no reason to stay at home. Her mother had passed away, and her older brother's spouse treated her poorly, forcing her to perform duties like those of a servant (Alsford 2010b). As a result, she made her first big move at the age of seventeen. Accompanied by a relative, she left for Haimen. They walked at night and slept during the day to avoid robbers. From Haimen, they continued to Ningbo, where they took a boat to Nanjing.

Jin lived in Nanjing for two years. In 1948, Zhang Zhaoze's Air Force Team 4 was sent to Taiwan (ROC Air Force n.d.). Chen, the children, and Jin were permitted to follow as military dependents. Following the order, they flew to Chiayi. Jin knew that a long stay in Taiwan would require registering through the household registration system. To legitimize living with her cousin, they faked Jin's identity, claiming she was Chen's sister. Jin had to change her family name to Chen, which she hated for the rest of her life. She specifically asked her son to change her family name back following her death. Her birthday was also changed (Alsford 2019b), adding six years to her age.

Jin Su-qin's story is Kafkaesque. When she boarded the plane in 1947, she had a history, a belonging. She exited the plane in disguise and placeless.

Her life in Taiwan did not start easily. Her role in her cousin's household was closer to that of a servant. Her main task was to look after the children. It was her job to take the children to school, where she met her future husband, Wang Hsi-chi, who was working as a janitor at the school. As the only son to a rich landlord and merchant who traded between Wuxi, Jiangsu, and Shanghai, Wang was spoiled. (The family suffered greatly later, during the Cultural Revolution, when landlords were targeted.) He lacked interest in anything academic, caring more about having fun. He did not attend school but instead had a private tutor at home. Wang's departure from home was not planned. He got into a dispute with his father's third wife and, in a fit of anger, threw a teacup at her. Unfortunately, she passed out, bleeding from the head. In that moment, Wang believed he had killed her. He escaped and went to Shanghai to stay with his aunt, who owned a hotel and a theater. During his stay in Shanghai, he joined the KMT army when Chiang Kai-shek campaigned in 1944 for the "100,000 young people, 100,000 soldiers" (*shiwan qingnian shiwan jun*; Alsford 2019b). Wang's troop was sent to Chiayi in 1948.

Between late 1948 and early 1949, the main group evacuated from the mainland comprised business elites, families, prominent statesmen, and some urban professionals—in other words, those who could finance the voyage themselves. The next group to migrate arrived in Taiwan starting in the summer of 1949 and was often referred to as the "forty-niners." Continuing into the 1950s, these migrants came from vastly different backgrounds, including the "raggedy" soldiers and "peasants," a number of whom had no idea that Taiwan would be their final destination (Dominic Yang 2021, 42). This included the fourteen thousand Chinese prisoners of war captured by US and UN troops in Korea during the Korean War, who entered Taiwan along with evacuees of the Dachen Islands (Dachen Zhudao). In 1955. Wang Hsi-chi left China with the forty-niners. For Jin Su-qin, as one of the early birds of late 1948 and early 1949, the crossing was largely accidental but not perilous. Her entry into Taiwanese society was not markedly different from those arriving on evacuation vessels. She, like all the others, including her future husband, would start again as a placeless person.

After arriving in Taiwan, Wang Hsi-chi did not want to stay in the military. For reasons unknown, he managed to get a three-month furlough from his company (Alsford 2019b). This was lucky, as his company was shortly after mobilized to fight against the Communists. None returned. He took a job as a janitor at the newly formed air force elementary school, where he met Jin and married her soon afterward. At that time, the KMT forbade soldiers to marry in Taiwan. Wang rationalized that "he was on a break" and was "not a soldier but a janitor" at the time (Alsford 2019b). They got married at Chaiyi District Court. Jin's decision was not entirely motivated by love, but rather was an opportunity to leave her cousin and live her own life. She remarked in an interview that her wedding day was the only time she had worn makeup in her entire life (Alsford 2010b).

In 1951–52, the KMT started to arrest soldiers who attempted to desert. Wang found himself in trouble. Nevertheless, as Zhang Zhaoze held a high rank in the air force, he was able to arrange a job for Wang at Chiayi Air Force Base in Shuishang. Wang thus migrated from the army to the air force. Shortly after moving into a house near the base, they welcomed their first son, Wang Hsu-kang. Following the birth of a second son, a third and a fourth were born in quick succession.

Wang was not an ideal husband (Alsford 2010b). He was often irresponsible and enjoyed gambling, and he could not apply for any benefits for his family, since he was not supposed to get married in the first place. As a result, Jin was often left to support the family all by herself. She sold food to those stationed at the base, ran a noodle stand outside of the Chiayi train station, and put her farming skills into practice by raising ducks and pigs. In her last job, she ran a small dumpling restaurant.

Wang Hsi-chi died in 1991 in a car accident. He always maintained a guest mentality, as if living Taiwan was merely temporary. He, like Jin and the others who came in the great exodus, were conditioned to believe in three ipseities: identification with the Kuomintang, identification with the province of their birth, and finally the cultural prejudice that marked them in Taiwan society as *waishengren* (Corcuff 2002, 173). Wang's imagined reality became complicated when he finally got the chance to return to China shortly before his death. He was shocked to find that the CCP had confiscated everything his family once owned and that the younger brother born after Wang left (by his father's third wife, who was the reason he left home) looked older than him. His brother told him that the Wang family had been badly tortured for being a landlord family and for having a son who had joined the KMT. The little brother and his children were denied an education and were allowed to perform only the lowest jobs as a result. Wang went back to Taiwan feeling extremely confused. He lost interest in returning to China. As for Jin, she never wanted to see her hometown again. She told me that the girl from the village had only negative memories (Alsford 2010b). As Edward Said puts it, the pathos of exile is the impossibility of return (Said 2012, xxxv).

Jin's cousin's family emigrated to the United States after all their children completed university. Chen asked Jin to join her in the United States, stating that she was lonely. Jin declined. She was no longer alone, as she had her own children and grandchildren (Alsford 2019b).

Jin lived in Taiwan for sixty-five years. She spoke Hokkien with a strong accent but had forgotten the language of her hometown. In 2012, she died of heart disease.

Jin Su-qin was a *waishengren*. She came to Taiwan during the great exodus. Although she came with the elites, Jin did not belong with them. Jin's relocation to Taiwan would shape the narrative of the island and would in return define her as being *waisheng,* outside. As an individual she had no role in the ill tidings brought about by her arrival. The year 1948 was monumental for Jin. It changed her life. She arrived in Taiwan not as a politically strong advocate for the Chinese Nationalists but as part of a complex social upheaval that had profound and wide-ranging repercussions in Taiwan, eventually leading to a period of terror.

MARTIAL LAW

1947–1987

18

A Tangwai's Tale

HUANG HSIN-CHIEH

Listen to the voice of the people.
LEE TENG-HUI · 1984

The year 2017 marked several important observances in the modern political history of Taiwan. It had been seventy years since the 228 Incident
and thirty years since the lifting of martial law. The four decades between
the 228 Incident and the lifting of martial law had witnessed remarkable
transformations on the island. Documentation of this change, however, has
for the most part focused on the island's economic and political transitions.
During the 1950s, Taiwan experienced a series of land reform and community development programs, primarily led by the Sino-American Joint
Commission on Rural Reconstruction. The notion of "developing agriculture by virtue of industry and fostering industry by virtue of agriculture" (*yi
nongye peiyang gongye, yi gongye fazhan nongye*) had by 1961 resulted in two
four-year economic plans. The period between 1963 and 1973, considered
"a golden age" of economic growth in Taiwan, saw the island become one
of the four Asian tigers (the others being South Korea, Singapore, and
Hong Kong; Kim 1998). This economic success story, often referred to as
the "Taiwan Miracle," arguably aided the island in its transformation into
a liberal democracy (Gold 1986, 130–31).

This economic shift, which opened up opportunities in the labor market,
sparked a significant rise in social mobility. By the late 1970s and early 1980s,

the new middle class of Taiwan and the free enterprise that had permitted its emergence become important markers in the people's demand for greater rights and more democratic processes. The development of civil society in Taiwan was a major turning point in the history of democracy on the island, the foundations of which can arguably be found in the Kaohsiung Incident on 10 December 1979.

To commemorate Human Rights Day, a date chosen to echo the United Nations General Assembly's adoption of the Universal Declaration of Human Rights, a demonstration was organized by *Formosa Magazine*, led by Huang Hsin-chieh and other members of the Tangwai, whose purpose was to promote democracy. The incident that occurred on 10 December had its roots a day earlier, when two campaign wagons (dispatched by *Formosa Magazine*) broadcast the Human Rights Forum. Police held up the procession, and two volunteers were arrested, prompting several of the Tangwai to gather outside the Gushan branch of the Police Security Bureau, where the two were being held. The outrage felt at the arrest prompted a number of the Tangwai and its followers to attend the following day's demonstration even though they had not previously planned to do so. On 10 December, four hours before the planned gathering (between 2 and 3 p.m.), the authorities—including the military police, the army, and the police—took up positions in the vicinity. As the event unfolded, military police began to close in on the demonstrators. Panic set in as demonstrators clashed with the authorities, and the Kuomintang (KMT) used the incident as an excuse to arrest well-known opposition leaders.

The subsequent military trials of the eight key defendants, known as the Kaohsiung Eight—Chang Chun-hung, Huang Hsin-chieh, Chen Chu, Yao Chia-wen, Shih Ming-teh, Lu Hsiu-lien, Lin Hung-hsuan, and Lin Yi-hsiung—took place along with thirty-three other civilian trials. Due to space constraints, a comprehensive analysis is not feasible at this juncture. Nonetheless, J. Bruce Jacobs's examination of the Kaohsiung Incident provides a significant perspective on the intellectual history of Taiwan's democratic movements (Jacobs 2016). This perspective allows for a deeper exploration of the knowledge generated, debated, documented, and notably put into action by Taiwanese intellectuals during the era of martial law. This is particularly noticeable in the identities of certain defense lawyers involved in the trials. Chief among those are the lawyer for Huang Hsin-chieh, Chen Shui-bian, who served as president in 2000–2008, and Yao Chia-wen's representative, Su Tseng-chang, who became chairman of the Democratic Progressive Party (2012–14).

———

Born on 20 August 1920 in Dalongdong, which is nestled between the Tamsui and Keelung Rivers north of Dadaocheng, Huang Hsin-chieh was the son of a rice mill owner. As was common then, Huang's father consulted a fortune teller to provide a suitable name for his son. The fortune teller said the boy would grow up to become an important official, so Chin-lung, meaning "Golden Dragon," would be most suitable. Huang changed his name in 1958 to Hsin-chieh when admiration for Japanese politician Kishi Nobusuke led him to take the kanji of Nobusuke as his new name.

Huang's mother, Lien Hao, was from a merchant family that owned and ran a shop on Dihua Street in Dadaocheng (Li Po-chuan 2003, 32). Her older brother Lien Wen-ching was a known activist during the Japanese period and participated in the Taiwanese Cultural Association. During the Second World War, Huang's father's business started to decline. Huang, who was only a teenager, decided to help the family by finding a job. He left school and began work as an intern at a metal factory, but he would later quit this occupation due to the meager wages. In 1940, he traveled to Tokyo to work at a printing factory. Meanwhile, he enrolled in a five-year middle and high school program, completing his degree at what is now Ueno High School.

In 1946, Huang returned to Taiwan and got a job as a print worker for Taiwan Bank. He studied Mandarin and took the university entrance exam for all universities in the Republic of China. Though offered a place at Peking University, he was unable to attend due to the outbreak of the Chinese Civil War. In 1949, he received an offer from the Taiwan Administration Junior College (Taiwan Xingzheng Zhuanke Xuexiao), which would later become part of National Chung Hsing University. During this period, he became passionate about politics. He joined the KMT and became a KMT student leader. The school encouraged him to support the independent candidate Wu San-lien for Taipei City mayor in February 1950 as the KMT had not selected a candidate that year. Huang graduated in 1951. In 1954, he married Chang Yueh-ching, whose family owned a textile shop in Dadaocheng (Li Po-chuan 2003, 34).

In the second Taipei City mayoral election in 1954, Huang supported the KMT candidate, who lost to Independent candidate Kao Yu-shu (Henry Kao). After this defeat, Huang reconsidered his membership in the KMT. Meanwhile, his father funded him in various businesses, but they never worked out. He told his father that he was passionate about politics, so his father introduced him to Li Fu-chun, who was one of Kao Yu-shu's main assistants. In 1957 Huang left the KMT and later that year joined Kao's reelection campaign team (Li Po-chuan 2003, 42–43). During this period Huang started to show his political potential. Despite his youth, he was considered a good speaker, and he had majored in politics. Lee Teng-hui had noticed Huang at the time (Huang Huang-hsiung 2018), impressed by the young man's promotion of democracy. Meanwhile, Huang became increasingly disappointed in the KMT, feeling that the party's political apparatus was corrupt (Li Po-chuan 2003, 42–45).

In 1961, when Huang was only thirty-three, he ran for Taipei City councilor and was elected. Three years later, he was reelected. In 1969, he successfully secured a seat in the Legislative Yuan. In 1975, Huang , along with Kang Ning-hsiang, a fellow non-KMT politician, founded *Taiwan Politics* magazine (Taiwan zhenglun). During the 1977–78 elections, Huang used his position to actively support non-KMT candidates in local elections. In August 1978, he established *Formosa Magazine* (Meilidao zazhi), which played a significant role in shaping a political party. However, following the Kaohsiung Incident in December of the same year, Huang was arrested.

In a trial in March 1980, Huang was sentenced to fourteen years. He was released on parole in 1987, the year martial law was lifted. The Democratic Progressive Party (DPP) had been established the year before his parole. One year after his release, Huang became a member of the newly established party. In October 1988, he was elected as party leader and successfully reelected the subsequent year. In 1989, the DPP introduced Taiwan independence policies in the run-up to the local government elections, and these policies were published in the *Independence Evening Post* (Chen Yi-shen 2010, 155). In spite of government threats to bring him to court, the DPP continued to push an independent agenda (DPP Huang Huang

Hsin-chieh Editorial Group 2000, 247–50). The DPP successes in the election of six mayors were especially important. Among the most important were Taipei County and Kaohsiung (Rigger 1999, 138–39).

In 1990, during the Wild Lily movement, Huang supported the student activists. The police, however, quickly had him removed. His treatment by the police was widely reported (Tsai Yu-jen 2003, 78–79), resulting in criticism by the general public of his treatment. As a result, Lee Teng-hui, who had claimed he had no idea what was happening, apologized and invited Huang to have a discussion at the presidential office (Tsai Yu-jen 2003, 79)—the first such meeting for an opposition leader. On 30 November 1999, Huang Hsin-chieh died of a heart attack. His final resting place is in Bali on the banks of the River Tamsui.

The Tangwai was a loosely knit group of political opponents to the authoritarian KMT government. The earliest figures in the movement were Huang Hsin-chieh and Kang Ning-hsiang in the 1970s. They began to collaborate more closely following the publication of the *Taiwan Politics* magazine in 1975. The chief aim of the movement was unity. Its goal was to unite the opposition in a quest for democracy. This alliance, most visible at the grassroots level, bore fruit in the 1977 election, a marked turning point in Taiwan's political development (Rigger 1999, 114), when the Tangwai won four local executive and twenty-one Provincial Assembly seats (Fell 2012, 25). The exposed deep-rooted support for the opposition revealed a rift between the KMT and local factions. Many in the Tangwai would interpret this as evidence of mass local support.

Like the political activism of Chiang Wei-shui (see chapter 14), the public sphere provided an important discursive arena. Yet the KMT's brutality toward members of the opposition meant that discussions needed to be secret. For the Tangwai, teahouses offered a critical site of intellectual exchange. They provided a space of political communication and opposition activism. In Taipei, locations such as the Wisteria Tea House, a two-story Japanese house in the Daan District close to National Taiwan University, occupied an important position in the political culture of Taiwan in the 1950s

(Alsford 2012, 286). Originally the residence of a Japanese official during the colonial period, the building was confiscated following the arrival of the Chinese Nationalists and turned into a residence for the KMT official Chou Te-wei. His son, Chou Yu, an artist, inherited the house in 1976.

Chou Yu, a political activist and a member of the Tangwai, opened up the premises for political discussion groups. As a teahouse, it provided a safe house for political dissidents, the avant-garde for revisionist expression, and Tangwai supporters (Chou Yu n.d.). The Wisteria Tea House became a hub for radical discussions, fostering a vibrant social environment that attracted new ideas, thinkers, and radicals, thus contributing to the development of a dynamic civil society. The tea house played a pivotal role in shaping the political perspectives of activists like Huang Hsin-chieh, while also serving as a regular meeting spot for prominent lawyers such as Chen Shui-bian and Hsieh Chang-ting. As a vital social institution, Wisteria Tea House became a catalyst for Taiwan's renewed nationalism and served as a caffeinated pathway to democratization.

Although the Tangwai were ultimately successful in forming the DPP in 1986, many saw the 1977 election as the moment when this confederation of academics and like-minded intellectuals split between moderates, such as Kang Ning-hsiang, and a more radical branch under Huang Hsin-chieh. The trigger was a violent episode at the Chungli polling station on 19 November 1977, when approximately one thousand people were protesting suspected election fraud. In the violence, one protestor died and the police station in Chungli was set on fire. Frictions within the Tangwai movement gave rise to divergent perspectives, with some contending that the violence served as evidence of widespread support, while others, adopting a more moderate stance, advocated for avoiding mass demonstrations (Rigger 1999, 115–16).

Divides in the Tangwai continued, and differences were again highlighted on 16 December 1978 when President Jimmy Carter announced a normalization of relations between the United States and the People's Republic of China. The timing was unfortunate, as the announcement came just days before local elections in Taiwan were to be held. The government postponed the election, saying that Taiwan could not afford instability. Moderates in the Tangwai, including Kang, agreed with the government. This position aggravated the radicals, and the divisions deepened. Tension was further exacerbated on 22 January 1979, when Yu Teng-fa, the Kao-hsiung County executive and a Tangwai-linked follower, was arrested for a planned protest over the election postponement. Many in the radical branch of the Tangwai gathered to protest his arrest and formed the core faction that would be named, after their magazine, Formosa.

19

A Prisoner's Tale

CHEN CHU

My beloved fellow Taiwanese, all of you with a
conscience, with compassion, my name is Lu Hsiu-lien.
I'm from Taoyuan. Today, December 10, is International
Human Rights Day. For hundreds of years, Taiwanese
have never had a chance like they have today.

LU HSIU-LIEN · 2014

Taiwan built its democracy at a time when the international community essentially turned its back on the island. For the Taiwanese people, democracy is not merely a static concept but an ongoing process, embodying both action and a tangible reality. To maintain a democracy requires sacrifice. And the challenge of legitimizing the detention of those who spoke critically of the KMT led to the use of the terms *political prisoner* (zhengzhifan), *thought-crime prisoner* (sixiangfan), and *political thought-crime prisoner* (zhengzhi sixiangfan). Penal practice in Taiwan, however, was not a product of the Chinese Nationalists. It was shaped by Japan, and prison designs marked the regime's militarization. Taiwan sat at the margins of empire but was at the forefront of Japan's colonial experimentation—a centralized system that has been termed a "colonial police sphere" (Ts'ai 2009, 68). For Hui-yu Ts'ai, the Japanese-controlled police systems held sway over the Taiwanese population during various stages of its colonial rule, while also effectively maintaining law, order, and governance (71). Japan's colonial engineering in the name of modernity adopted Western ideas of a "correctional facility," and this, importantly, occurred at a moment of reform that put Taiwan on a different penal track from China (Shu-mei Huang and Hyung Kyung Lee 2020, 95). The Manchus had built prison facilities following their colonization of the island in the seventeenth century, but these were short-term facilities for prisoners awaiting punishment or execution (Allee 1994, 236). Following its reform during the Japanese colonial period, the penal system in Taiwan became crucial not only for suppressing nationalistic anti-Japanese sentimentality but also for managing socialist movements. The Republic of China would adopt this system following the 228 Incident and when it imposed martial law on 20 May 1949.

Martial law in Taiwan lasted for thirty-eight years, ending on 14 July 1987. Only Syria had a longer period of martial law. The Order of Martial Law (Jieyan Ling) was enacted by Chen Cheng, chairman of the Taiwan Provincial Government after Chen Yi and Wei Tao-ming. The law included the Internal Security of the State in the Criminal Code, the Traitors' Punishment Act, and the Statute to Prevent Espionage. To police this, the KMT formed various secret agencies and military tribunals. This led to a climate of improper trials and eradication of civil liberties (H. W. Lin 2015, 265).

When President Jimmy Carter established formal diplomatic relations with the PRC on 16 December 1978, Chiang Ching-kuo postponed National Assembly and legislative elections, citing the need for stability in Taiwan. Former vice president Lu Hsiu-lien speculates in her biography that the timing of the US decision had conflicting explanations. She argues that the possibilities included that the United States felt "sorry" for the KMT and "did it a favor by announcing early to give them [KMT] an excuse to cancel the elections." A second theory was that Chiang Ching-kuo had asked the United States to announce the decision prior to the elections as a "token of goodwill." A third theory posits that Beijing was able to exert enough pressure to force Washington to make the unexpected announcement quickly (Lu and Esarey 2014, 94). The KMT's loss of seats a year earlier, in the 1977 municipal executive, municipal council, and Provincial Assembly elections, was a significant turning point in Taiwan's political development that triggered fears the KMT was losing political control (Rigger 1999, 114–15).

Elections became the crucial platform through which opposition politicians could showcase their cause. However, the postponement of the National Assembly and legislative elections exposed the deepening divisions within the Tangwai movement, specifically between moderates and radicals. The suspension of the elections forced the opposition to seek a new strategy to force political reform. Large-scale demonstrations and new political magazines were manifestations of a new populist front opposing KMT rule (Lu and Esarey 2014, 99). This would culminate a year later, in December 1979, with the prodemocracy demonstrations in Kaohsiung.

Nine weeks after the demonstrators' arrests, on 20 February 1980, the Taiwan Garrison Command announced that the Kaohsiung Eight would be tried in a military court, charged with *panluan* (rebellion or sedition; Jacobs 2016, 34). The trial began on 18 March, and a month later, three weeks after the conclusion of the trial, the judges delivered their verdict: Shih Ming-teh received a life sentence, Huang Hsin-chieh got fourteen years, and the remaining six were given twelve years each. Shih Ming-teh was incarcerated on Green Island, later joined by Lin Hung-hsuan.

Green Island (Ludao), known formally as Burnt Island (Huoshaodao), due to the visual display the island makes at sundown, lies just thirty-three kilometers off the southeast coast of Taiwan's main island. Its history as a prison, however, began with the Japanese. Built between 1911 and 1919, the Burnt Island Detention Center for Vagrants was chosen for its location. Much like Alcatraz, just off the coast of San Francisco, it was built to detain. As an island it was difficult to escape. The sea provided an additional boundary around the prisoners that was physical as well as mental. Following the arrival of the Chinese Nationalists, the prison was reestablished to hold prisoners of conscience. From 1951 to 1965 it was called the New Life Correction Center (NLCC), after which it became the Ministry of National Defense Green Island Reform and Reeducation Prison, also crudely known as Oasis Villa (Chen I-Shen 2008, 13). The island also became the headquarters of the Taiwan Garrison Command. The NLCC comprised both cell blocks and guard barracks. In the 1950s, the prisoners were divided into twelve teams, with one all-female group. A total of around three thousand prisoners could be held there at any one time (H. W. Lin

2015, 266). As more and more political prisoners were moved out of city and county prisons, most were sent to Green Island for hard labor and "thought reform" (Chen I-Shen 2008, 13–16). It has often been said that Green Island, as a prison for opposition intellectuals, had the highest density of doctors and the highest average educational level in all the ROC at the time (Chen I-Shen 2015, 9–18; Huang Jui-hung 2018).

In 2001, under the government of Huang Hsin-chieh's lawyer, Chen Shui-bian, the DPP opened Green Island Human Rights Culture Park (Ludao Renquan Wenhua Yuanqu), which later changed its name to Green Island White Terror Memorial Park (Baise Kongbu Ludao Jinian Yuanqu) to commemorate those who fought for Taiwan's democracy. Although the protagonist of this tale, Chen Chu, was not incarcerated at Green Island, context regarding the island is essential, as its location widely symbolizes the plight of political prisoners throughout the period of White Terror.

Born 10 June 1950 to a large farming family in Yilan, Chen Chu was deeply influenced by her mother, a woman she describes as having great perseverance and determination. Her mother, Chen Lin Lien-hua, was a *sim-pū-á*. The Japanese sent her father, Chen Atu, to the Philippines during the Second World War. Chen's mother was determined that her daughter be properly educated and insisted that Chen pursue her education beyond that of many of her peers. Chen was the first girl in her family to go to junior high school. She graduated from Shih Hsin Junior college, now Shih Hsin University, in 1968, with a degree in library and information science (Lin Hsing-fei 2017, 24–45; Wu Jen-chieh 2018).

Shortly after she arrived in Taipei in 1969, during her freshman year at college, Chen started work as a secretary for Kuo Yu-hsin. Kuo was then councilor on the Taiwan Provincial Council. When his former secretary left the job, he asked Chen to help him out on weekends until he could find a suitable replacement (Chieh Chu-shu 2018). Kuo was an important mentor to Chen. He was also from Yilan, and to many people there, Kuo was the spokesperson for the farming class (Chen Chu n.d). After graduating, Chen increased her hours to full-time. Although Kuo was not openly against the Republic of China, he firmly opposed the KMT dictatorship. In 1960, he had helped set up the China Democracy Party (Zhongguo Minzhudang) as a way to resist the KMT's single-party rule (Rigger 1999, 104–5). The attempt to establish an opposition failed, and many were arrested. Kuo escaped imprisonment but was continuously monitored by the secret service even after moving to the United States in 1977, where he established the Overseas Alliance of Taiwan Democracy Movement.

Chen had known Kuo since childhood, and she became his secretary not out of political ideology but to finance her education. As she began to learn more about her job and the people around her, she started to notice that she was being watched and Kuo was being followed. Several incidents she witnessed, including ballot stuffing, convinced Chen to join the Tangwai and become an activist. The KMT used the Kaohsiung Incident as an excuse to arrest all well-known opposition leaders. Kuo had left Taiwan for the United States before the incident; however, Chen was arrested as part of the Kaohsiung Eight, and in March–April 1980, she was tried at a military court.

Chen was jailed in Taiwan's Jen-ai Educational Experimental Institute (Taiwan Renai Jiaoyu Shiyansuo) in Taipei. She was sentenced to twelve years but only served six years and two months. During her imprisonment, her mother came to visit her every six months. She had supported Chen's participation in democracy despite not fully understanding exactly what it was all about (Lo 2011).

In 1994, Chen was made head of the Department of Social Welfare at the Taipei City government office. Six years later, following the DPP's election victory, she was appointed minister of the Council of Labor Affairs, the present-day Ministry of Labor. In 2006, she was elected major of Kaohsiung, winning by a small margin of 1,114 votes against the KMT candidate Huang Chun-ying (Lin Hsing-fei 2017, 46–55). Huang contested the result in court, but Chen prevailed. In 2010, Kaohsiung City and Kaohsiung County were combined, and Chen was elected mayor of the special municipality of Kaohsiung City. She was reelected in 2014 and served a total of twelve years as mayor of Kaohsiung before becoming secretary-general to the Tsai Ing-wen in 2018. In June 2020, Chen Chu was appointed president of the Control Yuan.

Though she was not imprisoned on Green Island, Chen Chu's name has been engraved on the memorial that pays tribute to the victims of the

White Terror period (Tang Shih 2018). Lee Teng-hui, who experienced detention and interrogation by the Taiwan Garrison Command in 1969, was later invited to join Chiang Ching-kuo's cabinet. As president, he established a public memorial dedicated to the victims of the White Terror and became the first to offer an apology on behalf on the KMT in 1995. In 2008, Ma Ying-jeou also extended an apology to the victims and their families.

Chen Chu, like many other Tangwai followers, survived martial law to help lead Taiwan on its journey to a consolidated and mature democracy. This, sadly, was not the case for all, as many sacrificed their lives for the democratic freedoms that Taiwan offers its people today. Concluding this tale, I leave you with a passage from Shawna Yang Ryan's novel, *Green Island*:

> A car pulled out from its spot beneath an oak tree and crawled toward him. He moved aside to let it pass, but instead the car stopped. He glanced around; there would be no witnesses.
>
> "Tang Jia Bao?" someone asked through the open window.
>
> "Hey," Jia Bao confirmed. *Run,* he thought. *Run.*
>
> *Run.*
>
> Jia Bao thought of his wife, standing next to the sofa, phone at her ear, unable to speak.
>
> . . .
>
> The man's hand was shaking. Jia Bao saw the tremor. *He's afraid.* If he had time enough to notice the twitch under the man's skin, he should have run.
>
> Even the bullet didn't speed up time. It tore through his chest.
>
> (Ryan 2016, 286)

Tang Jia Bao thus became the fictional representative of the Taiwanese sacrifice for democracy. Being Taiwanese is a cultural ideology that has been shaped by the country's political changes. The Kaohsiung Incident politicized Taiwanese history, and a consciousness rose to advocate opposition to authoritarianism (Hsiau 2000, 158). This resistance has remained constant, and Chen Chu with her twelve-year sentence and six years of imprisonment will forever be sketched not only on the Green Island wall but also on the consciousness of Taiwan's democracy.

PART THREE

Being Taiwan

20

An Anthropologist's Tale

ARTHUR P. WOLF

The final goal of which an ethnographer should never lose
sight . . . is, briefly, to grasp the native's point of view, his
relation to life, to realize his vision of his world.
BRONISLAW MALINOWSKI · 1992

Two years after Japan's colonization of Taiwan, a letter was published in
the *Journal of the Anthropological Society of Tokyo* calling for an ethnological survey of the cultures of the Taiwan Indigenous peoples. The letter,
written by Torii Ryūzō, initiated the first systematic anthropological study
of Taiwan. Together with other researchers, including Inō Kanori, Mori
Ushinosuke, Miyamoto Nobuhito, and Kanaseki Takeo, Torii contributed
to the field of Taiwan ethnology through his work at the Taiwan Museum. Constructed in 1908, the museum served as a repository for their
collections, expanding knowledge and understanding of Taiwan's cultural
heritage (Blundell 2009, 3–4).

The anthropology of these Japanese ethnologists included investigation
of material culture (clothing, tools, houses, and weapons) that they expected
might disappear as a result of colonial modernization projects. Like their
Euro-American counterparts, they sought to document rather than salvage cultural material. This continued in the immediate postwar period, as
Chinese nationalist pioneers, including Li Chi, founded the Department
of Archaeology and Anthropology at National Taiwan University in 1949.

The high tradition embedded in the ethos of the new department was heir to the research laboratories and a library of ethnological studies that had been established at what was known in 1928 as Taihoku University. Ethnographic research continued in the postwar period with academics such as Ruey Yih-fu, Ling Shung-sheng, Wei Hwei-lin, and Chen Shao-hsing. Collectively their sociocultural anthropology sought to understand, salvage, and document Indigenous cultures.

As expected, the lives of descendants of Taiwan's colonized peoples had been radically transformed, so the collected material proved vital in later cultural revitalization projects. Yet it was not just Indigenous communities that ethnologists such as Inō documented. They also conducted significant research into the belief systems and customs of the Han and Hakka settlers. Fulbright scholars arriving in the 1950s performed anthropology differently, seeking not to enhance their understanding of the island or its peoples, but rather to see it as a surrogate for China, which was officially closed to American scholarship following the Nationalist retreat to Taiwan in 1949 and US government support for Chiang Kai-shek. Yet their presence defined the field that we know today as Taiwan studies.

The purpose of this tale is to comprehend the development of a field of study and to recognize the importance of this early postwar study of the island in relation to some of the critical assessments made in this book, most notably that Taiwan's history of one of migration, displacement, democratization, and economic transformation. Key to this early development was the anthropology of Arthur P. Wolf.

Arthur P. Wolf was born on 2 March 1932 in Santa Rosa, California. His family was involved in ranching and logging, and Arthur worked in the family industry from a young age. While attending Santa Rosa Junior College, Wolf supported his studies by working as a miner and logger, with one summer spent in Alaska searching for gold. After receiving his degree, Wolf was honored with the much-coveted Telluride Fellowship to study anthropology at Cornell University. In 1964, he spent a year at the London School of Economics, and then a further year, a decade later, as a visiting fellow at All Souls College, Oxford University. Wolf settled at Stanford University, becoming a renowned scholar who spent years on Taiwan researching household demographics.

On 15 June 1958, Arthur, joined later by his then wife Margery Wolf, set off from his desk at Cornell to undertake research in Taiwan as part of the Fulbright Program. Both Arthur and Margery focused their studies on the southwestern regions of what is now New Taipei City's Tucheng District. As Arthur walked into Lower Xizhou on a path from Shulin, on the left majestically stood the large banyan tree pictured on the cover of Margery's book *House of Lim*, and on the right was the home of the Lim family—the largest in the village (Jing Xu 2019). The data collected there informed much of the work on Taiwanese anthropology in the postwar period.

Wolf spent his formative years doing field research in Taiwan and collected a vast archive of early twentieth-century household data. From 1968 to 2015 he passed this knowledge on to countless students studying anthropology at Stanford.

Both Arthur and Margery brought their graduate students along on fieldwork, and some of these scholars would go on to define the field of Taiwan studies: Emily Ahern, Steven Harrell, Steven Sangren, and Robert Weller. Wolf also influenced Myron Cohen as a graduate student at Columbia, David Jordon at Chicago, and Norma Diamond at Cornell. Each of them throughout their fieldwork in Taiwan came to recognize a distinctiveness in Taiwan after research opportunities on the Chinese mainland became more available.

Arthur P. Wolf's edited volume, *Religion and Ritual in Chinese Society*, in particular his chapter "Gods, Ghosts, and Ancestors," discussed how changes in worship were largely a result of the social context in which the worshippers lived (Arthur Wolf 1974). *Marriage and Adoption in China, 1845–1945*, cowritten with anthropologist Chieh-shan Huang, showed similar results and highlighted that marriage and adoption varied across the sinophone world. By examining records in nine districts in northern Taiwan from 1845 to 1945, they successfully show that "Chinese marriage and adoption practices were not the simple reflection of uniform ideals. Rather, they were the complex reflections of a variety of forces—demographic, economic, and psychological—that interacted to shape family organization" (Huang and Wolf 1980, 1). This point is important as it asserts that Taiwan studies is not a uniform subfield of China studies but an academic field in its own right. Furthermore, to give her anthropological study both historical depth and sense of place, Margery Wolf, in *Women and the Family in Rural Taiwan*, makes an important historical comparison between Taiwan's colonial history and that of North America, thereby opening a new field of inquiry (Margery Wolf 1972).

When the United States switched diplomatic recognition to the People's Republic of China on 1 January 1979, the way people studied Taiwan shifted as well, so that the field became a kind of study in and of itself and not as part of something else (Alsford 2020). In the following period, Taiwan and the Taiwanese began to stand alone. This transformation was critical in the development of Taiwan studies, which continues to grow globally. The decision of many scholars to specialize in Taiwan has had spillover effects as global media and its audience seek to understand the geostrategic importance of Taiwan and its relations with China and the wider region.

Arthur Wolf's career exemplifies how these social, political, and economic transformations began to shape a wider academic understanding of what Taiwan is and is not. In turn, this academic understanding of Taiwan subsequently shaped global narratives and policy concerning how Taiwan is understood in the world. For this reason, Taiwan invests significantly in academic outreach, providing scholarships and opportunities for students to study in Taiwan, and provides financial support to overseas universities for Taiwan-related programs.

21

A Businessman's Tale

CHANG YUNG-FA

At heart, it is clear, [Chang Yung-fa] remains a seaman. In
theory, of course, there is no reason why a shipping magnate
should be fascinated by ships, or an aircraft manufacturer
be captivated by aeroplanes, or a wine-grower by vintages.
In all these instances, a knowledge of markets and head
for finance should suffice. Yet for the really great business
figures it is usually otherwise. Dr Chang believes that
his early exposure to the rigours of shipboard life made a
fundamental contribution to his development.

MARGARET THATCHER · 1999

On 17 April 2021, it was reported that the United Kingdom was experiencing a national shortage of garden gnomes. The chief executive of the Garden Centre Association, Iain Wylie, reported to the British Broadcasting Corporation (BBC) that gardening had become popular during the coronavirus pandemic lockdown and that consequently "we've had difficult times where supply chains have been under pressure" (O'Reilly 2021). One of the principal causes was that the Suez Canal, one of the busiest sea lanes in the world, had been blocked by an Evergreen container ship.

The twenty-thousand-ton, four-hundred-meter-long container ship the *Ever Given* blocked the Suez Canal for six days after being buffeted by strong winds on the morning of the 23 March 2021. It ended up wedged across the waterway. Though Shoei Kisen Kaisha, a subsidiary of Japan's Imabari Shipbuilding, owned the vessel, its operator was Evergreen Marine Corporation, a Taiwanese company that registers its vessels in Panama. The *Ever Given* was managed by Bernhard Schulte Shipmanagement, based in Hamburg, Germany, and the vessel was crewed by a team of Indian nationals. A truly global enterprise.

The growth of Taiwan's Evergreen Marine, headquartered in Luzhu District of Taoyuan City in northern Taiwan, has its roots in Taiwan's postwar economic miracle and contributed significantly to the country's economic takeoff as an export-oriented economy. Taiwan is presently the seventh-largest economy in Asia and the twentieth-largest in the world in terms of purchasing power parity. Taiwan, like South Korea, transformed itself from an aid recipient in the 1950s and early 1960s to an aid donor from the 1990s. Land reform was the first step toward industrialization and a crucial step in the modernization of its economy. Unlike South Korea, which focused on the Choebols, or large conglomerates, Taiwan transformed its economy through the growth of the small and medium enterprise (SME) sector. Taiwan's economic transformation must be understood within a global and historic geopolitical framework. It exists in a world dominated politically by a superpower rivalry and economically by an international market that it neither controls nor can escape. Like South Korea and Japan, Taiwan was effectively economically rebuilt by the United States in the postwar period to contain the spread of Communism.

From the 1960s onward, Taiwan, with US aid and training, constructed economic institutions capable of competing effectively in that market system. The state was able to withdraw protection and force international competition among its industrialists in order to compete internationally. By the 1980s, Taiwan possessed a highly successful export industry. Similar to the "miracle on the Han River" in South Korea, Taiwan navigated this takeoff effectively as it imposed the kind of discipline associated with its authoritarian system of governance (Gold 1986, 72–73). The exercise of autocratic power led the dictatorial military regime in South Korea and the martial law regime in Taiwan—through individuals such as Park Chung-hee in South Korea and Chiang Kai-shek and later his son, Chiang Ching-kuo—to establish a centralized economic policy imposed through fear and oppression (Kwang 1998, 8). In Taiwan this was enforced by the

Council for Economic Planning and Development. By launching a series of planning agencies and initiatives, Taiwan was able to transform itself from a cheap, labor-intensive manufacturing hub in the 1950s and 1960s to an expansive base of heavy industry and infrastructure in the 1970s, and eventually an advanced electronic economy in subsequent decades.

Taiwan's strategy of combining export with direct foreign investment stimulated the industrialization process. As the economy took off, both government and industry engaged in an outward-looking development strategy, in a period when there were few global competitors. The developing countries in Latin America and Southeast Asia were still, at this time, following import-substitution policies. The 1950s land reform programs and the accompanying rice-fertilizer exchange system enabled the Taiwan government to offer a stable and affordable food source to urban workers, thereby reducing pressure for wage increases (Chow 2012, 598).

Developments such as these were promulgated across Taiwan by the KMT in response to shifting economic patterns. The Community Development Program, established in 1968, two years after the first export processing zone, housed three substantive areas: basic engineering and construction projects, social welfare projects, and ethics and morality enforcement projects. The aim of each project was to extend basic infrastructure into the local community, to diminish poverty and improve civilian life, and to advocate "traditional" (sinified) virtues (Hsiung 1996, 48). These programs included Living Rooms as Factories (Keting Ji Gongchang) and Mothers' Workshops (Mama Jiaoshi). Both initiatives involved the KMT's plan to incorporate women into the labor market while encouraging them to continue fulfilling family obligations.

The Living Rooms as Factories program was a key part of the government's effort to get surplus labor into employment. As family living rooms were converted into factories, mothers—who could use grandparents for childcare or make use of free day-care centers—became workers. The process began to domesticate employment in Taiwan, and the government's strategy for promoting Chinese values was to remedy social unrest by creating tightly knit families and fostering wider community identity. In the living room factories, women would do piecework for larger assembly at local manufacturing plants (Hsiung 1996, 47). Shawna Yang Ryan alludes to this program in *Green Island* when the unnamed protagonist, after returning to Taiwan from the United States in the 1980s, discusses how her mother was hired by a local doll manufacturer and turned their living room into a small factory (Ryan 2016, 316). The process was simple. Once the small components were assembled, like the painted dolls' heads in *Green Island*, they were packed up and sent to local factories, where the heads were attached to bodies. They were clothed in costumes that had been made in other living room factories. Once fully assembled, they were shipped worldwide. This "satellite factory system" encouraged a procapitalist orientation in the labor market that would contribute to the "economic miracle" (Gold 1986, 124). By the 1960s, high levels of export enabled Taiwan to begin its penetration into a third level of industry by exporting via its own vessels. Chief among these operators was Chang Yung-fa and the Evergreen Marine Corporation.

Suao, in southern Yilan Country on Taiwan's northeastern coastline, was established as Suō Town by the Japanese, and formed part of Taihoku Prefecture, created in 1920 to encompass modern-day Keelung, New Taipei City, Taipei, and Yilan County. Chang Yung-fa was born there on 6 October 1927, the third of six children. His father was a seaman, and his mother took charge of the family and home. In 1934, the family moved to Keelung. After graduating from Taipei Commercial High School, he began working in the Taipei office of the Minami Nippon Kisen Kabushiki Gaisha, a Japanese shipping company. At night he attended Taihoku College of Commerce (J. Taihoku Kōtō Shōgyō Gakkō) to continue his education. As a good filial child, he gave his salary to his family. To receive the benefit of the "national language family" (J. *kokugo katei*) policy, the Chang family changed their family name to Nagashima and Yung-Fa to Haruo, but Chang remembers everyone calling him Hatsu (Chang Yung-fa 1999, 23). After war broke out in the Pacific, Chang Yung-fa, or Nagashima Hatsu, as he was then known, enlisted as a kamikaze pilot but was not selected (ET Today News 2016). He later recalled that he enlisted partially due to peer pressure as he did not want to "let his friends down." Although he didn't pass the kamikaze test, he was put in the infantry of the Japanese Imperial Army. Fifteen days before he was due to depart for

Okinawa, the Japanese Empire surrendered. Chang's father died during the war after his ship, the *Shonan Maru*, was sunk by the Americans close to the Philippines (Chang Yung-fa 1999, 28).

After the war ended, Chang became a merchant sailor like his father. He began at the bottom as a cabin intern and rose to chief officer. Twenty years after his first internship, he established his own company. Chang married twice, meeting his first wife, Chang Lin Chin-chih, on a blind date. They had one daughter and three sons, before Chang Lin Chin-chih died in 2013. The following year, Chang Yung-fa, at eighty-seven, married his mistress, Li Mei-yu, with whom he had fathered another son, Chang Kuo-wei, in 1970. Chang Yung-fa favored this son, leaving him most of his wealth upon his death on 20 January 2016 (Yu-Huay Sun 2016). This subsequently led to a legal battle between Chang Kuo-wei and his half-siblings. Chang Kuo-wei registered Starlux Airlines shortly after his father's death in 2016, and the company was launched in January 2020.

In 1961, Chang Yung-fa, along with some close personal friends, established the shipping company Xintai Marine Corporation (Xintai Haiyun Gongsi; Chang Yung-fa Exhibition n.d). He withdrew from the company four years later following a disagreement with the shareholders and established a second company, Central Marine Corporation (Zhongyang Haiyun Gongsi). After helping this company develop, he branched out, establishing Evergreen Marine in 1968 with just one vessel: a fifteen-year-old, fifteen-thousand-ton freighter that he named *Central Trust*. Within four years, Chang had built a fleet of twelve ships (Chang Yung-fa Exhibition n.d). This remarkable increase was largely due to Taiwan's adapted strategy of combining an export orientation with direct foreign investment to simulate growth. The subsequent shift from an import substitution economy to an export-oriented one led to the economic and social transformations of Taiwan in the 1960s (Gold 1986, 74–75).

Evergreen opened a regular service to the Middle East, later dispatching ships to the Caribbean and thus enabling Taiwan to increase exports and compete with international companies that had previously held monopolies over these sought-after routes. In 1975, Chang saw a global opportunity to be part of the future of containerization and built four S-type container vessels. He then launched service to the US East Coast, and fifteen months later, he opened on the US West Coast. By 1985, Evergreen Marine had become the largest container ship operator in the world. By the end of the decade, Chang had begun to diversify his business and proposed to the Civil Aeronautics Administration the establishment of Eva Airways Corporation (Chang Yung-fa 1999, 172–73). In March 1989 this was approved, and the company began operations on 1 July 1991. The Evergreen Group also launched Evergreen International Hotels, which operates five-star properties throughout Taiwan and in other key locations overseas.

In 1985, Chang founded the Chang Yung-fa Foundation, which is committed to providing emergency and medical aid and promoting education and cultural exchange. Among its milestones are the formation of the Evergreen Symphony Orchestra and the launch of *Morals Monthly*, a magazine that is distributed free of charge to schoolchildren. The foundation also operates the Evergreen Maritime Museum in Taipei, which is dedicated to preserving Taiwan's maritime heritage.

Unlike other companies operating in Taiwan under martial law, Evergreen and the bulk of its operations were internationally oriented. This relieved pressure on the organization to join the KMT. Chang, despite funding Chen Shui-bian and the DPP, argued that it was unnecessary at the time to join a political party. Chang remembers that Lin Jin-shen, then KMT transport minister, had repeatedly encouraged him to join. His compromise was to become "a friend of the party": "It's easier for a friend of the party to maintain a politically neutral stand, which makes his words much more convincing to people. Besides, people might misconstrue me as a mouthpiece of the KMT if I became an official member" (Chang Yung-fa 1999, 274–75).

As the political landscape of Taiwan changed in the post–martial law period, Chang became more open about his political opinions. He was clear in his preference for Hokkien over Mandarin, and in his autobiography, he mentions persistent rumors of his support of pan-green politics due to the green corporate logo of his company. For Chang, democracy in Taiwan had proceeded too quickly, "so fast that in fact people did not understand the true essence of democracy" (Chang Yung-fa 1999, 276). In spite of his supposed political apathy, Chang worked for the government as a national policy adviser after the DPP took power in 2000. He later stepped down, after the Chen government refused to approve the direct cargo route across the Taiwan Strait (Tsai I-fang and Wu Kuei-yen 2016). In March 2006,

Chang purchased the former KMT headquarters at far below market value and repurposed the building into a museum and concert hall. The purchase was questioned by some DPP legislators, who suggested it was a means of assisting the KMT in clearing illegal party wealth (Li Hsin-fang 2018). During the 2012 presidential election, Chang supported KMT candidate Ma Ying-jeou.

In spite of Chang's attempt to be apolitical, there will always be links between industry and government. Governments are able to spur growth by creating an economic, legal, and regulatory environment in which businesses can thrive. Education and training contribute to producing the labor force necessary for business growth. In return, business leaders financially support candidates in democratic systems where they might receive preferential treatment.

Taiwan's current economic environment is vastly different from that in which Chang entered business in the 1960s. Today Taiwan's economy is a developed capitalist system. Among its most profitable industries is the information technology sector. One of the largest of these companies is the Taiwan Semiconductor Manufacturing Company (Taiwan Jiti Dianlu Zhizao Gufen Youxiangongsi), more commonly known by its acronym, TSMC. TSMC is the world's most valuable semiconductor company and the world's largest independent semiconductor foundry. It operates out of Hsinchu Science Park and is majority owned by foreign investment. Founded in 1897 by Morris Chang, the TSMC foundry is used by a wide range of fabless semiconductor companies such as Apple, Advanced Micro Devices, and Qualcomm. This strength in high-tech industries is vital to the power of states in the global international political economy (Chu 2012, 549). For Taiwan, it is critical, as China continues to seek ways to minimize Taiwan's global position. Innovative technology is crucial in a competitive global environment. Democracy and its institutions foster deeper innovation, and Taiwan's highly educated and skilled workforce allows it to push for a technologically oriented economy in the future. Areas that might become niches for Taiwan and its future economy are in green technology and artificial intelligence. Ethan Tu, the founder of Taiwan AI labs (and also founder of the PTT Bulletin Board System, the largest terminal-based bulletin board system in Taiwan), for example, sees Taiwan as being well positioned to become the "AI island of the word"

(Kuan-lin Liu and Po-sheng Chiu, 2018). Tu sees Taiwan as possessing multiple advantages. For example, Taiwan has a comprehensive medical industry through its national health insurance system and is a world leader in digitizing medical records. Tu believes that this network, coupled with big data, could incorporate AI technology to create a smart automated health care system.

The story of Chang Yung-fa is closely related to Taiwan's economic and social transformation in the postwar period. The 1950s saw Chang work mainly on ships moving between Japan and Taiwan (Chang 1999, 36). This tied him to the import substitution economy Taiwan had adopted in its immediate postwar industrialization. By the time Chang established his first shipping company, Taiwan was moving its economy to an export-oriented economy in which the label "made in Taiwan" became synonymous with cheap imports. That tag has come a long way in the intervening years. Taiwan has moved from low-cost production to original, innovative, high-value products and from a 1980s "made in Taiwan" label on cheap textiles, toys, and bikes to a "designed in Taiwan" mark of innovation, particularly around its domination of microchip production. Its current economic trajectory suggests enormous advances in future technology.

22

An Epidemiologist's Tale

CHEN CHIEN-JEN

The two most important questions in science are
What can I know? And How can I know it?
JOHN M. BARRY · 2021

On 30 December 2019, Li Wenliang, an ophthalmologist in Wuhan, China, sent a group message via WeChat warning his colleagues of the outbreak of a virus similar to the SARS virus that had appeared in China and spread worldwide in 2002. Li's message was shared the next day on the Taiwanese bulletin board system PTT. Taiwan's health authorities alerted the World Health Organization (WHO) as a warning to the rest of the world, but the warning was ignored. The new virus became known as COVID-19, and it would result in a pandemic that by November 2020 had infected over 58 million people and killed 1.4 million worldwide.

On the first day of 2020, the Taiwan government initiated health inspections and began to mobilize, while the WHO remained silent. Taiwan succeeded in keeping COVID out during the first waves of the pandemic that swept throughout Europe and North America. By May 2020, when most of the world was entering, or had already entered, strict lockdown measures, Taiwan had returned to relative normality. In October 2020, the island celebrated two hundred days without a single case, and thousands took to the streets for the annual Pride parade.

The success of Taiwan's response to the pandemic was partly due to previous experience with SARS in 2002 and 2003. This led to a culture of transparent data sharing, and the government was able to use big data to control the spread. The appointment of Audrey Tang (Tang Fang) Taiwan's youngest and first transgender minister, as digital minister, added credibility to the response and attracted the support of the younger, tech-savvy generation. The response was a collaborative effort among the private sector, civil society, and the government, utilizing digital innovations to combat disinformation and keep the public informed.

Vice President Chen Chien-jen had swung Taiwan into action in December 2019 as soon as he heard the report from Li Wenliang. His first call was to screen travelers coming into the country from China and to isolate those showing symptoms. On 21 January, Taiwan reported its first case, and Chen ordered the government to issue masks. His efforts, prior to the outbreak, to establish disease management centers, increase production of protective equipment, and revise infection law made Taiwan one of the countries in the world most prepared to manage a serious viral outbreak.

Chen Chien-jen was born in Cishan in Kaohsiung County in 1951. His father, Chen Hsin-an, served as Kaohsiung County magistrate until 1957, and his mother, Wei Lien-chih, managed a day-care center. Chen and his wife, Lo Fong-pin, both devout Catholics, have on a number of occasions been invited to the Vatican by Popes John Paul II, Benedict XVI, and Francis. Chen obtained a master's degree in public health from National Taiwan University and received his ScD in genetics and epidemiology from Johns Hopkins University in 1982. His research focused primarily on hepatitis B and was instrumental in raising awareness of vaccination needs in Taiwan. Chen discovered the link between arsenic and blackfoot disease, which led to revision of the international health standards for arsenic exposure.

The SARS virus of 2002–3 was first identified in Foshan, Guangdong. Over eight thousand people from twenty-nine countries are reported to have been infected, and at least 774 died globally. Taiwan's first confirmed case involved a Guangdong-based businessman returning to Taiwan in February 2003. In March 2003, he and his wife were admitted to National

Taiwan University Hospital with the illness. That month, a third case was confirmed in Yilan. Like the first case, the patient had traveled to Guangdong and transited via Hong Kong before arriving back in Taiwan. By the end of the month, Taiwan had six confirmed cases.

During the initial SARS outbreak, Chen collaborated with a team of experts from the Ministry of Health to contain its spread. Minister of the Executive Yuan Yu Shyi-kun asked Chen to lead the Ministry of Health after the previous minister resigned. Despite never having worked in government and initially hesitant, Chen accepted the position and served as Minister of Health from May 2003 to February 2005.

Taipei City mayor Ma Ying-jeou locked down Hoping Hospital in April, announcing to the city government that "if any of the medical professionals [in the hospital] tried to leave, it would be viewed as escaping from the frontline of a battlefield." In the end, fifty-seven hospital staff members were infected, and seven died. Of ninety-seven infected patients and family members, twenty-four died, including one case of suicide (Laura Li 2003).

Chen expressed relief that SARS had started to subside after he took office and came to an end shortly afterward. By 5 July 2003, the WHO announced that Taiwan was no longer one of the affected areas (Taiwan Centre for Disease Control 2003). Chen felt the success was mainly due to the strength and resolve of the Taiwanese people in addition to the hard work of his colleagues. Local governments and organizations worked together to set up temperature-checking points quickly and effectively. People willingly followed regulations concerning social distancing, washing hands, and wearing masks. Chen likened it to a social movement but on a grander scale.

Chen recalled an outbreak of SARS at the National Yang-Ming University Hospital on 5 June 2003. A group of experts entered the hospital and took control, and within twenty-four hours, the situation was under control. He believed that in the fields of human genetics and epidemiology, "the patients are the best teachers," as although the disease may be similar among patients, its occurrence can differ based on environment and personal background (Shih Wen-I 2004, 10). SARS taught professionals in Taiwan how to mobilize and how to work with the public. The robust antipandemic network that was established in Taiwan following the SARS outbreak demonstrated its effectiveness in combating swine flu in 2009 and avian flu in 2013. An essential element of Taiwan's success in combating pandemics was its prompt and proactive approach to "rumor surveillance," which involved monitoring unverified information circulating on social media platforms. The Centre for Disease Control utilized this approach to promptly identify the initial transmission of COVID-19.

Chen felt that public health awareness in Taiwan had increased following the SARS epidemic. He has continued to press for updated training for medical professionals and often uses the case at Hoping Hospital as an example. The medical professionals in the hospital protested because they were unaware of what they were fighting against and did not know how they could protect themselves (Shih Wen-I 2004, 11).

Chen recalled a conversation with a colleague about the difficulty faced by countries with authoritarian governments in controlling pandemics. Chen believed dictators would sacrifice people's health to maintain control. In contrast, democratic countries are supervised by the people. It may take time for the people to learn to deal with the situation, but the results are solid. He used boating as an example, comparing dictatorship to a canoe and democracy to a raft. The canoe may go faster, but it can capsize easily. A raft may be slower, and the paddlers need to learn to work together, but the chances that everyone will survive the journey are higher (Shih Wen-I 2004, 11). Thus, in learning to deal with SARS, over 60 percent of the Taiwanese population measured their temperature twice a day, and over 80 percent did it daily (Shih Wen-I 2004, 11). Chen felt this showed increased awareness of public health, which was just as important as medical care. As a result, he continued to push for education on public health after the epidemic.

During the pandemic, Chen gained an appreciation for the role of the media. He noticed that the press often received new information before medical professionals, and reporters sometimes failed to check their sources properly, wanting to publish before the competition or to increase readership (what is known in digital media as "clickbait"). This led to negative consequences and the spread of misinformation. For example, the nurses from Hoping Hospital protested for only ten minutes, but the footage was replayed nonstop over two days, which caused alarm among the general public and a belief that the protest was ongoing. As a result, the SARS team initiated a national broadcast across channels, so the companies of all these channels had to agree to announce the latest developments. This was the first national broadcast in the post–martial law period (Shih Wen-I

2004, 12). Through this medium, people received correct and up-to-date information.

Taiwan reported its first case of SARS to the WHO in March 2003, but the WHO did not reply until mid-May. Chen pointed out that the WHO had to get China's consent every time Taiwan asked for help, which caused delays in fighting the virus. In 2020, Taiwan was able to deal with the pandemic better than other countries mainly due to its experience with SARS. Following the outbreak of SARS, Taiwan took decisive action and implemented measures to strengthen its disease control capabilities. One key aspect was the reinforcement of governmental structures related to disease control, allowing for effective coordination with care homes and fostering collaboration with international health organizations. Furthermore, the Center for Disease Control was significantly restructured, enabling the involvement of experts, including individuals outside the civil service, in critical situations.

Another crucial development was the establishment of the Central Epidemic Command Centre, which played a pivotal role in keeping the public informed about the latest developments, thereby preventing group panic and curbing the spread of false information. This centralized office acted as a reliable source of up-to-date information, ensuring the dissemination of accurate and timely updates.

Recognizing the importance of preparedness, continuous training programs were implemented for medical professionals, ensuring they remained knowledgeable and well equipped to effectively respond to various disease outbreaks. Moreover, great emphasis was placed on ensuring an adequate supply of personal protective equipment (PPE), a vital resource for safeguarding health and safety of healthcare workers and the general population. The implementation of these comprehensive measures enabled Taiwan to bolster its resilience and readiness in combating disease effectively.

Although attention to public health was a clear driver for Taiwan's successes in managing the spread of infectious diseases, it constitutes only 3 percent of the health care budget. Chen has campaigned for this to increase to 30 percent, arguing that Taiwan should concentrate more on prevention than cure (Shu-feng Teng 2003). In 2020, Taiwan enacted the Public Health Specialist Act, considered the first of its kind in Asia. The legislation, considered a notable achievement for Vice President Chen, awards

Taiwanese citizens who have successfully passed the exam with a Public Health Specialist certificate, enabling them to work in various healthcare organizations, facilities, or nursing homes, thus significantly enhancing the nation's ability to address future health challenges by expanding its pool of qualified professionals.

Taiwan's campaign to improve the effectiveness of disease control is central in its public health initiative. The informed advice given to communities at the onset of a health crisis has aided in preventing the spread of disease. For this to be effective, Taiwan, through its continued revision of policy, has garnered the reliable knowledge needed to advise the public. The establishment of institutes such as the Central Epidemic Command Centre has also generated valuable information, which has led in turn to trust in the government. The public has been open to health surveillance and put its trust in government on matters critical to the well-being of the nation. Taiwan's continued campaign for admittance to the WHO, met by the WHO's rebuffs, may also have impacted the level of trust given to the government in matters relating to health. There is no contradiction between the advice of the WHO and implementation of necessary measures. Taiwan acted early during the COVID-19 pandemic in spite of the WHO's response.

Chen Chien-jen has been instrumental in fostering widespread trust in effective governance, which is one of the greatest successes of Taiwan's democratization. However, this confidence may prove to be situational and dependent on people such as Chen.

Chen argues that despite Taiwan's substantial progress, lack of access to vital international information due to exclusion from the WHO is challenging. Taiwan continues to demonstrate that, nonetheless, there is much that it can contribute to the international system.

23

An Indigenous Tale

ICYANG PAROD

We are the Indigenous peoples of Taiwan, and we've lived in
Taiwan, our motherland, for more than 6,000 years. We are not
the so-called "ethnic minorities" within the Chinese nation. . . .
Taiwan is the sacred land where generations of our ancestors lived
and protected with their lives. It doesn't belong to China.

Once called "barbarians," we are now recognized as the
original owners of Taiwan. We the Indigenous peoples of
Taiwan have pushed this nation forward towards respect
for human rights, democracy, and freedom. After thousands
of years, we are still here. We have never given up our
rightful claim to the sovereignty of Taiwan.

JOINT DECLARATION BY THE REPRESENTATIVES OF
THE INDIGENOUS PEOPLES OF TAIWAN · 2019

The rights of Taiwanese Indigenous peoples are firmly woven into the
history of democracy in Taiwan, particularly due to significant advance-
ments made during the 1980s and early 1990s. These gains brought about
lasting changes that prioritized Indigenous interests, including adoption of
the term *yuanzhumin* (Indigenous peoples) instead of the now pejorative
term *shanbao* (mountain compatriots) in official nomenclature, a revival
of Indigenous personal names, and the establishment of government-level
structural institutions. However, prior to these developments, the postwar

period and the arrival of the Chinese Nationalists introduced new stigmatized identities for Indigenous communities.

These stigmatized identities can be characterized by two primary factors: The first, an external factor, involves a traditional Chinese perception of Han (Hua) versus non-Han (Yi) peoples, prominently demonstrated in the Han myth of Wu Feng, who "sacrificed himself" to oppose Indigenous headhunting practices (Roy 2003, 26). Stereotyping of indigeneity, similar to Orientalism, was both overt and implicit in the Han labeling of Indigenous peoples as violent, primitive, and alcoholic (Chang Hsin-ping 1997, 124). This labeling affects the representation of Indigenous peoples and contributes to the second factor: internal experiences shared by Taiwan's Indigenous communities, including historical events (such as the conquest of "mountain people"), loss of sociocultural traditions and heritage, and situational reactions, such as feelings of inferiority (Shih-Chung Hsieh 1994, 407). Changes in Taiwan's economic structure—the shift from an agricultural and import substitution economy to an export-oriented industrial economy—created competition for work across ethnic divides in Taiwan. The ramifications would raise the average household income of Indigenous peoples from NT$3,930 in 1953 to NT$112,668 in 1978 (Hsu and Li 1989, 197). The industrial sectors by the end of the 1970s were thus a critical site of Indigenous employment and a major migratory pull factor (Mutsu Hsu and Yih-Yuan Li 1989, 197). This tale illustrates how the development of Taiwan's contemporary democratic society impacted and continues to impact Taiwan's Indigenous peoples.

Expressions of indigeneity in contemporary Taiwan are often articulated in specific ritual practices. For instance, the young men of the E'tolan village (Dulan), in the Amis Indigenous group, use a form of "modern" dance as an expression of their sociocultural concepts, thus maintaining a living society (Tsai Cheng-liang 2006). Tradition is thus not simply a remnant left behind by an ever-advancing modernity but rather embraces a process of modernity, the discourse of which is seen as a social fact of self-realization among the men of the E'tolan village. The notion of tradition among Taiwan's Indigenous groups encompasses a multifaceted practice of rituals and ideology that is shaped by the contemporary perspectives of the Indigenous communities themselves. These communities are not trapped in a bygone era practicing "tradition," but rather live out their traditions in a twenty-first-century world shaped by a range of colonial and postcolonial dynamics. In the case of Taiwan, Indigenous peoples are contemporary because they are shaped by the fabric of colonization that Taiwan has been subjected to. In the process of dance, tradition is embedded in the culture. This is important. As Indigenous communities—tribes, villages, and even households—become displaced, the ability to practice culture and tradition alongside modernity is vital to the survival of cultural heritage. A good example was the release of a music album in May 2010, with complete lyrics in Amis, by Amis artist Suming. Although not the first album of Amis music, it was the first to combine pop culture and Indigenous melodies. One song, "Kapah," presents Amis tradition as modern. Suming writes, "We Indigenous peoples in Taiwan are living in modern times. In the future, I don't want to have to visit a museum to learn about our culture" (Friedman 2010).

The practice of modern dance thus acts as a social fact—a practice that affects the behavior of individual members of that society—for each age-grade set, or *kapot*. As members of each *kapot* use symbols of modernity to express themselves, they set the foundations of historical visual representation. Each *kapot* maintains a sociological perspective throughout their lives, and one can observe not only the tradition in the culture but also how those in each *kapot* identified themselves at different stages in their past. The notion that tradition, in its nascent sense, is simply anything transmitted from the past to the present makes no proclamation about what is handed down from one generation to another. There is no mention of the length of time it has been passed down, or the method used, whether it was verbally communicated or recorded in writing (Shils 2006, 12). Neither does it say whether it is a material artefact or a cultural construction. The idea of transmitting does not indicate that the presence of something from the past logically necessitates acceptance, appreciation, repetition, or incorporation of any normative or compulsory proposition (Shils 2006, 12). This is perhaps best understood with an analogy. An artefact, for example, that sits on the wall of a museum or gallery has for the most part remained the same since it was collected; though the object has been subjected to deterioration and maintenance by physical substances, it remains partially untouched. However, the interpretation of the artefact does not remain the same for all who encounter it. As culture modernizes, so does the interpretation of material tradition. The object remains traditional, but the analysis modernizes. As each culture interprets its sense of space and meaning in a ritualized context, tradition remains the same, while exposition differs. Therefore, tradition changes by the "internal process of cultural invention" (Otto 1993, 9). For the Indigenous peoples of Taiwan, the social, economic, and political transformations since the island's colonization—first in the seventeenth century and then through the various layers of coloniality that followed—forced people to continually reinvent what it means to be Indigenous and to navigate notions of tradition to fit colonial agendas.

Tradition is, thus, not simply a belief system or material culture handed down intact from one generation to another; it is ubiquitous and forever changing. A tradition remains habitual in the interpretation of the actor who uses it. Modern concepts of tradition ignore key components of what is regarded as customary. Tradition does not need to be old, nor does it need to be followed by everyone in the community; it flourishes by retaining a certain stability and integrity from past community life. Rituals and customs handed down in the ethnographic present, as in the case of *Amis Hip Hop*, a form of contemporary dance among the Amis (see Tsai Cheng-liang 2006), have as much reverence as those handed down over many generations. For the many Indigenous groups in Taiwan, their rituals and customs are not in the past tense but forever in the present; they are products of their living history. Tradition represents the historical existence of a people.

Shifting demographic patterns of Indigenous settlement continue to prompt actualization of new forms of community identity. Expressions of indigeneity are not limited to Indigenous communities; they can be demonstrated in locations with limited or no Indigenous identity. Practice of "tradition" enables a pan-Indigenous identity whereby the collective 2 percent of Indigenous peoples in Taiwan are able to come together in a cooperative unity. Whether Amis or Bunun, people identify with each other under the umbrella of "Indigenous," distinct and separate from the dominant Han Chinese settler cultures with whom they share space.

By the 1960s, Indigenous communities began to form in Taiwan's cities, and by 1985 these constituted 6.9 percent of the total Indigenous population. By 1991 this had grown to 14.4 percent, and by 1995 to 24.6 percent. By 2003 this number had jumped to 34.07 percent, and to 45 percent in 2012 (Council of Indigenous Peoples 2013). This remarkable increase from rural "traditional" communities to urban centers is a clear indication of an economic push and pull (Alsford 2021, 18). According to the Council of Indigenous Peoples, throughout this period of growth, Indigenous communities residing in urban areas remained particularly vulnerable to the Asian financial crisis in 1997 and the financial crisis in 2007–8 in comparison to their non-Indigenous counterparts. According to the report, the average non-Indigenous household income decreased by 0.7 percent between 2006 and 2010, but for Indigenous households the decrease was 2.4 percent. It is clear that the Indigenous peoples of Taiwan have faced numerous challenges since colonization began in the seventeenth century. There is no single story of indigeneity. The development of multiple identities, both pan and poly, since the 1990s has, to a certain extent, eroded senses of differing identities, and thus it is often left to material culture and language to speak for distinctive Indigenous nations.

Taiwan's postauthoritarian period has seen a shift toward recognizing a polyethnic sense of self while accepting pan-Indigenous identities—a collective sense of indigeneity. Two important moments were the establishment of the Council of Aboriginal Affairs in 1996 and the incorporation of the Aboriginal Affairs Commission in 1999, which has been known since 2002 as the Council of Indigenous Peoples and is headed by a minister who is recommended by the premier and appointed by the president. This puts the council on par with other cabinet-level bodies under the Executive Yuan. The council's main objective is to assist the Indigenous populations on the island by advocating for laws that promote language revitalization and provide support for self-governing Indigenous communities. It also bestows recognized status upon Indigenous groups. In determining this status, the council considers various factors such as member genealogies, linguistic identity, and the historical background of the groups. However, some groups face challenges in obtaining official recognition due to a lack of documentation and the extinction of their languages. Since its establishment, the council has granted Indigenous status to seven groups, but there are still at least thirteen groups that remain unrecognized. Among these thirteen, three have received recognition at the local government level. Regaining lost Indigenous identity became an important factor in the 2001 Declaration of Taiwan's Plain Indigenous Peoples: "Today, we stand up and speak out, solemnly telling the people and government of Taiwan that we are Indigenous peoples and that we have not disappeared! We were forced to conceal ourselves. Under the conditions of national humiliation, our people's flame has continued and become another kind of identity survival in Taiwan society. . . . From today onward, Taiwan's various Indigenous peoples must not be separated from each other" (Jolan Hsieh 2018, 12).

The Indigenous movements have emphasized three demands: (1) name rectification, including personal, peoples, land, territory, and the use of romanized script as opposed to Chinese characters; (2) return of land and land rights; and (3) establishment of self-government (Jolan Hsieh 2018, 14–15). Survival of Indigenous activism depends on focusing on collective rights and recognizing Indigenous (singular) identity and values. Evaluating cultural values entails examining concepts such as hospitality, success, and equality. Values, like tradition, are not fixed and self-evident; values are relative. Such Indigenous declarations draw on issues of equality as a collective value for all Indigenous peoples. The sense of a lack of equality draws them together. The dramatic geographical movement from traditional communities to metropolitan areas has had a significant effect on how Indigenous peoples understand and recognize inequality.

The percentage of urban-dwelling Indigenous peoples shows that rural-to-urban migration is considerable. Between 1991 and 2018 the percentage of Indigenous peoples residing in metropolitan districts had risen from 14 to 47 percent (Huang Shu-min and Ying-Hwa Chang 2010). The largest source of migration is along the eastern Hualien-Taitung corridor, and the principal destinations are the Taipei-Taoyuan metropolitan areas, Taichung, and Kaohsiung. All three areas house major industrial hubs where a significant portion of Taiwan's labor-intensive manufacturing takes place (Shu-min Huang and Shao-hua Liu 2016, 299). The dramatic geographical movement from traditional communities to metropolitan areas has had a significant effect on how Indigenous people understand and recognize inequality. This inequality is often most acutely felt when people become minorities in specific social structures: education, the labor market, and representation in local and national government. For Taiwan's Indigenous peoples this sense of becoming a minority is particularly acute when they migrate to urban centers. Many reside in communities on the outskirts of the city. Unable to afford the higher rents of the central districts, they are forced many to reside illegally on riverbanks, adding spatial as well as ethnic stratification (Fu Yangchih 2002, 60; Lin Ji-ping et al. 2010, 104). Chain migration, a pattern of migration in which family members who have already migrated assist in bringing other family members to join them, is an important factor in the motivation for Indigenous people to move to the cities (Su Yihju 2007, 160).

The beginning of demands for Indigenous rights in Taiwan by young Indigenous activists was evident in the Wild Lily sit-in in March 1990. That generation of activists campaigned for many of the democratic institutional frameworks that exist in Taiwan today. An overnight sleep-in by Indigenous activists in March 2021 outside the Judicial Yuan, over Tama Tulum—a Bunun man arrested in 2013 for hunting wild game—demonstrates that equality for Indigenous peoples in Taiwan is still some way off.

On 2 December 1960, Icyang Parod was born into an Amis-speaking Lohok family in Yuli, Hualien. Parod became politically active as a political science major at National Taiwan University. He was made head of the Association of Taiwan Indigenous Rights Promotion (Taiwan Yunzhuminzu Quanli Cujinhui) in 1986, two years after it was established in 1984 by young Indigenous people from across the island. His political campaigning focused on two important movements. The first, Huanwuo Tudi Yundong (Return Our Land Movement), was part of a wider Indigenous rights movement that saw numerous Indigenous activists, from across the various Indigenous nations in Taiwan, taking to the streets to protest over land rights. In three main protests, in 1988, 1989, and 1993, Indigenous activists urged the government to return Indigenous land that had been occupied by the government or private enterprises. The second, Yuanzhumin Zhengming Yundong (Indigenous Name Rectification Movement), was a movement in the 1990s initiated by the Association of Taiwan Indigenous Rights Promotion to change the Chinese term *shanbao* to *yuanzhumin* and restore traditional names, as well as pushing to include Indigenous rights in the constitution. Their demands were met in 1994.

As early as 1989, Icyang Parod sought a political position in government. Like other activists, his first attempt to join the Legislative Yuan failed. In November 1995, Parod was jailed for eight months as a consequence of violating the Assembly and Parade Act when he organized a protest to change the collective name for Indigenous peoples from *shanbao*. Following his release, Parod worked for Fan Sun-lu, a legislator in the DPP. In 2000, the Department of Indigenous People was established in the Taipei County government, and Parod was elected director-general. He maintained this role until his promotion to minister of the Council of Indigenous Peoples in 2007. In 2008, with the election of Ma Ying-jeou and the KMT, Parod was removed from his position. In 2010 he was elected councilor of New Taipei City as a DPP candidate, and then reelected in 2014. When Tsai Ing-wen of the DPP won the presidential election in 2016, Parod returned to his post as minister for the council. As part of the Indigenous Historical Justice and Transitional Justice Committee, he was given an executive secretary position to oversee three core foci of the committee: (1) traditional territory; (2) Indigenous language (in May 2017, the committee oversaw passage of the Taiwan Indigenous Languages Development Act); and (3) residential rights of urban Indigenous peoples (Suqluman 2018.

The flexibility of indigeneity is important for the survival of cultural heritage. In societies such as Taiwan, where migration plays a key role in the complex processes of social change, its impact on communities, economies, and polities has undoubtedly affected how this information is transmitted and how the narratives of the past are told. In contemporary society, these constraints are largely socioeconomic. Indigenous people who have migrated from traditional communities to larger metropolitan areas have done so to improve their social and economic circumstances. However, it then becomes important for them to foster notions of tradition (linguistically, creative industries, and storytelling) and maintain values that are compatible with multiple identities, whether community-based, pan-Indigenous, or part of a wider Taiwanese identity.

Some have chosen to return to ancestral homelands. Better transportation and communication between rural and urban communities have meant that divisions between the two have diminished. Many of those who have chosen to return have done so because of rising costs in metropolitan areas and increasing competition for work with foreign labor (Liao and Li 2000). It is clear that many young Taiwan Indigenous peoples are "coming home" to help rebuild their *buluo*, or community, for future generations.

Taiwan's history is one of settler colonialism, and the principles of the state are based on Han-centric ideologies. Inherent in the myth of Chinese primacy has been widespread acceptance and embrace of that settler past. This persists less out of a lack of awareness of the Indigenous past than from a desire to find a single national narrative. Indigenous history and the story of Icyang Parod are thus entwined with the history of migration, economic transformation, and democratization that has informed the wider Taiwanese narrative.

24

A President's Tale

TSAI ING-WEN

He was a shepherde and noght a mercenarie.
And thogh he hooly were and vertuous,
He was to synful men nat despitous,
Ne of his speche daungerous ne digne,
But in his techyng discreet and benynge.
GEOFFREY CHAUCER · 1870

So, we have come to our final tale. For Chaucer this was the Parson. Unlike the tales of other pilgrims, this one was neither story nor poem but rather a treatise on penitence. The Parson divides penitence into three parts: contrition of the heart, confession of the mouth, and satisfaction. The Parson, since Chaucer first penned him, has often been portrayed as a man who practices what he preaches. He was, after all, "a shepherd and not a mercenary."

This tale, about a president, also functions as a conclusion. In contradistinction to the first tale, of a male British sojourner in 1864, it features a female president in the twenty-first century. This president is in office not because she comes from a wealthy or powerful family but because she appeals to the electorate. As we conclude, Tsai Ing-wen is in her second term, having been reelected despite strong opposition, misinformation, and foreign interference. She shook off populism and then, less than a month later, demonstrated her prowess by minimizing the impact of COVID-19.

Despite a history of settler colonialism, violence, and conflict, the people who make up this island of 24 million have come together under an umbrella of democracy—a civic identity that they fought for, which emerged first after their betrayal in 1945 and then transformed into a democracy when the world disregarded them. To get here, the island has endured layers of coloniality. Although Taiwan arguably still exists within a framework of colonization, the majority of its people have managed to carve out a postcolonial identity. Therefore, identity reflects the impact that colonial exploitation and domination had on colonized people. There may be one Taiwan, but there is no single Taiwan story.

Taiwan belongs to various groups, and the identity of being from Taiwan holds different levels of significance to different people. Throughout the past four hundred years of colonial settlement, Taiwan has been imagined by numerous individuals or lives. The people of Taiwan have a rich history of reshaping their nation, including its culture and identity, economy and society, politics and status (Rigger 2011, 196). For some, Taiwan, particularly its democracy, has gained a sacred status. Democracy came to Taiwan after four decades of authoritarian rule by a government that had assumed jurisdiction over the island in 1945 and would settle its entire government upon it, in exile, four years later. Movement toward popular rule was fragmentary and negotiated. Democracy was completed in 1996 and consolidated in 2008, when it had gone through four direct presidential elections and a second ruling party transition. With the reelection of the DPP in 2016, Taiwan demonstrated to the world that, in its fourth transition of power, its democracy was both robust and mature.

Despite this maturity, democracy continues to be challenged. The People's Republic of China's economic position and growing international influence has meant that Taiwan is frequently denied access to the global stage. Canadian World Health Organization (WHO) adviser Bruce Aylward's dodging of questions on Taiwan's response to the COVID-19 pandemic in March 2020 indicates Beijing's latitude in dictating how the world discusses Taiwan.

Since its first democratic milestone with the lifting of martial law in 1987 and its first direct presidential election in 1996, Taiwan has achieved what political scientist Dafydd Fell terms "a series of political miracles" (Fell 2012, 240). After years of enduring cross-strait tension, Taiwan remains a healthy democracy with strong democratic institutions.

The pathway to consolidating democracy has not always been easy. Following the election of Chen Shui-bian in 2000, the DPP administration was accused of supporting a growing Taiwanese nativist movement that was consolidating identity by purging the island of its Chinese past in a process of desinicization. But this view amounted more to a perceived challenge to the KMT's version of *Chinese* nationalism in Taiwan (Hughes 2011, 51). What was actually happening was that this *nativist* movement was shifting an identity, gradually, toward something that was both participatory and civic. Taiwan has, I argue, done this successfully. Nativist movements with notions of nation-state building have tended to be used to legitimize ultranationalist ideology and, in some cases, militarism. The breakup of the former Yugoslavia would be a good point of reference here. Yet, by focusing on civic culture, the Taiwanese were able, in spite of the raw political cleavages in domestic politics, to navigate this danger and come together in celebration of its democratic institutions. One need only be on the streets of Taiwan during election season to witness the extent to which its people see democracy as sacred. Flags and banners of candidates flutter in the breeze, and heated discussions and debates echo out from TV sets and radios in workplaces and homes.

Taiwan is a multiparty representative republic headed by a president. The structure of its government is based on the principles of Sun Yat-sen's *Three Principles of the People*. There are five branches of government, known as *yuan*: executive, legislative, judicial, examination, and control. The president and vice president are elected through a popular vote system every four years with a maximum of two four-year terms. The current elected president is Tsai Ing-wen, with Lai Ching-te as her vice president and Su Tseng-chang as premier, the head of the executive branch.

<hr />

On 31 August 1956 at the George Mackay Hospital in Taipei, Chang Chin-feng gave birth to her final child, Tsai Ing-wen. Tsai's father, Tsai Chieh-sheng, was originally from Fangshan in Pingtung County, Hakka on his father's side and Paiwan on his mother's. Tsai's Paiwan name is Tjuku, meaning "round like the sun, a daughter of a chief." Tsai Chieh-sheng's early

life was similar to that of the *shōnenkō*, although his motivation differed. At eighteen, during the Second World War, he went to Dalian—then part of the Japanese puppet state of Manchukuo—where he trained as a mechanic to repair aircraft (Tsai Ing-wen 2011). Unlike the *shōnenkō*, he went to Dalian to avoid being sent to Southeast Asia. After the war, he returned to Pingtung and established a delivery company and auto repair shop. In 1968, he expanded his business and moved to Taipei. Aside from his established trades, Tsai began trading in secondhand automobiles. During this time, he had noticed a demand for cars in the American expat and military communities. He hired English teachers for his staff, and by 1979, he had accumulated enough capital to invest in real estate. Tsai purchased land in the Zhongshan District of Taipei City, which proved to be very profitable. Toward the end of the martial law period, Tsai donated significantly to the Tangwai, and following the establishment of the DPP, he contributed financially to the party.

Tsai had four wives and eleven children. Tsai Ing-wen's mother was his fourth wife, with whom he parented four children. As the youngest of eleven siblings, Tsai Ing-wen was the most pampered. Tsai entered National Taiwan University in 1974 to study law. After graduation she left for the United States and graduated with an LLM from Cornell Law School in 1980. Following this, she moved to London to study for a PhD in law at the London School of Economics (LSE). After graduating from the LSE in 1984, she returned to Taiwan and began lecturing in the Department of Law at National Chengchi University (NCCU). In 1991, she left NCCU, although she remained an adjunct professor, for Soochow University School of Law.

During her university years, Tsai had a number of suitors, but she chose to focus on her studies. During her Cornell years, Tsai had a boyfriend whom she planned to marry. Sadly, he died in a mountain-climbing accident. Her long-term single status led to unfortunate questions concerning her sexuality during her presidential election bid in 2012, which Tsai refused to comment on (Lin Nan-sen 2011). By 2016, the topic no longer came up publicly.

Tsai joined the DPP in 2004 and became a legislator the following year. In 2006, she was invited to serve as vice premier, a position she held until the end of 2007. Following the success of Ma Ying-jeou and the KMT in

2008, in opposition, Tsai was elected as the first female chairperson of the DPP for two consecutive terms (2008–10 and 2010–12). Following her defeat by Ma in the 2012 presidential election, she returned to being chairperson in 2014. She held this position until 2016, when she was elected president.

Often seen as the president of the status quo, she appeals to the middle-ground electorate. In her first inauguration speech, she stated her policies, including a controversial pension reform plan, care for the elderly, transitional justice, and judicial reform (Tsai Ing-wen 2016). Her economic plan was all about diversification. She prioritized innovative industries and core development via a new Southbound Policy that aimed to enhance cooperation and exchange with eighteen countries in Southeast Asia, South Asia, and Australasia. Her cross-strait policy was clear. She acknowledged that her predecessor had framed relations under the so-called 1992 Consensus (an acceptance that there is one China but there are different interpretations; *yizhong gebiao, yige zhongguo gezi biaoshu*), but she could not agree to it. Instead, she reiterated the importance of continued dialogue.

Under Tsai's administration, the DPP has shifted from being the issue-based party of the Tangwai movement to a more liberal progressive party, putting Taiwan's politics on a more common left-right spectrum. Tsai's government favors action to reduce unemployment by introducing incentives for entrepreneurship among the youth. It also pursues an agenda to expand public housing and mandate childcare support (Tsai Ing-wen 2017). She has proactively engaged with Taiwan Indigenous issues—the Indigenous Languages Development Act took effect in June 2017—and has shown support for LGBTQ rights. Under her presidency, same-sex marriage was legalized in 2018. Debates surrounding immigration—Taiwan does not yet have a refugee policy—and issues of crime and punishment, particularly the death penalty, remain relatively conservative in Taiwanese society but are continually discussed.

Tsai Ing-wen has had a profound impact on Taiwan through her tenure as seventh president of the ROC on Taiwan. She has demonstrated remarkable determination and resilience in navigating a range of complex domestic and international challenges, particularly in light of shifting geopolitical dynamics and China's increasingly assertive stance. As leader, she has been steadfast in upholding democratic values, human rights, and social justice, evident through various policy initiatives and reforms. Tsai has positioned the DPP as a progressive force in cross-strait relations and has sought to establish Taiwan as a world leader in sustainable development. Her strong commitment to the status quo has left an indelible mark on Taiwan's political landscape. Tsai's vision and integrity as president will undoubtedly shape the trajectory of the country's future.

A Conclusion

The history of Taiwan is made up by its people. Although the tales presented here are separated by as much as a hundred years, crossing colonial layers, they congregate in certain areas of Taiwan. Dadaocheng in Taipei shaped multiple narratives. As a hub of radical thought, it has been globally situated since the late nineteenth century. It is a place of migration, a home to the semi-exiled. It is a site of marginality and of nostalgia. In a sense, it is the Canterbury to many in this set of tales.

The course of Taiwan from the late nineteenth century to the present has passed through the three phases (Gennep 2019). The first phase marked a period of separation. It is not part of China, but it does have a connection to a Chinese sociocultural heritage. It is not part of Japan, but it has a Japanese colonial heritage. It is a thing-in-itself. Martial law and the White Terror that accompanied it constituted its transitional, or liminal, phase. Having completed this metaphorical rite, Taiwan has assumed its new identity. Its task now is to enter the international community with its new status. The only force that presently stands in its way is the PRC, which falsely believes that for it to complete its own quest to assume a new identity, a mission that it has assumed since 1949, it must include Taiwan. With the passage of time, however, the people of China might realize that even as an independent country, Taiwan can offer China bright prospects (Roy 2003, 246). It, too, can pass through the three phases without Taiwan.

I end by borrowing again from Shawna Yang Ryan. The scene: a warm day in March under a perfectly blue sky, as a small group of friends sit on the banks of Taiwan's most northernly mountain range. Dr. Tsai, switching to Taiwanese as there is a Japanese family picnicking under the tree beside him, whispers to his future wife, "We are curious creatures, we Taiwanese.

Orphans. Eventually orphans must choose their own name and write their own stories. The beauty of orphanhood is the blank slate" (Ryan 2016, 372). And so, different people with different tales (many more than the twenty-four depicted here) have chalked their presence upon this slate.

As such, for the peoples of Taiwan, this book of tales belongs to you.

Glossary

Unless noted otherwise, names and terms represent Standard Chinese (Mandarin) pronunciation in Hanyu Pinyin (HP) romanization or in an individual's preferred spelling. Pronunciations in other Chinese dialects or other languages are indicated as follows:

J · Japanese (standard Revised Hepburn system)

K · Korean (standard Revised Romanization transcription)

TH · Taiwanese Hokkien (Tâi-gí; HP Taiyu)

Aiai Ryou (J) 愛愛寮 a hostel for homeless people

Akashi Motojirō (J) 明石 元二郎

Andō Rikichi (J) 安藤 利吉

Anping 安平

Ataabu 霧峰 Hoanya Indigenous name for Wufeng, a suburban district in southern Taichung

Bai Longfa 白隆發

baihua 白話 vernacular literature

Baise Kongbu 白色恐怖 White Terror

Baise Kongbu Ludao Jinian Yuanqu 白色恐怖綠島紀念園區 Green Island White Terror Memorial Park

Baishanjun 白衫軍運動 White Shirt Army

baojia 保甲 community-based system of law enforcement and civil control

Beipu Shijian 北埔事件 Beipu Incident

benshengren 本省人 Han settlers in Taiwan that arrived prior to the Japanese colonization

bianjiang wenxue 邊疆文學 literature of borders

Buchanzuhui 不纏足會 Foot Emancipation Society

buluo 部落 Indigenous community

Cai Yuanpei 蔡元培

Chang Chin-feng 張金鳳

Chang Chun-hung 張俊宏

Chang Kuo-wei 張國煒

Chang Liang-Tse 張良澤

Chang Lin Chin-chih 張林金枝

Chang Yueh-ching 張月卿

Chang Yung-fa 張榮發

Changrenkeng Chedao 長仁坑車道 Chengrenkeng Cable Car Trail

Chen Atu 陳阿土

Chen Cheng 陳誠

Chen Chieh 陳傑
Chen Chien-jen 陳建仁
Chen Chu 陳菊
Chen Duxiu 陳獨秀
Chen Fuqian 陳福謙
Chen Hsin-an 陳新安
Chen Jingwen 陳甜
Chen Lin Lien-hua 陳林連花
Chen Mao-ping (Sanmao) 陳懋平
Chen Meixiang 陳美香
Chen Pi-Kuei 陳碧奎
Chen Shao-hsing 陳紹馨陳
Chen Sheng 陳聖
Chen Shui-bian 陳水扁
Chen Suching 陳嗣慶
Chen Tienshin 陳田心
Chen Yi 陳儀
Chen Yunlin 陳雲林
Chenghuang Miao 城隍廟
Chenghuang Temple in Yilan 宜蘭
Chiang Hong-zhang 蔣鴻章
Chiang Kai-shek 蔣介石
Chiang Wei-chuan 蔣渭川
Chiang Wei-shui 蔣渭水
Chiayi 嘉義
Chou Te-wei 周德偉
Chou Tzu-yu 周子瑜
Chou Wen-yao 周婉窈
Chou Yu 周渝
Chu Feng-min 朱馮敏
chulsaengji (K) 출생지 birthplace
Chung Yi-ren 鍾逸人
cizi zhushui 刺字逐水 a form
    of punishment

Daan Yiyuan 大安醫院 Taian Hospital
Dabu Zijiuhui 大埔自救會 Dapu Self-
    Help Organization
Dachen Zhudao 大陳諸島 Dachen
    Islands
Dahehang 大和行 Dahe Company

Daichaochun Shijian 戴潮春事件 Tai
    Chao-chuen Incident
Dajiang dahai 大江大海 *Big River, Big
    Sea* by Lung Ying-tai
Dalongdong 大龍峒
Dangwai 黨外 lit. "outside the party"
Dapenkeng 大坌坑文化
Den Kenjirō (J) 田 健治郎
Dihuajie 迪化街 Dihua Street
dingcuo 頂厝 the upper mansion family
    (reference to Wufeng Lin family)
dōjō 道場 (J) a hall for immersive learning
dōka (J) 同化 assimilation
Dulan 都蘭 also known as E'tolan in Amis

Erlin 二林 a township in Changhua
    County, Taiwan.
Erqi budui 二七部隊 27 Brigade

Fan Guoguang Shihua 反國光石化
    Anti Guo-Kuang Petroleum Plant
    social movement
Fan Sun-lu 范巽綠
Fan Yun 范雲
fanshi lizaichun 番勢李仔春 lit.,
    "ally of the barbarians" or "man
    empowered by the foreigners"
Fengtian Yimin Cun 豐田移民村
    Fengtian/Toyota Village

Gao Gongqian 高拱乾
Gaw Bun-sui (TH) Wu Wenshui
    吳文水
geta (J) 下駄 type of Japanese platform
    sandal
Gongmin Zuhe 公民組合 Taiwan Citizen
    Union
Gongyihui 公益會 Gongyi Association
Gouqu zhulai 狗去豬來 "Out with the
    dogs and in with the pigs"
Gu Liansong 辜濂松 Jeffrey Koo Sr.

Guandi 關帝 historical name of Chinese military general Guan Yu (160–220 AD)

guangfu 光復 retrocession

gukjeok (K) 국적 nationality

Gungun hongchen 滾滾紅塵 *Red Dust*; movie script by Sanmao

Guoli Taiwan Daxue Xuesheng Zizhi Guizhang 國立臺灣大學學生會自治規程 NTU Student Association Autonomous Regulations

haijin 海禁 overseas trade

haiwai yiyi fenzi 海外異議分子 overseas dissidents

Hallyu (K) 한류 Korean Wave

Hatazō Adachi (J) 安達 二十三

Heishuigou 黑水溝 Black Trench, colloquially used to refer to the Taiwan Strait

Heito (J) 屏東 present-day Pingtung

Hongji Yiyuan 宏濟醫院 Hongji Hospital

Hou Hsiao-hsien 侯孝賢

Hsieh Chang-ting 謝長廷

Hsieh Hsueh-hung 謝雪紅

Hua 華 Han people

Huaguang Shequ 華光社區 Huaguang Community

Huanan Yinhang 華南銀行 Hua Nan Bank

Huang An 黃安

Huang Chiau-tong 黃昭堂

Huang Chin-lung 黃金龍 birth name of Huang Hsin-Chieh

Huang Chun-ying 黃俊英

Huang Hsin-chieh 黃信介

Huang Jui-niang 黃瑞娘

Huang Nanqiu 黃南球

Huang Shou-li 黃守禮

Huang Xing 黃興

Huang Yujie 黃玉階

Huang Yu-shu 黃玉書

Huang Zhanghui (Shoki Coe) 黃彰輝

Huanjing Baohu Shu 環境保護署 Environmental Protection Administration (EPA)

Huanwuo Tudi Yundong 還我土地運動 Return Our Land Movement

Hubu 戶部 Ministry of Revenue

Huihua Yanjiusuo 繪畫研究所 Research Institute of Painting

Humaozhuang 虎茅莊 present-day Taoyuan City

Huo 惑 "Confusion"; article by Sanmao

Hyōgikai (J) 評議会 Advisory Council

Icyang Parod 夷將·拔路兒

Inō Kanori 伊能 嘉矩

Insa-dong (K) 인사동

Ji Qiguan 季麒光

Jianchang houjie 建昌後街 Jianchang Back Street

Jianchangjie 建昌街 Jianchang Street

Jiang Yuying 蔣毓英

jianmin 賤民 lit., "filthy people"

jiao 郊 guild system

jiao pu 郊鋪 type of guild

jiao shang 郊商 guild members

Jiaobanian Shijian 噍吧哖事件 Tapani Incident

jieshou 劫收 robber

Jieyan Ling 臺灣省戒嚴令 Order of Martial Law

Jin Su-qin 金素琴

Jinguashi 金瓜石

jinshi 進士 an imperial scholar or recipient of the highest imperial exam

Jiye Yimin Cun 吉野移民村 Chiye/Yoshino Village

Juan Mei-shu 阮美姝

GLOSSARY *237*

Kanaseki Takeo 金関丈夫

Kao Chun-ming 高俊明

Kao Yu-shu 高玉樹 Henry Kao

Keelung 基隆

Keting Ji Gongchang 客廳即工廠 Living Rooms as Factories

Kikuchi Kan (J) 菊池寬

Kizoku-in (J) 貴族院 the House of Peers, or the Upper House of the Japanese Diet

Kobayama Sukenori (J) 樺山資紀

Kobayashi Seizō (J) 小林 躋造

kōgakkō (J) 公学校 mixed common school

kokugo katei (J) 国語家庭 national language family

kōminka (J) 皇民化 imperial subjects

Koo (Ku) Kwang-ming 辜寬敏

Koza (J) 高座

Ku Chin 辜琴

Ku Fu-sheng 顧福生

Ku Hsien-chung 辜顯忠

Ku Hsien-jung 辜顯榮

Ku Jui-yun 古瑞雲

Kuangren riji 狂人日記 Diary of a Madman by Lu Xun

Kukutsu (J) 久々津 POW camp in Xindian 新店, Taipei City

Kuo Yu-hsin 郭雨新

Lan Yinding 藍蔭鼎

Laoyuzai 老芋仔 lit., "old taro," indicating a waishengren male; Lāu-ōo-á (TH)

Li Chi 李濟

Li Chunsheng 李春生

Li Desheng 李德生

Li Dazhao 李大釗

Li Fu-chun 李福春

Li Hsien-wen 李憲文

Li Wenliang 李文亮

Li Yen-Hsi 李延禧

Liao Chinlin 繆進蘭

Liao Wen-I 廖文毅

Lien Hao 連好

Lien Heng 連橫

Lien Wen-ching 連溫卿

Lifayuan 立法院 Legislative Yuan

Lim Chông-gī (TH) Lin Zongyi 林宗義

Lin Chao-hsuan 林朝選

Lin Chao-tung 林朝棟

Lin Cheng-tang 林澄堂

Lin Chiang-mai 林江邁

Lin Chia-yin 林甲寅

Lin Ching-wu 林精武

Lin Chiung-yao 林瓊瑤

Lin Hsien-tang 林獻堂

Lin Hsiung-cheng 林熊徵

Lin Hung-hsuan 林弘宣

Lin Jiang-mai 林江邁

Lin Jin-shen 林金生

Lin Lantian 林藍田

Lin Ming-chu 林明珠

Lin Pao-lo 林苞螺

Lin Qianguang 林謙光

Lin Qingyue 林清月

Lin Shih 林石

Lin Shuangwen Shijian 林爽文事件

Lin Shuguang 林曙光

Lin Sun 林遜

Lin Tien-kuo 林奠國

Lin Tin-pang 林定邦

Lin Weiyuan 林維源

Lin Wen-cha 林文察

Lin Wen-chin 林文欽

Lin Wen-ming 林文明

Lin Wen-shan 林文山

Lin Xiong-zheng 林熊徵

Lin Yi-hsiung 林義雄

"Linchuang jiangyi: Guanyu Taiwan zhege huanzhe" 臨床講:關於台灣

這個患者 "Clinical Notes: A Patient Named Taiwan"; essay by Chiang Wei-shui

Ling Shung-sheng 凌純聲

Lintian Yimin Cun 林田移民村 Lintian/ Hayashida Village

Liu Cheng-hung 劉政鴻

Liu Yongfu 劉永福

Liuguanjie 六館街 Liuguan Street

Liusi, sanliu, yihuitou 六死,三 留,一回 頭 "Six in ten die, three stay, and one is sent back"

liuwang 流亡 "To drift away and die"

Lo Fong-pin 羅鳳蘋

Lu (Annette) Hsiu-lien 呂秀蓮

Lu Xun 魯迅

Ludao Renquan Wenhua Yuanqu 綠島 人權文化園區 Green Island Human Rights Culture Park, former name of Green Island White Terror Memorial Park

Lugouqiao 盧溝橋 Marco Polo Bridge

Lung Ying-tai 龍應台

Ma Ying-jeou 馬英九

Ma Yung-cheng 馬永成

Madou 麻豆 Mattau in Sirayan language

Mai liteul telebijeon (K) 마이 리틀 텔레비전 *My Little Television*

Mama Jiaoshi 媽媽教室 Mothers' Workshop

Mao Zedong 毛澤東

Mazu 媽祖 Chinese sea goddess

Meilidao Shijian 美麗島事件 Kaohsiung Eight

Meilidao zazhi 美麗島雜誌 *Formosa* magazine

Mengjia 艋舺 Banka

Minami Nippon Kisen Kabushiki Gaisha (J) 南日本汽船株式会社 MKK, a Japanese shipping company

Miyamoto Nobuhito 宮本延人

Mori Ushinosuke 森丑之助

naichijin (J) 内地人 homelander

Nanyang Cangku Zhushi Huishe 南洋 倉庫株式會社 Southern Warehouse Company

Ng Bú-tong (TH) 黃武東 Huang Wudong

Ng Leng-kiat (TH) 黃能傑 Huang Nengjie

Ng Siok-eng (TH) 黃淑英 Huang Shuying

Ni Jianghui 倪蔣懷

Nihonjin (J) 日本人 Japanese people

nikkyō (J) 日僑 overseas Japanese

Oka (J) 岡 POW camp in Shilin District 士林區 of Taipei City

Okamura Yasuji (J) 岡村 寧次

Pai Hsien-yung 白先勇

panluan 叛亂 rebellion or sedition

Peng Ching-kao 彭清靠

Peng Ming-min 彭明敏

Pudu 普渡 Universal Salvation Festival

Qian jiao 塹郊 Zhuqian Guild

Qianqiujie 千秋街 Qianqiu Street

Qigai Pumie Xiehui 乞丐撲滅協會 Association for the Care of Homeless

qingnian tuan 青年團 Youth Patrol Group

Qinmindang 親民黨 People First Party

Qiu Fengjia 丘逢甲

Qiyiwu Shengming 715 聲明 715 Announcement

Quan jiao 泉郊 Quanzhou Guild

Quanmei Taiwan Duli Lianmeng 全美 台灣獨立聯盟 United Formosans in America for Independence

Quanmin Qiangjiu Danshuihe Xingdong

Lianmeng 全民搶救淡水河行動聯盟 National Alliance for the Rescue of the Tamsui River

Quanzhou Sanyi 泉州三邑 name of clan

Quanzhou Tongan 泉州同安 name of clan

Renjiyuan 仁濟院 Jen-Chi Relief Institution

Rikugun Nakano Gakkō (J) 陸軍中野学校 Nakano School

ru bantu 入版圖 "entered the map"

Ruey Yih-fu 芮逸夫

Ruicheng 瑞澂 viceroy of Huguang 湖廣

Sahala de gushi 撒哈拉的故事 *Stories of the Sahara*; collection of stories by Sanmao

Samil Undong (K) 삼일 운동 Sam-il Movement

sangyō (J) 産業 industrial workers

Sanmao 三毛

Sanmao liulangji 三毛流浪記 *The Adventures of Sanmao*; comic by Zhang Leping

Sanmaore 三毛熱 Sanmao Craze

Sannian yixiaofan, wunian yidafan 三年一小反, 五年一大反 "Every three years there was an uprising and every five years a rebellion"

Sann-kha-á (TH) 三腳仔 sanjiaozai; lit., "three-legged management"; a reference to lower-level management that was considered neither animal nor human

seishōnen (J) 青少年 young people

shanbao 山胞 lit., "mountain compatriots," used to describe Taiwan Indigenous peoples

she 社 Indigenous settlement

Shehui Minzhu Dang 社會民主黨 Social Democratic Party

shengfan 生番 "raw" Indigenous groups

shi 石 unit of measure; one shi is equivalent to 103.6 liters

Shi Jiuduan Shijian 施九緞事件 Shih Chiutuan Incident

Shih Hsiu-feng 施秀鳳

Shih Ien 施乾

Shih Ming-teh 施明德

Shih Wu-ching 施武靖

Shih You 石有

Shijian haizhanzai women zhebian ma? 時間還站在我們這邊嗎 *Is Time Still on Our Side?* (documentary)

Shimizu Teruko (J) 清水照子

Shinchiku (J) 新竹州 Japanese colonial administrative division of Taiwan, including present-day Hsinchu City 新竹市, Hsinchu County 新竹縣, Taoyuan City 桃園市, and Miaoli County 桃園縣

Shinchinmi (J) 新珍味 New Gourmet (restaurant)

shiwan qingnian shiwan jun 十萬青年十萬軍 "100,000 young people, 100,000 soldiers"; campaign proposed by Chiang Kai-shek in 1944

shōgakkō (J) 小学校 Japanese-only primary school

Shoki Coe 黃彰輝

shōnenkō (J) 少年工 child laborer

shufan 熟番 "cooked" Indigenous groups

shuinsen (J) 朱印船

Shulin 樹林

sì-kha-á (TH) 四腳仔 sijiaozai; lit., "four-legged management"; a reference to management acting like animals rather than humans

Sikseutin (K) 식스틴 *Sixteen*

sim-pū-á (TH) 童養媳 tongyangxi; adoption of a preadolescent girl for future marriage

sixiangfan 思想犯 thought-crime prisoner

Sòng Chôan Sēng (TH) Song Quansheng 宋泉盛

Song Jiaoren 宋教仁

Su Beng 史明

Su Tseng-chang 蘇貞昌

Sun Yat-sen 孫中山

Taehwagwan (K) 태화관 restaurant in Seoul

Taibei Tianranzu Hui 台北天然足會 Taipei Natural Foot Association

Taichū (J) 臺中 present-day Taichung

Taihoku (J) 台北 present-day Taipei

Taihoku Kōgyō Gakkō (J) 台北工業学校 Taihoku Industrial School

Taihoku Kōtō Shōgyō Gakkō (J) 台北高等商業学校 Taihoku College of Commerce

Taimin 臺民 Taiwanese people

Tainan 台南

Taiwan Duli Jianguo Lianmeng 台灣獨立建國聯盟 World United Formosans for Independence

Taiwan Gongheguo Linshi Zhengfu 台灣共和國臨時政府 Provisional Government of the Republic of Formosa

Taiwan Jinshu Kuangye Gongsi 臺灣金屬礦業公司 Taiwan Metal Mining Company

Taiwan Jintong Kuangwuju 臺灣金銅礦務局 Taiwan Gold and Copper Mining Bureau

Taiwan Jiti Dianlu Zhizao Gufen Youxiangongsi 台灣積體電路製造股份有限公司 Taiwan Semiconductor Manufacturing Company (TSMC)

Taiwan qingnian 台灣青年 *Taiwanese Youth* magazine

Taiwan Qingnian Duli Lianmeng 台灣青年獨立聯盟 United Young Formosans for Independence

Taiwan Qingnianhui 台灣青年會 Formosa Association

Taiwan Renai Jiaoyu Shiyansuo 台灣仁愛教育實驗所 Taiwan's Jen-ai Educational Experimental Institute

Taiwan Renmin Zijue Yundong 台灣人民自決運動 Formosan Christians for Self Determination

Taiwan Renquan Weiyuanhui 臺灣人權委員會 Taiwan Human Rights Commission

Taiwan tongshi 臺灣通史 *The History of Taiwan*, book by Lien Heng

Taiwan Wenhua Xiehui 台灣文化協會 Taiwan Cultural Association

Taiwan Xingzheng Zhuanke Xuexiao 台灣行政專科學校 Taiwan Administration Junior College

Taiwan Yunzhuminzu Quanli Cujinhui 臺灣原住民族權利促進會 Association of Taiwan Indigenous Rights Promotion

Taiwan zhenglun 台灣政論 *Taiwan Politics* magazine

Taiwan Zhumin Zijue Lianmeng 台灣住民自決聯盟 League for Self-Determination of Formosans

Taiyang Kuangye Shiwu Suo 台陽礦業事務所 Taiyang Gold Mine Office

Taiyanghua Xueyun 太陽花學運 Sunflower Movement

Takao 打狗 lit., "bamboo forest" in Sirayan; present-day Kaohsiung 高雄

Takasago Giyūtai (J) 高砂義勇隊 Takasago Volunteers

Tang (Audrey) Fang 唐鳳

tang jiao 糖郊 sugar guild

Tang Jingsong 唐景崧

GLOSSARY 241

Tang Yu 唐羽

Tiandao Yimen 天道 儀門 Entry Door to the Heavenly Way

Tianma Chafang 天馬茶房 Tianma Tea House

Tok-phīnn-á-liâu (TH) 啄鼻仔寮 Zhuobizailiao; lit., "the hut for the tall nose"

Tok-phīnn-á-lōo (TH) Zhuobizailu 啄鼻仔路; lit., "Tall Nose Road"

tongzhi 同知 subprefect

Torii Ryūzō 鳥居龍藏

Tsai Cheng-liang 蔡政良

Tsai Chieh-sheng 蔡潔生

Tsai Ing-wen 蔡英文

Tsai Pei-huo 蔡培火

Tuanjie zai linian zhixia, zhiyao chixu, jiuneng chansheng gaibian 團結在理念之下，只要持續，就能產生改變 "We shall unite under our belief. If we carry on, changes can happen"

Tucheng 土城 district in New Taipei City

Tudigong 土地公 lit., "spirit of the earth," "territory god," or "tutelary deity"

Tzuyu (K) 쯔위

Un-tsiu-liâu (TH) 溫州寮 Wenzhouliao; lit., "the hut for the Wenzhou people"

waisheng 外省 lit. "outside"

waishengren 外省人 mainlanders; lit., "people from outside"

wakō (J) 倭寇 pirate

Wang Hsi-chi 王錫祺

Wang Hsu-kang 王旭康

Wang Kuei-jung 王桂榮

Wei Hwei-lin 衛惠林

Wei Lien-chih 魏蓮芷

Wei Tao-ming 魏道明

Wei Te-sheng 魏德聖

wen miao 文廟 temple of Confucius

wenwu miao 文武廟 temple of literature and martial arts

Wu Den-yih 吳敦義

Wu Feng 吳鳳

Wu Zhenchen 吳振臣

Wushe Shijian 霧社事件 Musha Incident

Xia jiao 廈郊 Xiamen guild

xiacuo 下厝 lower mansion family (reference to Wufeng Lin family)

Xiandai wenxue 現代文學 *Contemporary Literature* magazine

Xin qinqnian 新青年 *New Youth* magazine

Xindang 新黨 New Party

Xingzhengyuan 行政院 Executive Yuan

Xintai Haiyun Gongsi 新台海運公司 Xintai Marine Corporation

Xinwenhua Yundong 新文化運動 New Cultural Movement

Xu Huaizu 徐懷祖

Xuchun 許春

Xunzhao ererba de chenmo muqin 尋找二二八的沉默母親 *Looking for the Silent Mother of the 228 Incident* (documentary)

Yamamoto Isoroku (J) 山本 五十六

Yang Du 楊渡

Yang Nan-chun 楊南郡

Yang Sanlang 楊三郎

Yao Chia-wen 姚嘉文

Ye Baihe Xue Yun 野百合學運 Wild Lily movement

Ye Caomei 趁怴愩 Wild Strawberries

Yen Yun-nian 顏雲年

yi 夷 barbarian

Yi nongye peiyang gongye, yi gongye fazhan nongye 以農業培養工業，以工業發展農業 E "Developing agriculture by virtue of industry and fostering industry by virtue of agriculture"

Yizhong gebiao, yige zhongguo gezi

biaoshu 一中各表, 一個中國各自表述 1992 Consensus, acceptance that there is one China, but there are different interpretations

Yizhu Jiangli Yaoling 移住獎勵要領 Essentials to Encourage and Reward Immigration; a Japanese colonial plan for migration to Taiwan from Japan proper.

Yoshimura Tadashi (J) 吉村務 Ro'eng (Amis)

You tangshangong, wu tangshanma 有唐山公, 無唐山媽 "There were only Chinese grandfathers, not Chinese grandmothers"

Yu Qingfang 余清芳

Yu Shyi-kun 游錫堃

Yu Yonghe 郁永河

yuanzhumin 原住民 Indigenous peoples

Yunzhumin Zhengming Yundong 原住民族正名運動 Indigenous Name Rectification Movement

yutingtang 育嬰堂 orphanages

yuyong shenshi 御用紳士 gentleman hired by the Japanese emperor

Zhang Jingguang 張鏡光

Zhang Leping 張樂平

Zhang Zhaoze 章肇澤

Zhanghua Yinhang 彰化銀行 Chang Hwa Bank

Zheng Chenggong 鄭成功

zhengzhi sixiangfan 政治思想犯 political thought-crime prisoner

zhengzhifan 政治犯 political prisoner

zhixian 知縣 county governor

"Zhongguo fandian" 中國飯店 "The Chinese Restaurant"; article by Sanmao

Zhongguo Kangri Zhanzheng 中國抗日戰爭 War of Resistance against Japanese Aggression

Zhongguo Minzhudang 中國民主黨 China Democracy Party

Zhongxin Jituan 中信集團 CTBC Financial Holding Company

Zhongyang Haiyun Gongsi 中央海運公司 Central Marine Corporation

Zhunan Kexue Yuanqu 竹南科學園區 Jhunan Science Park

Zhuqian 竹塹 present-day Hsinchu 新竹

zhuzai zaohua shangdi sheng dian 主宰 造化 上帝 聖 殿 the sacred palace of the High God who created the world

zili jiaohui 自立教會 self-supporting church

Zitenglu 紫藤廬 Wisteria Tea House

References

Ahn, Ji-Hyun, and Tien-wen Lin. 2019. "The Politics of Apology: The 'Tzuyu Scandal' and Transnational Dynamics of K-Pop." *International Communication Gazette* 81 (2):158–75.

Allee, Mark. 1994. *Law and Local Society in Late Imperial China: Northern Taiwan in the Nineteenth Century*. Stanford, CA: Stanford University Press.

Allen, Herbert J. 1877. "Notes of a Journey through Formosa from Tamsui to Taiwanfu." *Proceedings of the Royal Geographical Society of London* 21:259.

Alsford, Niki J. P. 2010a. *The Witnessed Account of British Resident John Dodd at Tamsui*. Taipei: SMC.

———. 2010b. Interview with Jin Su-qin, 5 March 2010.

———. 2012. "Tea of Taiwan: Contemporary Adaptation." In *Taiwan since Martial Law*, edited by David Blundell, 263–97. Berkeley: University of California Press.

———. 2015. *Chronicling Formosa: Setting the Foundation for the Presbyterian Mission, 1865–1876*. Taiwan: Shung Ye Museum of Formosan Aborigines.

———. 2018. *Transitions to Modernity in Taiwan: The Spirit of 1895 and the Cession of Formosa to Japan*. London: Routledge.

———. 2019a. "The City within the City: A Glimpse of Elite Formation in Deptford-London and Dadaocheng-Taiwan." *Journal of Urban History* 47 (1):123–29.

———. 2019b. Interview with Wang Hsu-kang, 13 April 2019.

———. 2020. "Finding the Threads in Taiwan History and Historiography." *European Journal of East Asian Studies* 19 (1):13–47.

———. 2021. "Population Movements and the Construction of Modern Tradition within Contemporary Taiwan Indigenous Society." In *Taiwan's Contemporary Indigenous Peoples*, edited by Chia-yuan Huang, Daniel Davies, and Dafydd Fell, 18–34. London: Routledge.

Alsford, Niki J. P., and Bernhard Fuehrer. 2017. "Carstairs Douglas (1830–1877) and His Chinese-English Dictionary of the Vernacular or Spoken Language of Amoy (1873)." *Translation Studies* 1 (1):137–82.

Amae, Yoshihisa. 2008. "Pioneers in Taiwan's Human Rights and Democracy: The Role of the Foreign Missionaries of the Presbyterian Church in Taiwan." In *A Borrowed Voice: Taiwan Human Rights through International Networks, 1960–1980*, edited by Linda Gail Arrigo and Lynn Miles, 176–90. Taipei: Social Empowerment Alliance.

Ambaras, David R. 2004. "Juvenile Delinquency and the National Defense State: Policing Young Workers in Wartime Japan, 1937–1945." *Journal of Asian Studies* 63 (1):31–61.

Andrade, Tonio. 2005. "Pirates, Pelts, and Promises: The Sino-Dutch Colony of Seventeenth-Century Taiwan and the Aboriginal Village of Favorolong," *Journal of Asian Studies* 64 (2):295–321.

———. 2009. *How Taiwan Became Chinese*. New York: Columbia University Press.

Anthony, Robert J. 2003. *Like Froth Floating on the Sea: The World of Pirates and Seafarers in Late Imperial South China Sea*. Berkeley: Institute of East Asian Studies, University of California.

———. 2009. "Mingqing shidai, changjue de Zhongguo haidao" 明清時代, 猖獗的中國海盜 (Outrageous Chinese pirates during the Ming and Qing period). *World Vision* 4:10.

Arendt, Hannah. 1943. "We Refugees." *Menorah Journal* 31 (1):66–77.

Arrigo, Linda Gail. 2019. "Su Beng and Taiwan National Liberation: Where Is the Colonial Oppressor?" *New Bloom,* 24 October 2019. https://newbloommag.net /2019/10/24/su-beng-commemoration-linda-arrigo/.

Bakewell, Sarah. 2016. *At the Existentialist Café: Freedom, Being and Apricot Cocktails*. London: Vintage.

Band, Edward. 1947. *Working His Purpose Out: The History of the English Presbyterian Mission 1847–1947*. London: Publishing Office of the PCE.

Barclay, George W. 1954. *Colonial Development and Population in Taiwan*. Princeton, NJ: Princeton University Press.

Barclay, Paul D. 2018. *Outcasts of Empire: Japan's Rule on Taiwan's "Savage Border," 1874–1945*. Oakland: University of California Press.

Becker, Ernest. 1997. *Denial of Death*. New York: Simon and Schuster.

Bellwood, Peter. 2009. "Formosan Prehistory and Austronesian Dispersal." In *Austronesian Taiwan*, edited by David Blundell, 336–65. Taipei: Shung Ye Museum of Formosan Aborigines.

Berry, Michael, ed. 2022. *Musha Incident: A Reader on the Indigenous Uprising in Colonial Taiwan*. New York: Columbia University Press.

Bhabha, Homi K. 1994. *The Location of Culture*. London: Routledge.

Bickers, Robert A. 1996. "To Serve and Not to Rule: British Protestant Missionaries and Chinese Nationalism." In *Missionary Encounters: Sources and Issues*, edited by Robert A. Bickers and Rosemary Seton, 211–40. Richmond: Curzon Press.

Blundell, David, ed. 2009. *Austronesian Taiwan*. Taipei: Shung Ye Museum of Formosan Aborigines.

Blust, Robert. 2014. "Some Recent Proposals Concerning the Classification of the Austronesian Languages." *Oceanic Linguistics* 53 (2):300–391.

Boehm, Lise. 1906. *Formosa: A Tale of the French Blockade of 1884–1885*. Shanghai: Kelly and Walsh.

Booth, Ann. 2007. *Colonial Legacies: Economic and Social Development in East and Southeast Asia*. Honolulu: University of Hawai'i Press.

Burns, Islay. 1870. *Memoir of the Rev. Wm. C. Burns, MA: Missionary to China from the English Presbyterian Church*. London: James Nisbet.

Campbell, William. 1910. *Handbook of the South Formosa Mission*. Hastings: F. J. Parsons.

———. 1915. *Sketches from Formosa*. London: Marshall Brothers.

Chang, Doris T. 2009. *Women's Movements in Twentieth-Century Taiwan*. Chicago: University of Illinois Press.

Chang Hsin-ping 張信平. 1997. "Doushi wufeng haide" 都是吳鳳害的 (It was all Wu Feng's fault). In *Yaoqiu mingzi de zhuren* 要求名字的主人 (The owner seeking for one's name back), edited by Hsia Mei-kuan 夏美寬, 124. Tainan: Jen Kuang.

Chang, Jonas. 2001. "The Untold Story: An Overview." In *Shonenko: Taiwanese Child Laborers in World War II Japan*, edited by Liang-Tse Chang, 8–17. Taipei: Avanguard.

———. 2012. *Shoki Coe: An Ecumenical Life in Context*. Translated by Ching-fen Hsiao. Geneva: WCC Publications.

Chang, Jung. 2019. *Big Sister, Little Sister, Red Sister: Three Women at the Heart of Twentieth-Century China*. London: Jonathan Cape.

Chang, WoongJo, and Shin-Eui Park. 2016. "The Fandom of Hallyu, a Tribe in the Digital Network Era: The Case of ARMY of BTS." *Kritika Kultura* 32:260–87.

Chang, Yung-fa. 1999. *Tides of Fortune: Memoirs of Chang Yung-Fa*. Singapore: Times Books.

Chang Yung-fa Exhibition. n.d. *Changrong jituan pian* 長榮集團篇 (The chapter of Evergreen Group). Accessed 23 November 2020. https://www.cyff.org.tw/exhibition/exh-01.html.

Chatani, Sayaka. 2018. *Nation-Empire: Ideology and Rural Youth Mobilization in Japan and Its Colonies*. Ithaca, NY: Cornell University Press.

Chen, Chiukun. 1999. "From Landlords to Local Stongmen: The Transformation of Local Elites in Mid-Ch'ing Taiwan, 1780–1862." In *Taiwan: A New History*, edited by Murray Rubinstein, 147–59. Armonk, NY: M. E. Sharpe.

Chen Chu 陳菊. n.d. "Guoyuxin yu Taiwan zhanhou minzhu yundong" 郭雨新與台灣戰後民主運動 (Kuo Yu-Hsin and postwar democratic movements in Taiwan). Wu Sanlien Taiwan Foundation. Accessed 15 November 2020. http://www.twcenter.org.tw/thematic_series/history_class/history04.

Chen, Edward I-te. 1973. "Japan: Oppressor or Modernizer?" In *Korea under Japanese*

Colonial Rule, edited by Andrew Nahm, 251–60. Kalamazoo: Center for Korean Studies, Institute of International and Area Studies, Western Michigan University.

Chen Hsiao-I 陳曉宜, Liu Jung 劉榮, and Cheng Hsueh-yung 鄭學庸. 2007. "Huanyuan ererba, yi Zhongguo zanzhu" 還原228，疑中國贊助 (The film to restore the truth of 228 is suspected to be funded by the Chinese). *Liberty Times*, 28 February 2007. https://news.ltn.com.tw/news/focus/paper/117877.

Chen I-Shen 陳儀深. 2008. *Luzhou shanzhuang (Bagualou) lishi ziliao diaocha yanjiu* 綠洲山莊(八卦樓)歷史資料調查研究 (Historical research into the Oasis Villa [Bagua Building]). National Human Rights Museum. Accessed 11 November 2020. https://humanrightstory.nhrm.gov.tw/home/zh-tw/museumreport/300805.

Chen, Ketty. 2013. "Dapu Villagers' Protest—Three Years Later." *The Participant Observer: Soaking and Poking—between Inside and Outside* (blog), 5 July 2013. http://theparticipantobserverblog.blogspot.co.uk/2013/07/dapu-villagers-protest-three-years-later.html.

Chen Pi-Kuei 陳碧奎. 1998. *Chishou kongquan: Yige shaoniangong de gushi* 赤手空拳：一個「少年工」的故事 (Empty-handed: Story of a teenage laborer). Taipei: Avanguard.

Chen Po-Tsung 陳柏棕. n.d. "Taiwan nanzai zaofeiji: Taiwan shaoniangong" 臺灣囝仔造飛機：臺灣少年工 (Taiwanese children building airplanes: Taiwanese shonenko). *National Taiwan Library*. Accessed 26 March 2020. https://www.ntl.edu.tw/public/Attachment/45141084128.pdf.

Chen Tsui-lien 陳翠蓮. 2016. "Taiwan zhanhou chuqi de lishi qingsuan (1945–1947)" 台灣戰後初期的歷史清算 (1945–1947) (The historical rectification in postwar Taiwan [1945–1947]). *Historical Inquiry* 58:195–248.

Chen Yi-shen 陳儀深. 2010. "Taidu zhuzhang de qiyuan yu liubian" 臺獨主張的起源與流變 (The origins and development of advocacy for an independent state of Taiwan). *Taiwan Historical Research* 17 (2):155.

Cheng Chin-yao 鄭進耀. 2019. "Laole danxin shandaoyao. Fan Yun: Shazi caiyou jihui gaibian shijie" 老了擔心閃到腰。范雲：傻子才有機會改變世界 (You only worry about damaging your waist when you are old. Fan Yun: Only the fools have the opportunity to change the world). *Mirror Media*, 26 August 2019. https://www.mirrormedia.mg/story/20190826web001/.

Cheng Chung-lan 鄭仲嵐. 2016. "Haowu xuannian! Caiyingwen chengwei Taiwan shishang shouren nuzongtong" 毫無懸念！蔡英文成為台灣史上首任女總統 (No chance of losing! Tsai Ing-Wen became the first female president in Taiwan history). *BBC Chinese*, 16 January 2016. https://www.bbc.com/zhongwen/trad/china/2016/01/160116_taiwan_tsai_elected.

Cheng Hsi-fu 鄭喜夫. 1977. "Jiqiguang zaitai shiji ji yizuo huiji" 季麒光在臺事蹟及遺作彙輯 (Ji Qiguang in Taiwan and a collection of his works). *Taiwan Historica* 28 (3):11–39.

Chewytzuyu. n.d. "How to Support Tzuyu." Tumblr. https://arunningspy.tumblr.com/post/137399077747/how-to-Thisupport-tzuyu.

Chiang, Frank. 2017. *The One-China Policy: State, Sovereignty, and Taiwan's International Legal Status*. London: Elsevier.

Chiang Wei-shui. (1921) n.d. "Linchuang jiangyi: Guanyu Taiwan zhege huanzhe" 臨床講: 關於台灣這個患者 (Clinical notes: A patient named Taiwan). Chiang Wei-shui Cultural Foundation. Accessed 14 November 2020. http://www.weishui.org/p/portfolio.html.

Chieh Chu-shu 簡竹書. 2018. "Chenju zhuanfang er" 陳菊專訪二 (Interviewing Chen Chu II). *Mirror Media*, 21 November 2018. . https://www.mirrormedia.mg/premium/20181120pol003.

Ching, Leo T. S. 2001. *Becoming "Japanese."* Berkeley: University of California Press.

Chou Wan-yao 周婉窈. 2011. "Taiwan yihui shezhi qingyuan yundong zaitantao" 臺灣議會設置請願運動再探討 (Revisiting the petition movement to establish the Taiwan Parliament). *Taiwan Historical Materials Studies* 臺灣史料研究. 37:2–31.

———. 2015. *A New Illustrated History of Taiwan*. Taipei: SMC Publishing.

Chou Yu 周渝. n.d. "Zitenglu, jidairen de gongtong jiyi" 紫藤廬, 幾代人的共同記憶 (Wistaria Tea House, a memory shared by generations). *Wistaria Tea House* (blog). Accessed 10 March 2021. https://www.wistariateahouse.com/mainssl/modules/MySpace/BlogInfo.php?xmlid=53205.

Chow, Peter C. Y. 2012. "Economy of Taiwan after the Lifting of Martial Law: A Waning Development State?" In *Taiwan since Martial Law*, edited by David Blundell, 597–631. Berkeley: University of California Press.

Chu, Ming-Chin Monique. 2012. "Globalization and Economic Security: The Case of the Taiwanese Semiconductor Industry." In *Taiwan since Martial Law*, edited by David Blundell, 549–97. Berkeley: University of California Press.

Chung Yi-ren 鍾逸人. 1993. *Xinsuan liushinian* 辛酸六十年 (Sixty years of hardship). Taipei: Avanguard.

Coe, Shoki. 1991. *Recollections and Reflections*. Taipei: Formosan Christians for Self-Determination.

Cole, J. Michael. 2014. "Taiwan Rocked by Anti-Nuclear Protests." *The Diplomat*, 28 April 2014.

Collingwood, Cuthbert. 1867. "A Boat Journey across the Northern End of Formosa, from Tam-Suy, on the West, to Kee-Lung, on the East; With Notices of Hoo-Wei, Mangka, and Kelung." *Proceedings of the Royal Geographical Society of London* 11:168.

Cooper, Helen. 1991. *Oxford Guides to Chaucer: The Canterbury Tales*. Oxford: Oxford University Press.

Corcuff, Stephane. 2002. "Taiwan's 'Mainlanders': New Taiwanese?" In *Memories of the Future*, edited by Stephane Corcuff, 163–96. Armonk, NY: M. E. Sharpe.

Costello, John. 1982. *The Pacific War 1941–1945*. New York: Harper.

Council of Indigenous Peoples. 2013. "Xingzhengyuan Yuanzhumin weiyuanhui dushi Yuanzhumin fazhan fiwuqi (yilinger-yilingwu nian) shishi jihui" 行政院原住民族委員會都市原住民發展第五期 (102年-105年) 實施計畫 (Implementation plan for the development of urban Indigenous communities by the Council of Indigenous Peoples [Year 102-105]). Accessed 12 April 2019. https://www.cip.gov.tw/portal/getfile?source=79ADDDD9195DB0E52610217BBF0B058FA9DAB2A97BBE1DD0E0C44C38ED9E0AD234F5ED525735ACA3EF4C72610176E3B6931AECF44104A51F3B91B9DF71659F0C&filename=ED6A9EB1BCF5E2C9B0B6BB88E5078 21092EC7637D3A65CE913E115E5FCC30CADF890C31FFA8549B309DCCB8329 897E11A852238F00A7C162.

Cowan, Brian William. 2005. *The Social Life of Coffee: The Emergence of the British Coffeehouse.* New Haven, CT: Yale University Press.

Crouch, Archie R., Steven Agoratus, Arthur Emerson, and Debra E. Soled. 1989. *Christianity in China: A Scholars' Guide to Resources in the Libraries and Archives of the United States.* Armonk, NY: M. E. Sharpe.

Damm, Jens. 2005. "Same Sex Desire and Society in Taiwan, 1970–1987." *China Quarterly* 181:67–81.

Davidson, James W. 2005. *The Island of Formosa: Past and Present.* Taipei: SMC Publishing.

Dawley, Evan. 2015. "Closing a Colony: The Meanings of Japanese Deportation from Taiwan after World War II." In *Japanese Taiwan: Colonial Rule and Its Contested Legacy,* edited by Andrew D. Morris, 115–33. London: Bloomsbury.

———. 2019. *Becoming Taiwanese: Ethnogenesis in a Colonial City, 1880s–1950s.* Cambridge, MA: Harvard University Press.

DeGlopper, Donald R. 1995. *Lukang: Commerce and Community in a Chinese City.* Albany: State University of New York Press.

Diamond, Jared. 2000. "Taiwan's Gift to the World." *Nature* 403:709.

Dluhosova, Tana. 2010. "Taiwan and Taiwanese Literature: 1945–49." In *Becoming Taiwan: From Colonialism to Democracy,* edited by Ann Heylen and Scott Sommers, 181–99. Wiesbaden: Harrassowitz Verlag.

Dodd, John. 1882a. "A Few Ideas of the Probable Origin of the Hill Tribes of Formosa." *Journal of the Straits Branch of the Royal Asiatic Society* 9:69–86.

———. 1882b. "A Few Ideas of the Probable Origin of the Hill Tribes of Formosa." *Journal of the Straits Branch of the Royal Asiatic Society* 10:95–212.

———. 1895. "Formosa." *Scottish Geographical Journal* 11 (11):569.

DPP Huang Hsin-chieh Editorial Group. 2000. *Huangxinjie jinian wenji* 黃信介紀念文集 (Collection in memory of Huang Hsin-chieh). Taipei: DPP.

Edwards, Jack. 1988. *Banzai You Bastards.* Hong Kong: Corporate Communications.

Election Study Center, National Chengchi University. 2021. "Taiwanese/Chinese Identity (1996/06–2023/06)." https://esc.nccu.edu.tw/PageDoc/Detail?fid=7800&id=6961.

Eskildsen, Robert. 2005. "Taiwan: A Periphery in Search of a Narrative." *Journal of Asian Studies* 64 (2):281–94.

ET Today News. 2016. "Gansi budui luoxuan, Zhang Tongfa taiji ribenbin shengya molian xinzhi" 敢死隊落選, 張榮發台籍日本兵生涯磨心志 (Unfit for the death squad, Chang Yung-Fa became tougher through his experience of being a Taiwan-Japanese soldier). *ET Today News,* 2 January 2016. https://finance.ettoday.net/news/634351.

Fan, Joshua. 2011. *China's Homeless Generation: Voices from the Veterans of the Chinese Civil War, 1940–1990s.* London: Routledge.

Fan Yun 范雲. 2010. "Shuogushi yu minzhu taolun: Yige gongmin shehui neibu zuqun duihua luntan de fenxi" 說故事與民主討論:一個公民社會內部族群對話論壇的分析 (Story-telling and democratic discussion: An analysis of ethnic dialogue workshops in civil society). *Taiwan Democracy Quarterly* 7 (1):65–105.

Fanon, Frantz. 1952. *Black Skin, White Masks.* New York: Grove Press.

Fell, Dafydd. 2012. *Government and Politics in Taiwan.* London: Routledge.

Feuchtwang, Stephan. 1977. "School-Temple and City God." In *The City in Late Imperial China,* edited by G. William Skinner, 581–609. Stanford, CA: Stanford University Press.

Firth, Stewart. 1997. "The Pacific since 1941." In *The Cambridge History of the Pacific Islanders,* edited by Donald Denoon, 291–324. Cambridge: Cambridge University Press.

Fraser, Nancy. 1990. "Rethinking the Public Sphere: A Contribution to the Critique of Actually Existing Democracy." *Social Text* 25 (26):56–80.

Friedman, Kerim. 2010. "Kapah (Young Me): Alternative Cultural Activism in Taiwan." *Savage Minds,* 4 August 2010. https://savageminds.org/2010/08/04/kapah-young-men/.

Fu Yangchih 傅仰止. 2002. *Taibeixian Yunzhuminzu shenghuo zhuangkuang diaocha baogao* 臺北縣原住民族生活狀況調查報告 (An investigation into the living conditions of Indigenous people in Taipei County). Taipei: Taipei County Government.

Gao Gongqian 高拱乾. 1987. *Taiwanfu Zhi* 臺灣府志 (The Taiwan Prefecture Gazetteer). Taipei: Datong Bookstore, 1987.

Gardella, Robert. 1994. *Harvesting Mountains: Fujian and the China Tea Trade, 1757–1937.* Berkeley: University of California Press.

———. 1999. "From Treaty Ports to Provincial Status, 1860–1894." In *Taiwan: A New History,* edited by Murray Rubinstein, 163–201. Armonk, NY: M. E. Sharpe.

Garver, John W. 2011. "Introduction." In *Taiwan's Democracy: Economic and Political Challenges,* edited by Robert Ash, John W. Garver, and Penelope B. Prime, 1–35. London: Routledge.

Gates, Hill. 1987. *Chinese Working-Class Lives: Getting By in Taiwan.* Ithaca, NY: Cornell University Press.

Gennep, Arnold van. 2019. *The Rites of Passage*. Chicago: University of Chicago Press.

Goddio, Franck, and Gabriel Casal. 2002. *Lost at Sea: The Strange Route of the Len Shoal Junk*. London: Periplus.

Gold, Thomas B. 1986. *State and Society in the Taiwan Miracle*. Armonk, NY: M. E. Sharpe.

———. 1988. "Colonial Origins of Taiwanese Capitalism." In *Contending Approaches to the Political Economy of Taiwan*, edited by Edwin A. Winckler and Susan Greenhalgh, 111. Armonk, NY: M. E. Sharpe.

Graeber, David. 2013. *The Democracy Project: A History, a Crisis, a Movement*. Oakland, CA: AK Press.

Grano, Simona. 2015. *Environmental Governance in Taiwan: A New Generation of Activists and Stakeholders*. London: Routledge.

Grano, Simona, and Ping-lan Tu. 2012. "Development vs. Environment in Taibei." *Journal of Current Chinese Affairs* 41 (2):130–33.

Gu Biling 古碧玲. 1999. *Taiwan houlai haosuozai* 臺灣後來好所在 (Taiwan: A good place after all). Taipei: Commercial Press.

Habermas, Jurgen. 1989. *The Structural Transformation of the Public Sphere: An Inquiry into a Category of Bourgeois Society*. Cambridge, MA: MIT Press.

Hanioğlu, M. Şükrü. 1997. "Garbcılar: Their Attitudes toward Religion and Their Impact on the Official Ideology of the Turkish Republic." *Studia Islamica* 86:133–58.

Harper, Tim. 2020. *Underground Asia: Global Revolutionaries and the Assault on Empire*. London: Allen Lane.

Harrell, Stevan, and Huang Chün-chieh. 2018. *Cultural Change in Postwar Taiwan*. London: Routledge.

Harrison, Henrietta. 2005. *The Man Awakened from Dreams*. Stanford, CA: Stanford University Press.

He Cai-man 何彩滿. 2009. "Guxianrong de duochong shenfen rentong" 辜顯榮的多重身份認同 (Ku Hsien-Jung's multiple self-identities). *Twenty-First Century* 二十一世紀 112:102–13.

Heylen, Ann, and Scott Sommers. 2010. *Becoming Taiwan: From Colonialism to Democracy*. Wiesbaden: Harrassowitz Verlag.

Hirohito. (1945) n.d. "The Jewel Voice Broadcast." Atomic Heritage Foundation, accessed 6 July 2023. https://ahf.nuclearmuseum.org/ahf/key-documents/jewel-voice-broadcast/#:~:text=On%20August%2015%2C%201945%2C%20Japanese,the%20speech%20formal%2C%20florid%20Japanese.

Ho, Ming-sho. 2003. "The Politics of Anti-Nuclear Protest in Taiwan: A Case of Party-Dependent Movement (1980–2000)." *Modern Asian Studies* 37 (3):683–708.

———. 2005a. "Taiwan's State and Social Movements under the DPP Government, 2000–2004." *Journal of Asian Studies* 5:401–25.

———. 2005b. "Weakened State and Social Movement: The Paradox of Taiwanese Environmental Politics after the Power Transfer." *Journal of Contemporary China* 14 (43):339–52.

———. 2010. "Understanding the Trajectory of Social Movements in Taiwan (1980–2010)." *Journal of Current Chinese Affairs* 39 (3):3–22.

———. 2014a. "The Fukushima Effect: Explaining the Resurgence of the Anti-Nuclear Movement in Taiwan." *Environmental Politics* 23 (6):1–19.

———. 2014b. "The Resurgence of Social Movements under the Ma Ying-Jeou Government: A Political Opportunity Structure Perspective." In *Political Changes in Taiwan under Ma Ying-Jeou: Partisan Conflict, Policy Choices, External Constraints and Security Challenges*, edited by Jean-Pierre Cabestan and Jacques deLisle, 100–120. London: Routledge.

———. 2019. *Challenging Beijing's Mandate of Heaven*. Philadelphia: Temple University Press.

Ho, Samuel P. 1978. *Economic Development of Taiwan, 1860–1970*. New Haven, CT: Yale University Press.

Ho Yi. 2013. "Refugees 'Squatting' on a Gold Mine." *Taipei Times*, 3 July 2013. https://www.taipeitimes.com/News/feat/archives/2013/07/03/2003566212.

Horwitz, Josh. 2016. "Why a Washed-up Pop Star Is Suddenly the Most Hated Man in Taiwan." *Quartz*, 20 January 2016. https://qz.com/597272/why-a-washed-up-pop-star-is-suddenly-the-most-hated-man-in-taiwan/.

Hsiau, A-Chin. 2000. *Contemporary Taiwanese Nationalism*. London: Routledge.

Hsieh, Jolan. 2018. "The Changing Identities of Taiwan's Plains Indigenous Peoples." In *Changing Taiwan Identities*, edited by Bruce J. Jacobs and Peter Kang, 12–27. London: Routledge.

———. 2021. "Restoring Pingpu Indigenous Status and Rights." In *Taiwan's Contemporary Indigenous Peoples*, edited by Chia-yuan Huang, Daniel Davies, and Dafydd Fell, 239–56. London: Routledge.

Hsieh, Shih-Chung. 1994. "From Shanbao to Yuanzhumin: Taiwanese Aborigines in Transition." In *The Other Taiwan*, edited by Murray Rubinstein, 404–21. Armonk, NY: M. E. Sharpe.

Hsieh, Yu-Wei. 1967. "Filial Piety and Chinese Society." In *The Chinese Mind: Essentials of Chinese Philosophy and Culture*, edited by Charles Alexander Moore, 167–87. Honolulu: University of Hawai'i Press.

Hsiung, Ping-Chun. 1996. *Living Rooms as Factories: Class, Gender, and the Satellite Factory System in Taiwan*. Philadelphia: Temple University Press.

Hsu Hsueh-chi 許雪姬. 1998. *Wufeng Linjia xiangguan renwu fangtan jilu* 霧峰林家相關人物訪談記錄 (Interview record with members of the Wufeng Lin family). Taichung: Taichung County Culture Centre.

Hsu Ju Lin 徐如林. 2017. *Lianfeng zongzuo: Yangnanjun de chuanqi yisheng* 連峰縱走：楊南郡的傳奇一生 (Walking across the peaks: The legendary life of Yang Nan-Chun). Taipei: Morning Stars Publishing.

Hsu, Mutsu, and Yih-Yuan Li. 1989. "Paradise in Change: The Dilemma of Taiwanese Aborigines in Modernization." In *Anthropological Studies of the Taiwan Area*, edited by Kwang-Chih Chang et al., 197. Taipei: NTU Press.

Hu, Jackson. 2012. "Retrieving Ancestral Power from the Landscape: Cultural Struggle and Yami Ecological Memory on Orchid Island." In *Taiwan since Martial Law*, edited by David Blundell, 183–211. Berkeley: University of California Press.

Huang Chih-huei 黃智慧. 2011. "Jiedu gaosha yiyongdui de dahehun: Jianlun Taiwan houzhimin qingjing de fuzaxing" 解讀高砂義勇隊的「大和魂」：兼論台灣後殖民情境的複雜性 (Interpreting the Japanese spirit of the Takasago volunteers: Postcolonial resistance to two successive periods of colonization). *Journal of the Taiwan Indigenous Studies Association* 1 (4):139–74.

Huang Deshi 黃得時. 1965. "Liang Chi-Tsau's Tour in Taiwan." *Taiwan Historica* 16 (3):1–68.

Huang Fu-san 黃富三. 2004. "Shijiu shiji zhi wailai tiaozhan yu Taiwan xinshangye" 十九世紀之外來挑戰與台灣新商業 (The foreign challenges and new business in nineteenth-century Taiwan). *Historical Monthly* 201:60–73.

Huang Hsiu-cheng 黃秀政. 1997. *Zhuanji yu zhanhou Taiwanshi yanjiu* 傳記與戰後台灣史研究 (Biographies and the study of Taiwan history in the postwar period). *Journal of Taichung Evening School, NCHU* 3:281–96.

Huang Huang-hsiung 黃煌雄. 2018. "Huangxinjie: Zhanhou Taiwan minzhu yundong deyi lingdaozhe" 黃信介：戰後台灣民主運動第一領導者 (Huang Hsin-chieh: The pioneer of the democratic movement in postwar Taiwan). *Storm Media*, 18 August 2018. https://www.storm.mg/article/476599?page=1.

Huang Jui-hung 黃瑞弘. 2018. "Ludao chuileibei: Jianzheng baba xielei renquanshi" 綠島垂淚碑：見證斑斑血淚人權史 (The weeping monument of Green Island: A witness account of the human rights history). *Central News Agency*, 16 May 2018. https://www.cna.com.tw/news/firstnews/201805160040.aspx.

Huang, Shu-mei, and Hyung Kyung Lee. 2020. *Heritage, Memory, and Punishment: Remembering Colonial Prisons in East Asia*. London: Routledge.

Huang, Shu-min, and Shao-hua Liu. 2016. "Discrimination and Incorporation of Taiwanese Indigenous Austronesian Peoples." *Asian Ethnicity* 17 (2):294–312.

Huang Shu-min and Ying-Hwa Chang. 2010. "Taiwan Yuanzhumin de qianxi ji shehui diwei zhi bianqian yu xiankuang" 臺灣原住民的遷移及社會經濟地位之變遷與現況 (The current movement and socioeconomic status of Taiwanese Indigenous peoples). In 臺灣原住民政策變遷與社會發展 *Taiwan Yuanzhumin zhengce bianqian yu shehui fazhan* (Social development and policy transformation regarding

Taiwanese Indigenous peoples), edited by Shu-min Huang and Ying-Hwa Chang, 51–120. Taipei: Institute of Ethnology, Academia Sinica.

Hughes, Christopher R. 2011. "Negotiating National Identity in Taiwan: Between Nativization and De-Sinicization." In *Taiwan's Democracy: Economic and Political Challenges*, edited by Robert Ash, John W. Garver, and Penelope B. Prime, 51–75. London: Routledge.

Huntington, Samuel P. 1991. *The Third Wave: Democratization in the Late Twentieth Century*. Norman: University of Oklahoma Press.

Hurst, Michael. 1998. "The Camps." Never Forgotten website. Accessed 21 June 2023. http://www.powtaiwan.org/The%20Camps/index.php.

Hwang, Kyung Moon. 2017. *A History of Korea*. London: Palgrave.

Itō, Kiyoshi. 2004. *Taiwan lishi* 臺灣歷史 (History of Taiwan). Taipei: Avanguard.

Jacobs, J. Bruce. 2008. "Taiwan's Colonial History and Postcolonial Nationalism." In *The 'One China' Dilemma*, edited by Peter C. Y. Chow, 37–56. Basingstoke: Palgrave Macmillan.

———. 2016. *The Kaohsiung Incident in Taiwan and Memoirs of a Foreign Big Beard*. Leiden: Brill.

Jennings, Ralph. 2013. "Tipping Point for Taiwan's Environmental Movement." *Forbes*, 17 December 2013. http://www.forbes.com/sites/ralphjennings/2013/12/17/tipping -point-for-taiwans-environmental-movement/.

Joint Declaration by the Representatives of the Indigenous Peoples of Taiwan. 2019. "Indigenous Peoples of Taiwan to President Xi Jinping of China." *Medium*, 8 January 2019. https://chihaoyo.medium.com/indigenous-peoples-of-taiwan-to- president-xi-jinping-of-china-4469d1a3bde6.

Juan Mei-Shu 阮美姝. 1994. *Guji jianao sishiwunian: Xunzhao ererba shizong de baba ruanchaori* 孤寂煎熬四十五年：尋找二二八失踪的爸爸阮朝日 (Forty-five years of loneliness: Looking for my father Juan Chao-Jih who disappeared after the 228 Incident). Taipei: Avanguard.

———. 2007. "Ererba jilupian: Linjiangmai de zhenzhenjiajia" 二二八紀錄片：林江邁 的真真假假 (The 228 Documentary: The truths and lies of Lin Chiang-Mai). *Liberty Times*, 9 February 2007. https://talk.ltn.com.tw/article/paper/115590.

Kafka, Franz. 1995. "A Country Doctor." In *Kafka: The Complete Short Stories,* edited by Nahum N. Glatzer, 220–26. London: Random House.

Kao Fei-yao 高飛鶴. 2016. "Beiju shidai jianzhengren de yunluo: Wei Jiangweichuan pingfan de jianxin guocheng. Gaojiangliyun nushi de fuwen" 悲劇時代見證人的殞 落：為蔣渭川平反的艱辛過程。高蔣梨雲女士的訃聞 (The fall of a witness in the troubled era: The difficult process of addressing Jiang Wei-Chuan's grievance. Obituary of Mrs. Kao Chiang Li-Yun). *People Media*, 20 October 2016. https://www .peoplemedia.tw/news/4455751a-8907-4e04-8691-7e73ff05e5a8.

Kaplan, Steven. 1986. "The Africanization of Missionary Christianity: History and Typology." *Journal of Religion in Africa* 16 (3):166–86.

Katz, Paul R. 2005. *When Valleys Turned Blood Red: The Ta-Pa-Ni Incident in Colonial Taiwan.* Honolulu: University of Hawai'i Press.

Keliher, Macabe. 2003. *Out of China or Yu Yonghe's Tale of Formosa.* Taipei: SMC Publishing.

Kerr, George H. 1966. *Formosa Betrayed.* London: Eyre and Spottiswoode.

———. 1974. *Formosa: Licensed Revolution and the Home Rule Movement, 1895–1945.* Honolulu: University of Hawai'i Press.

Kim, Eun Mee, ed. 1998. *The Four Asian Tigers: Economic Development and the Global Political Economy.* San Diego: Academic Press.

Knapp, Ronald G. 1976. "Chinese Frontier Settlement in Taiwan." *Annals of the Association of American Geographers* 66 (1):43–59.

———. 1980. "Settlement and Frontier Land Tenure." In *China's Island Frontier: Studies in the Historical Geography of Taiwan,* edited by Ronald G. Knapp, 55–69. Honolulu: University of Hawai'i Press.

———. 1999. "The Shaping of Taiwan's Landscape." In *Taiwan: A New History,* edited by Murray Rubinstein, 3–27. Armonk, NY: M. E. Sharpe.

Koreaboo. 2016. "Tzuyu Releases Apology Video for Scandal." *Koreaboo,* 15 January 2016. https://www.koreaboo.com/news/tzuyu-releases-apology-video-for -taiwanese-flag-incident/.

Ku Jui-yun 古瑞雲. 1990. *Taichung de fenglei* 台中的風雷 (Wind and thunder of Taichung). Taipei: Renjian Publishing.

Kuo, Ya-pei. 2017. "The Dawn of Indigenous Consciousness—a 'Chinese' Convert's Criticism of the Western Missionary." In *Shaping Christianity in Greater China,* edited by Paul Woods, 41–55. Oxford: Regnum Books.

Kwang, Yeong-Shin. 1998. "The Political Economy of Economic Growth in East Asia: South Korea and Taiwan." In *The Four Asian Tigers: Economic Development and the Global Political Economy,* edited by Eun Mee Kim. 3–33. San Diego, CA: Academic Press.

Lai Liang-yang 賴兩陽. 2008. "Taiwan Qingling zhi rizhi shiqi de shehui fuli fazhan" 臺灣清領至日治時期的社會福利發展 (Development of the social welfare system between the Qing Dynasty and Japanese Period). *Kongda xuexun* 空大學訊 394:80–86.

Laws and Regulations Database of the Republic of China. 2020. Public Health Specialists Act, 3 June 2020. https://law.moj.gov.tw/ENG/LawClass/LawAll.aspx ?pcode=L0020216.

Li Hsin-fang 李欣芳. 2018. "Guomindang zhuanshou jiudangbu gai zhangrongfa jijinhui, dangchanhui zhuizheng shiyidiansiyi" 國民黨轉售舊黨部給張榮發基金會, 黨產會追徵11.4 億 (KMT sold its old headquarter to the Chang Yung-Fa Foundation, the Ill-Gotten Party Assets Settlement Committee seeks to recover the 11.4

billion profit). *Liberty Times*, 24 July 2018. https://news.ltn.com.tw/news/politics/breakingnews/2498027.

Li, Laura. 2003. "SARS Wars: Taiwan Fights a Battle It Cannot Afford to Lose." *Taiwan Panorama*, June 2003. https://www.taiwan-panorama.com/Articles/Details?Guid=6ffb68fd-61ac-47a5-b49a-b06235e46b7b&langId=3&CatId=10.

Li Po-chuan 李柏泉. 2003. "Huangxinjie yu Taiwan minzhu yundong zhi yanjiu" 黃信介與台灣民主運動之研究 (Research into Huang Hsin-chieh and the Democratic Movement in Taiwan). MA diss., National Taiwan Normal University.

Liao Benquan 廖本全 and Li Chengjia 李承嘉. 2000. "Dushi Yuanzhumin—Yi ili" 都市原住民遷移因素與居住現象之探討—以居住在台北市的排灣族為例 (A discussion on the cause of migration among urban Indigenous peoples: A case study of Paiwan in Taipei City). Paper presented at Dushi Yuanzhumin Zuqun yu Zhuzai Wenti Yantaohui 都市原住民族群與住宅問題研討會 (Conference on Urban Indigenous Communities and Housing Issues).

Lim Iong-iong. 2012. "Huang zhanghui rongyan jilupian?" 黃彰輝容顏紀錄片 (Is time still on our side?). *Shoki Coe Blog* 黃彰輝 (blog), 3 September 2012. http://shokicoe.blogspot.co.uk/2012/09/is-time-still-on-our-side.html.

Lin Cheng-jung 林呈蓉. 2001. "Ribenren de Taiwan jingyan: Rizhi shiqi de yimincun" 日本人的臺灣經驗: 日治時期的移民村 (The Japanese experience in Taiwan: The immigrant village during the Japanese Period). *Wusanlian Taiwan Shiliao Jijinhui* 吳三連台灣史料基金會 (The Wu San-lien Foundation of Historical Materials), 30 July 2001. http://www.twcenter.org.tw/thematic_series/history_class/tw_window/e02_20010730.

———. 2006. "Ribenren de Taiwan jingyan: Rizhi shiqi de yimincun" 日本人的臺灣經驗: 日治時期的移民村 (The Japanese experience in Taiwan: The immigrant village during the Japanese period). In *Taiwan lishi de jing yu chuang* 台灣歷史的鏡與窗 (The mirror and the window of Taiwan history), edited by Tai Pao-tsun, 136–45. Taipei: Guojia Zhanwang Wenjiao Jijinhui 國家展望文教基金會.

Lin Ching-hu 林慶弧. 2011. "Linzhifang jiazu yu Taiping diqu de kaifa" 林志芳家族與太平地區的開發 (Lin Zhi-Fang family in the development of the Tai-Ping region). *Taiwan Historica* 台灣文獻 63 (2):227–72.

Lin Chiung-hua 林瓊華. 2013. "Cong yiwang dao daixiang: Xiexuehong de lishi zai Taiwan yu Zhongguo de Yixu" 從遺忘到再現：謝雪紅的歷史在臺灣與中國的影響與遺緒 (From disappearance to reappearance: Influence and legacy of Hsieh Hsueh-Hung in Taiwan and China). *Journal of Taiwan Historical Association* 15:33–72.

Lin, Christine Louise. 1999. "The Presbyterian Church in Taiwan and the Advocacy of Local Autonomy." In *Sino-Platonic Papers* 92, edited by Victor H. Mair, 1–236. Philadelphia: Department of East Asian Languages and Civilizations, University of Pennsylvania.

Lin, H. W. 2015. "Re-Constructed Unitary History on Green Island, Taiwan: The Former Political Prison / Oasis Village." *International Journal of Social Science and Humanity* 5 (3):265–71.

Lin Hsing-fei 林倖妃. 2017. *Huama xinneihua: Chenju siqiantian* 花媽心內話: 陳菊四千天(Words from Huama's heart: Four thousand days of Chen Chu). Taipei: Common Wealth Magazine Group.

Lin Ji-ping, Chang Ying-Hwa, and Liu Chien-Chia. 2010. "Taiwan Yuanzhumin de qianxi ji shehui jingji diwei zhi bianqian yu xiankuang" 台灣原住民的遷移及社會經濟地位之變遷與現況 (The current migration and socioeconomic development of Taiwanese Indigenous people). In *Taiwan Yuanzhumin zhengce bianqian yu shehui fazhan* 台灣原住民政策變遷與社會發展 (The policy and social development of Taiwanese Indigenous people), edited by Chang Yinghwa 章英華 and Huang Shumin 黃樹民, 51–120. Taipei: Institute of Ethnography, Academia Sinica.

Lin Man-houng 林滿紅. 1979. "Maoyi yu Qingmo Taiwan de jingji shehui bianqian, 1860–1895" 貿易與清末臺灣的經濟社會變遷, 1860–1895 (Trade, economic, and social change in Late Qing Taiwan). *Shihuo Yuekan* 9 (4):18–31.

Lin Nansen 林楠森. 2011. "Shimingde zhiyi caiyingwen xingxiang guangshou piping" 施明德質疑蔡英文性向廣受批評 (Shih Ming-Te is heavily criticized for questioning Tsai Ing-wen's sexuality). *BBC Chinese*, 15 April 2011. https://www.bbc.com /zhongwen/trad/china/2011/04/110415_taiwan_tsai.

———. 2013. "Taiwan Dapu zhengdian mianlin qiangchai" 台灣大埔徵地案面臨強拆 (Residential houses in Dapu, Taiwan to be forcibly demolished). *BBC Chinese*, 7 July 2013. http://www.bbc.co.uk/zhongwen/trad/taiwan_letters/2013/07/130707 _taiwan_land.

———. 2014. "Taiwan shushiwan minzhong zongtongfuqian shiwei fanfumao" 台灣數十萬民眾總統府前示威反服貿 (Hundreds of thousands of protesters gathered against the Cross-Strait Service Trade Agreement outside the Taiwan Presidential Office). *BBC Chinese*, 30 March 2014. http://www.bbc.co.uk/zhongwen/trad /china/2014/03/140330_taiwan_protest.

Lin Yuju 林玉茹. 1995. *Qingdai Taiwan gangkou de kongjian jiegou* 清代臺灣港口的空間結構 (The spatial structure of the ports in Taiwan during the Qing Dynasty). Taipei: Zhishufang.

Liu, Kuan-lin, and Po-sheng Chiu. 2018. "Artificial Intelligence Could Be Taiwan's Niche in the World." *News Agency*, 18 February 2018. https://www.taiwannews.com .tw/en/news/3366571?fbclid=IwAR0woLuaX9ZVd93w1Psb823R5sjfeGkAXAUU 5Q7BGRZ3YPBeLjPp4CeR8bs.

Liu Yen-Chi 劉晏齊. 2016. "Weishemo yao baohu weichengnianren? Ershao fuli, falv yu lishi de fenxi" 為什麼要保護未成年人? 兒少福利、法律與歷史的分析 (Why do we protect children? Children's welfare and an analysis of history and the law in postwar Taiwan). *Chengchi Law Review* 147:83–157.

Lo Hung-hsu 羅弘旭. 2011. "Chenju: Muqin de jianren tezhi luoyin wode shengming" 陳菊：母親的堅忍特質烙印我的生命 (Chen Chu: My mother's perseverance has lightened up my life). *Business Today*, 5 May 2011. https://www.businesstoday.com .tw/article/category/154769/post/201105050011.

Lu, Hsiu-lien, and Ashley Esarey. 2014. *My Fight for a New Taiwan: One Woman's Journey from Prison to Power*. Seattle: University of Washington Press.

Lung Ying-tai 龍應台. 2009. *Dajiang dahai yijiusijiu* 大江大海一九四九 (Big river, big sea: Untold stories of 1949). Taipei: Common Wealth Magazine.

Mackay, George Leslie. (1896) 2002. *From Far Formosa*. London: Oliphant Anderson and Ferrier. Reprint, Taipei: SMC Publishing.

MacMillan, Margaret. 2001. *Paris 1919: Six Months That Changed the World*. New York: Random House.

Malinowski, Bronislaw. 1922. *Argonauts of the Western Pacific*. New York: E. P. Dutton.

Marchand, Sandrine. 2010. "Silence in Postwar Taiwan." In *Becoming Taiwan: From Colonialism to Democracy*, edited by Ann Heylen and Scott Sommers. 165–81. Wiesbaden: Harrassowitz Verlag.

Matheson, Donald. 1886. *Narrative of the Mission to China of the English Presbyterian Church*. London: James Nisbet.

Mazumdar, Sucheta. 1998. *Sugar and Society in China: Peasants, Technology, and the World Market*. Cambridge, MA: Harvard University Asia Center.

Meskill, Johanna Menzel. 1979. *A Chinese Pioneer Family: The Lins of Wu-Feng, Taiwan 1729–1895*. Princeton, NJ: Princeton University Press.

Mishima, Yukio. 2016. *Confessions of a Mask*. Taipei: VME Books.

Mitter, Rana. 2004. *A Bitter Revolution*. Oxford: Oxford University Press.

———. 2014. *Forgotten Ally*. Boston, MA: Mariner Books.

Moody, Campbell N. 1912. *The Saints of Formosa*. London: Oliphant, Anderson and Ferrier.

Murphy, Kevin C. 2003. *The American Merchant in Nineteenth Century Japan*. London: Routledge.

National Archives Administration. 1947. *Minguo sanshiliunian zhenzi sijiuyihao sharenan* 民國三十六年偵字四九一號殺人案 (Murder case no. 491, 1947). Online exhibition of the 228 Incident archives. Accessed 3 March 2021. https://atc.archives.gov .tw/228/228online/Type2/000025825/index.html.

Nengliang Media Official Channel. 2016. "Laoyouji zhi xunfang Sanmao zuji" 老友記之尋訪三毛足跡 (Friends: Seeking Sanmao's footprints). YouTube, 25 July 2016. https://youtu.be/hG7wWTXkjXg.

O'Reilly, Luke. 2021. "UK Experiences Garden Gnome Shortage due to Suez Canal Blockage and Lockdown." *Evening Standard*, 16 April 2021. https://www.standard .co.uk/news/uk/uk-garden-gnome-shortage-suez-canal-b930123.html.

Otness, Harold. 1990. *One Thousand Westerners in Taiwan, to 1945: A Biographical and*

Bibliographical Dictionary. Taipei: Institute of Taiwan History, Preparatory Office.

Otto, Ton. 1993. "Empty Tins for Lost Traditions? The West's Material and Intellectual Involvement in the Pacific." In *Pacific Islands Trajectories: Five Personal Views*, edited by Ton Otto, 1–29. Canberra: Australian National University.

Ou Suying 歐素瑛. 2010. "Zhanhou chuqi zaitai riren zhi qianfan yu liuyong" 戰後初期在臺日人之遣返與留用 (The sending back of the Japanese People in Taiwan in the beginning years after the Second World War and those who remained). *Taiwan Wenxian* 61 (3):287–329.

Park, Robert Ezra. 1950. *Race and Culture*. Glencoe, IL: Free Press.

Peng, Ming-min. 1972. *A Taste of Freedom: Memoirs of a Formosan Independence Leader*. New York: Holt, Rinehart and Winston.

Phillips, Steven E. 2003. *Between Assimilation and Independence: The Taiwanese Encounter Nationalist China, 1945–1950*. Stanford, CA: Stanford University Press.

Phillon, Stephen. 2010. "The Impact of Social Movements on Taiwan's Democracy." *Journal of Current Chinese Affairs* 39 (3):149–63.

Porter, Andrew. 2002. "Church History, History of Christianity, Religious History: Some Reflections on British Missionary Enterprise since the Late Eighteenth Century." *Church History* 71 (3):555–84.

———. 2004. *Religion versus Empire? British Protestant Missionaries and Overseas Expansion, 1700–1914*. Manchester: Manchester University Press.

Rigger, Shelly. 1999. *Politics in Taiwan: Voting for Democracy*. London: Routledge.

———. 2001. *From Opposition to Power: Taiwan's Democratic Progressive Party*. Boulder, CO: Lynne Reiner.

———. 2011. *Why Taiwan Matters: Small Island, Global Powerhouse*. Lanham, MD: Rowman and Littlefield.

Robert, Dana L. 2009. *Christian Mission: How Christianity Became a World Religion*. Chichester: John Wiley and Sons.

Robinson, Neville K. 1981. *Villagers at War: Some Papua New Guinean Experiences in World War II*. Canberra: Australian National University Press.

ROC Air Force. n.d. "Silianduai yange" 四聯隊沿革 (History of Air Force Team 4). Accessed 4 March 2021. https://air.mnd.gov.tw/TW/Unit/AirUnit_Detail.aspx?FID=4&CID=12&ID=24.

Rooney, Maurice A. n.d. "The Road Back to Kinkaeseki." COFEPOW. Accessed 3 January 2020. https://www.cofepow.org.uk/stories-poems/the-road-back-to-kinkaeseki.

Roy, Denny. 2003. *Taiwan: A Political History*. Ithaca, NY: Cornell University Press.

Rubinstein, Murray A. 1991a. "Mission of Faith, Burden of Witness: The Presbyterian Church in the Evolution of Modern Taiwan, 1865–1989." *American Asian Review* 9 (2):70–108.

———. 1991b. *The Protestant Community on Modern Taiwan: Mission, Seminary, and Church*. Armonk, NY: M. E. Sharpe.

Ryan, Shawna Yang. 2016. *Green Island*. New York: Alfred A. Knopf.

Said, Edward W. 2000. *Reflections on Exile*. London: Granta.

———. 2012. *Reflections on Exile and Other Literary and Cultural Essays*. London: Granta.

Sangren, Steven. 1984. "Traditional Chinese Corporations: Beyond Kinship." *Journal of Asian Studies* 43 (3):391–415.

Sanmao 三毛. 1991. *Beiying* 背影 (Looking from behind). Taipei: Crown Publishing.

———. 2019. *Stories of the Sahara*. London: Bloomsbury.

Sebastian, Elsa, Kavitha Gopalakrishnan, and Viju Kurian. *Hallyu Nameste: Korean Waves on the Indian Shores*. Kerala: Co-Text Publishing.

SET News. 2016. "Zaolu fengsha! Huang An jiemu weibo jie bojian zongying, zichao yingxiong biangouxiong" 遭陸封殺!黃安節目、微博皆不見蹤影,自嘲英雄變狗熊 (Being banned by China! Huang An claims he is being treated like a loser instead of the hero he should be, as his shows and Weibo have been removed). *SET News*, 17 January 2016, https://www.setn.com/News.aspx?NewsID=119078.

Shepherd, John R. 1995. *Statecraft and Political Economy on the Taiwan Frontier 1600– 1800*. Taipei: SMC Publishing.

———. 1999. "The Island Frontier of the Ch'ing, 1684–1780." In *Taiwan: A New History*, edited by Murray Rubinstein, 107–33. Armonk, NY: M. E. Sharpe.

Shih Chien 施乾. 1925. "Qigai pumeilun" 乞丐撲滅論 (A discussion on how to remove the problem of homelessness). In "A hand up for the down and out: Social pioneer Shih Chien," by Jackie Chen, *Taiwan Panorama*, July 1994. https://www.taiwan -panorama.com.tw/en/Articles/Details?Guid=eedf5059-c9ad-4301-8f46-3f65e4f 4c4c4&langId=3&CatId=11&postname=A%20Hand%20Up%20for%20the%20 Down%20and%20Out%3A%20Social%20Pioneer%20Shih%20Chien.

Shih Wen-I, ed. 2004. *Kang SARS guanjian jilu* 抗 *SARS* 關鍵紀錄 (Key records against the SARS epidemic). Taipei: Taiwan Centers for Disease Control.

Shils, Edward. 2006. *Tradition*. Chicago: Chicago University Press.

Shin, Gi-Wook, and Michael Robinson. 1999. "Introduction: Rethinking Colonial Korea." In *Colonial Modernity in Korea*, edited by Gi-Wook Shin and Michael Robinson, 1–21. Cambridge, MA: Harvard University Press.

Shu, Wei-der. 2002. "Who Joined the Clandestine Political Organisation?" In *Memories of the Future*, edited by Stephane Corcuff, 47–73. Armonk, NY: M. E. Sharpe.

Solheim, Willhelm. 1996. "The Nusantao and North-South Dispersals." *Bulletin of the Indo-Pacific Prehistory Association* 15:101–9.

Standaert, Nicolas, and R. G. Tiedemann. 2010. *Handbook of Christianity in China*. Leiden: Brill.

Stanley, Brian. 1990. *The Bible and the Flag: Protestant Missions and British Imperialism in the Nineteenth and Twentieth Centuries*. Leicester: Apollos.

———. 2003. "Christianity and the End of Empire." In *Missions, Nationalism, and the End of Empire*, edited by Brian Stanley, 1–11. Grand Rapids, MI: Wm. B. Eerdmans.

Stonebridge, Lyndsey. 2018. *Placeless People: Writings, Rights, and Refugees*. Oxford: Oxford University Press.

Stonequist, Everett. 1937. *The Marginal Man: A Study in Personality and Culture Conflict*. New York: Scribner's.

Su Beng Interviewing Group. 2013. *Shiming koushushi (san)* 史明口述史(三) (Su Beng oral history [3]). Taipei: Flâneur Culture Lab.

Su Yihju 蘇羿如. 2007. "Qianxizhong de Taiwan dushi Yuanzhumin" 遷移中的台灣「都市」原住民 (The migration of Taiwan's urban Indigenous people). *Journal of Social Science* 15:153–74.

Sun I-Hsuan 孫伊萱. 2019. "Nanhan junzhong qingrenbang chulu! Twice de ta dabai ziyu duode guanjun" 南韓軍中情人榜出爐！TWICE的她打敗子瑜奪得冠軍 (The result of ranking of the most popular female artist is out! Another girl from TWICE defeated Tzuyu to become the champion). *SET News*, 10 November 2019. https://www.setn.com/News.aspx?NewsID=633195.

Sun, Yu-Huay. 2016. "Chang Yung-Fa, Taiwan's Evergreen Group Founder, Dies at 88." *Bloomberg*, 20 January 2016. https://www.bloomberg.com/news/articles/2016-01-20/chang-yung-fa-founder-of-taiwan-s-evergreen-group-dies-at-88.

Sun, Yu-Huay. 2013. "Taiwan Anti-Nuclear Protests May Derail $8.9 Billion Power Plant." *Bloomberg*, 11 March 2013. https://www.bloomberg.com/news/articles/2013-03-11/taiwan-anti-nuclear-protests-may-derail-8-9-billion-power-plant#xj4y7vzkg.

Suqluman, Umas. 2018. "Yijiang: Baluer zhang yuanminhui, jin shangren shouri" 夷將‧拔路兒掌原民會，今上任首日 (Icyang Parod's first day as the new minister of CIP). Taiwan's Indigenous Peoples Portal, 23 May 2016. http://www.tipp.org.tw/news_article.asp?F_ID=71078&FT_No=1.

Swinhoe, Robert. 1864. "'Notes on the Island of Formosa.'" *Journal of the Royal Geographical Society of London* 34:7–8.

Tai, Pao-tsun. 2007. *The Concise History of Taiwan (Bilingual Edition)*. Nantou: Taiwan Historica.

Taiwan Centre for Disease Control. 2003. "Huibie SARS, Taiwan jiankang qibuzou" 揮別SARS, 台灣健康起步走 (Waving goodbye to SARS, Taiwan marching forward)." Taiwan Centre for Disease Control, 6 July 2003. https://www.cdc.gov.tw/Category/ListContent/AHwuigegBBBmuDcbWkzoGQ?uaid=aGNhTomCVt4pYDa2rJOn_w.

Tang Shih 唐詩. 2018. "Shoudu yu meiti chaxu: Chenju fenxiang dangnian zhengzhefan yu jinri mishuzhang xinqing" 首度與媒體茶敘: 陳菊分享當年「政治犯」與今日「秘書長」心情 (First tea chat with the press: Chen Chu shares her feelings as a "political prisoner" and as the "secretary-general" to the president). *People Media*, 17

May 2018. https://www.peoplemedia.tw/news/1395663e-ceb8-4f86-9ed9
-c7213a7408fc.

Tang Yu (tông-ú) 唐羽. 2005. "Taipingyang zhanzheng zhong yingfu zai Jinguashi de shengsi suiyue: Yiming dangdi xiaotong kandao tingdao de fuluying" 太平洋戰爭中英俘在金瓜石的生死歲月: 一名當地小童看到聽到的俘虜營 (The lives and death of POWs in Jinguashi during the Pacific War: The witness account of a local child). *Taiwan Folkways* 台灣風物55 (2):9–44.

Tawney, R. H. 1932. *Land and Labour in China*. London: George Allen and Unwin.

Teng, Emma Jinhua. 2004. *Taiwan's Imagined Geography: Chinese Colonial Travel Writing and Pictures, 1683–1895*. Cambridge, MA: Harvard University Press.

Teng, Shu-feng. 2003. "An Interview with Chen Chien-Jen, Minister of the Department of Health." *Taiwan Panorama*, August 2003. https://www.taiwan-panorama.com/Articles/Details?Guid=f9712158-611a-4f26-9674-43d3681b4855&langId=3&CatId=10.

Thomas, Norman E. 1995. *Classic Texts in Mission and World Christianity*. Maryknoll, NY: Orbis Books.

Titherington, Arthur. 1993. *One Day at a Time*. Hanley Swan: SPA.

Tong, Yanqi. 2005. "Environmental Movements in Transitional Societies: A Comparative Study of Taiwan and China." *Comparative Politics* 37 (2):167–88.

Ts'ai, Caroline. 2009. *Taiwan in Japan's Empire Building: An Institutional Approach to Colonial Engineering*. London: Routledge.

Tsai Cheng-liang 蔡政良. 2006. "Amis Hip Hop: The Body Exhibitions of Contemporary Amis Youth in Taiwan." *TsingHua Anthropological and Area Studies Paper Series 2*.

———. 2011. *Cong Dulan dao Xinjineiya* 從都蘭到新幾內亞 (From Dulan to New Guinea). Taipei: Taiwan Interminds Publishing.

Tsai, Henry Shih-shan. 2005. *Lee Teng-Hui and Taiwan's Quest for Identity*. New York: Palgrave Macmillan.

———. 2009. *Maritime Taiwan: Historical Encounters with the East and the West*. Armonk, NY: M. E. Sharpe.

Tsai Hui-ping 蔡惠萍. 2006. "Linjiangmai zhi nu: Yunbao renwu tan ererba chongtu" 林江邁之女: 原爆人物談228衝突 (Discussing the 228 Incident with Lin Chiang-mai's daughter). *United Daily News*. Accessed 4 March 2021. http://udn.com/NEWS/NATIONAL/NAT1/3196932.shtml.

Tsai Hui-yu 蔡慧玉. 1996. "Taiwan minjian duiri suopei yundong chutan: Panduola zhi xiang" 臺灣民間對日索賠運動初探: 潘朵拉之箱 (The postwar compensation movement in Taiwan: A Pandora's box)." *Taiwan Historical Research* 3 (1):173–228.

Tsai I-fang 蔡依芳 and Wu Kuei-yen 吳奎炎. 2016. "Youlu zhuanlan? Zhangrongfa ceng liting Chenshuibian, queyin zhezhengce touma" 由綠轉藍?張榮發曾力挺陳水扁, 卻因「這政策」投馬 (Turning from pro-Green to pro-Blue? Chang Yung-Fa once supported Chen Shui-Bien but turned to Ma due to "this policy"). *SET News*, 20 January 2016. https://www.setn.com/News.aspx?NewsID=119803.

Tsai Ing-wen. 2011. *Yancong chaodan dao Xiaoying biandang* 洋蔥炒蛋到小英便當 (From stir-fried onions and eggs to Little-Ying's bento). Taipei: Eurasian Press.

———. 2016. "Inaugural Address." *Office of the President of ROC Taiwan*, 20 May 2016. https://english.president.gov.tw/Page/252.

———. 2017. "President Tsai Holds 2017 Year-End Press Conference." *Office of the President of ROC Taiwan*, 29 December 2017. https://english.president.gov.tw/news/5313.

———. 2021. "#Taiwan is a vibrant democracy." Twitter, 30 April 2021, 4:55 a.m. https://twitter.com/iingwen/status/1388099630529880065.

Tsai Yu-jen 蔡裕仁. 2003. "Huangxinjie yu zhanhou Taiwan minzhu yundong" 黃信介與戰後台灣民主運動 (Huang Hsin-Chieh and the Democratic Movement in postwar Taiwan). MA diss., Tunghai University.

Tseng, Yu-chin, Isabelle Cheng, and Dafydd Fell. 2014. "The Politics of the Mainland Spouses' Rights Movement in Taiwan." In *Migration to and from Taiwan*, edited by Kuei-fan Chiu, Dafydd Fell, and Ping Lin, 205–66. London: Routledge.

Tu Tsung-ming 杜聰明. 1963. "Taisheng chaye zhi fu—Lichunsheng de shengping" 臺省茶葉之父—李春生的生平 (Father of Taiwanese tea—Biography of Li Chunsheng). *News Taiwan*, 21 September 1963. http://www.laijohn.com/archives/pc/Li/Li,CSeng/brief/Tou,Cbeng.htm.

Tzuyu Support Union. 2016. "Because this lovely girl don't deserve this hate." Twitter, 15 January 2016, 11:35 p.m. https://twitter.com/Supportyoutzuyu/status/688263323859554304.

UNICEF. 2005. "The State of the World's Children." Geneva: UNICEF.

Vermeer, Eduard B. 1999. "Up the Mountains and Out to the Sea: The Expansion of the Fukienese in the Late Ming Period." In *Taiwan: A New History*, edited by Murray Rubinstein, 45–84. Armonk, NY: M. E. Sharpe.

Wagener, Albin. 2020. "The Postdigital Emergence of Memes and GIFs: Meaning, Discourse, and Hypernarrative Creativity." *Postdigital Science and Education* 3:831–50.

Wei Te-sheng, dir. 2011. *Warriors of the Rainbow: Seediq Bale*. Taipei: View Vision Pictures.

Weller, Robert P. 1985. "Bandits, Beggars, and Ghosts." *American Ethnologist* 12 (1):46–61.

Wheeler, Ray. 2002. "The Legacy of Shoki Coe." *International Bulletin of Missionary Research* 26 (2):77–80.

Wilkinson, Rupert. 2014. *Surviving a Japanese Internment Camp*. Jefferson, NC: McFarland.

Wills, John E., Jr. 1999. "The Seventeenth-Century Transformation: Taiwan under the Dutch and the Cheng Regime." In *Taiwan: A New History*, edited by Murray Rubinstein, 84–107. New York: M. E. Sharpe.

Wolf, Arthur P., ed. 1974. *Religion and Ritual in Chinese Society*. Stanford, CA: Stanford University Press.

Wolf, Arthur P., and Chieh-Shan Huang. 1980. *Marriage and Adoption in China, 1845–1945*. Stanford, CA: Stanford University Press.

Wolf, Margery. 1972. *Women and the Family in Rural Taiwan*. Stanford, CA: Stanford University Press.

World United Formosans for Independence. n.d. "Taidu Lianmeng Meiguo Benbu" 台獨聯盟美國本部 (United Formosans in America for Independence). Accessed 1 March 2020. https://www.wufi.org.tw/%E5%8F%B0%E7%8D%A8%E8%81%AF%E7%9B%9F%E7%BE%8E%E5%9C%8B%E6%9C%AC%E9%83%A8/.

Wu Jen-chieh 吳仁捷. 2018. "Sishisi nianqian de Huama zhangzheyan! Chenju qingchun moyang puguang, 44" 年前的花媽長這樣! 陳菊青春模樣曝光 (Huama looked like this forty-four years ago! Photos of young Chen Chu discovered). *Liberty Times*, 1 July 2018. https://news.ltn.com.tw/news/NewTaipei/breakingnews/2474059.

Wu Micha 吳密察. 2005. *Taiwan tongshi: Tangshan guohai de gushi* 臺灣通史: 唐山過海的故事 (The general history of Taiwan: Stories of the heroic pioneers). In *Taiwan sibainian de bianqian* (Four hundred years of transformation in Taiwan). Taipei: Shibao.

Wu Wen-hsing 吳文星. 2012. "Guxianrong yu Lugang gujia zhi jueqi" 辜顯榮與鹿港辜家之崛起 (Ku Hsien-Jung and the rise of the Ku family from Lukang). *Academia Historica Research Newsletter* 國史研究通訊 2:29–35.

Wu Yingtao 吳瀛濤. 1980. *Taiwan minsu* 臺灣民俗 (Taiwan folkways). Taipei: Jong Wen.

Xu, Jing. 2019. "The Mischievous, the Naughty, and the Violent in a Taiwanese Village: Peer Aggression Narratives in Arthur P. Wolf's 'Child Interview' (1959)." *Cross Currents* 33:143–65.

Xu Xueji 許雪姬. 2005. "Qingdai de jiazu yu zhengzhi fazhan" 清代的家族與政治發展 (Family and political development in the Qing Dynasty). In *Taiwan sibainian de bianqian* (Four hundred years of transformation in Taiwan), edited by Xueji Xu, 193–215. Zhongli: National Central University.

Xu Yaxiang. 2013. *Sounds from the Other Side: The Operatic Interaction between Colonial Taiwan and China during the Early Twentieth Century*. Taipei: SMC Publishing.

Yang, Dominic Meng-Hsuan. 2021. *The Great Exodus from China*. Cambridge: Cambridge University Press.

Yang Tu 楊渡. 2015. "Xunzhao ererba de chenmo muqin" 尋找二二八的沉默母親 (Looking for the silent mother of the 228 Incident). Commonwealth Publishing, 24 November 2015. https://bookzone.cwgv.com.tw/topic/details/1900.

Yu Bingsheng 余炳盛. 2011. *Zhonghua minguo kuangye xiejinhui chuanghui bainian tekan* 中華民國鑛業協進會創會百年慶紀念特刊 (The hundredth anniversary of the ROC Mining Association Special Publication). Taipei: ROC Mining Association.

Yu Yonghe 郁永河. 1959. *Pihai jiyou* 裨海紀遊 (Small sea travelogue). Taipei: Taiwan Bank. https://tcss.ith.sinica.edu.tw/browse-ebook.html?id=EB0000000044.

Yuan, Aiai. 2021. "Shiqian yu qingshuizhaozi zhuanqu" 施乾與清水照子專區 (Section of Shih Chien and Shimizu Teruko). https://aiai.org.tw/?FID=16.

Zhang Canhu 張燦鍙. 1991. *Taiwan duli yundong sanshinian* 台灣獨立運動三十年 (Thirty years of the Taiwan independence movement). Taipei: Avanguard.

Zhou, Yiqun. 2013. "Honglou Meng and Agrarian Values." *Late Imperial China* 34 (1):28–66.

Index

Aboriginal Affairs Commission, 221

activism, 133, 151, 153; community-led, 127; cultural, 150; digital, 137, 140; elitism and, 112; Indigenous, 12, 222, 223; political, 111, 113, 187; social, 136; student-led, 128

Advanced Micro Devices, 209

Adventures of Sanmao, The (Sanmao liulangji) (Zhang), 124

Advisory Council (Hyōgikai), 54

African Americans, 6, 154

agriculture, 33, 34, 35, 55; developing, 183; traditional, 55

Ahern, Emily, 201

Aia Ryou (Aiailiao), 53, 159

Aitape-Wewak campaign, 67

Akashi Motojirō, 82

Amae, Yoshihisa, 107

American Liaison Group, 94, 96, 97

Amis, 64, 65, 218, 219, 220

Amis Hip Hop, 220

Amnesty International, 109

Amoy, 24, 25, 33, 101, 102

Anderson, Boris, 107

Andō Rikichi, 94

Anping, Dutch in, 60–61

anthropology, 129, 199, 200, 201

Anti Guo-Kuang (Guoguang) Petroleum Plant, protest at, 139

Anti-Rightist Movement, 114

Apple, 209

Arendt, Hannah, 109, 110, 171

Aron, Raymond, 148

Arrigo, Linda, 107, 116

Article 100, revision of, 116

Asian tigers, 183

A-Siok (Ng Siok-eng), 106

assimilation, 47–48, 61, 63; education and, 83; Indigenous, 60; social/political, 83

Association for Relations across the Taiwan Straits, 128

Association for the Care of Homeless People (Qigai Pumie Xiehui), 159

Association of Taiwan Indigenous Rights Promotion (Taiwan Yunzhuminzu Quanli Cujinhui), 223, 224

Ataabu, 45

Atayal Indigenous group, 114

Australian Army, PIB and, 66

Australian Sixth Division, 67

Austro-Hungarian Empire, 145

Austronesian expansion, 8, 12, 63

authenticity, 114, 148; cultural, 63; Han-centric narratives of, 99

authoritarianism, 126, 195

Aylward, Bruce, 227

Bai Longfa, 156

Ballard, J. G., 81

Bank of Taiwan, 52

Banka, 23, 25, 32, 36, 53, 152, 159;
development of, 35
Banka Lin, 36–37
Banqiao Lin family, funding from, 159
Banzai You Bastards (Edwards), 79
baojia system, 34, 48
Barclay, Paul, 63
Barry, John M., 211
BBC (British Broadcasting Corporation),
203
Beauvoir, Simone de, 148
Becker, Ernest, 145
Beckwith-Smith, Merton, 79
Becoming "Japanese" (Ching), 47
Becoming Taiwan (Heyler and Sommers), 48
Beeby, Daniel, 107
Beijing, 149, 173, 191, 227
Beipu Incident (Beipu Shijian) (1907), 49,
150
Benedict XVI, Pope, 212
benshengren, 98, 99, 130, 131, 164, 169;
waishengren and, 166, 168
Bernhard Schulte Shipmanagement, 204
Bhabha, Homi: on colonization, 89
Big River, Big Sea (Dajiang dahai) (Lung),
95
Black Death, 1
Black Skin, White Masks (Fanon), 89
Black Trench (Heishuigou), 4, 42, 44
Blake, Ralph, 96
Bourdieu, Pierre, 119
bourgeois public sphere (*Öffentlichkeit*), 150
Boxer Rebellion, 49
Boyd and Company, 155
British Broadcasting Corporation (BBC),
203
British Broadcasting Corporation (BBC)
World Service, 105
British Dependent Territories Citizenship,
79
British Legion, 79

Buddhism, 5
Bun, Elder, 103. *See also* Gaw Bun-sui
(Wu Wenshui)
Bunun, 65, 220, 223
Bureau Branch Office, 169
Burns, William Chalmers, 101
Burnt Island (Huoshaodao), 192
Burnt Island Detention Center for
Vagrants, 192

C Aircraft Factory (Koza), 85
Cai Yuanpei, 149
Campbell, William, 102, 103
Camus, Albert, 148
Canterbury Tales, The (Chaucer), 1
capitalism, 33, 125, 209
Carter, Jimmy, 188, 191
Cass and Company, 152
CCP (Chinese Communist Party), 112, 114,
115, 173, 174, 179
Centers for Disease Control, 215
Central Epidemic Command Centre, 76,
215
Central Marine Corporation (Zhongyang
Haiyun Gongsi), 207
Central Trust (freighter), 207
Centre for Disease Control, 214
Cevdet, Abdullah, 147
Chang, Jonas, 87
Chang, Morris: TSMC and, 209
Chang Chin-feng, 228
Chang Chun-hung, 184
Chang Hwa Bank (Zhanghua Yinhang), 36
Chang Kuo-wei, 207
Chang Liang Tse, 116
Chang Lin Chih-chih, death of, 207
Chang Woongjo, 136
Chang Yung-fa, 203, 207, 210;
diversification by, 208; politics and, 209;
youth of, 206
Chang Yung-fa Exhibition, 207

Chang Yung-fa Foundation, 208

Changhua, 23, 36, 46, 104

Changi Prison, 76

Chao, Y. (Zhao Youyuan), 107

Chaucer, Geoffrey, 1, 226

Chen, Edward I-te, 47

Chen, Ms., 44

Chen Atu, 193

Chen Cheng, 191

Chen Chieh, 121

Chen Chien-jen, 12, 215–16; effective governance and, 216; public health awareness and, 214; SARS and, 213; WHO and, 215; youth of, 212

Chen Chu, 12, 184, 193, 194–95; imprisonment of, 194; Kuo and, 194

Chen Duxiu, 149, 173

Chen Fuqian, 156

Chen Hsiao, 36

Chen Hsin-an, 212

Chen Lin Lien-hua, 193

Chen Mao-ping, 121–22, 123. *See also* Echo Chen; Sanmao

Chen Meixiang, 177

Chen Pi-Kuei, 84

Chen Shao-hsing, 200

Chen Sheng, 121

Chen Shui-bian, 128, 185, 188, 193, 208; election of, 228; protest against, 132

Chen Suching, 121

Chen Tian (Chen Jingwen), 151

Chen Tienshin, 121

Chen Yi, 95, 97, 151, 163, 164, 169, 191

Chen Yunlin, 128

Chenghuang Temple (Chenghuang Miao), 153

Chiang Ching-kuo, 107, 191, 195, 204

Chiang Hong-zhang, 151

Chiang Kai-shek, 80, 116, 174, 178, 204; "big four" and, 79; consolidation of power by, 110; Ku and, 37; martial law and, 106;

Peng and, 109; protests and, 7; Soong and, 98, 104; Su and, 112; Taiwan and, 6; US support for, 200

Chiang Wei-chuan, 151

Chiang Wei-shui, 37, 146, 147, 153, 154; activism of, 187; existentialism and, 148–49; Petition Movement and, 46; story of, 155; youth of, 151

Chiang Yueh-ching, 186

Chiayi, 177–79

Chiayi Air Force Base, 179

China Democracy Party (Zhongguo Minzhuadang), 194

China Inland Mission, 101

China Youth League, 114

Chinese Civil War, 88, 185

Chinese Communist Party (CCP), 112, 114, 115, 173, 174, 179

Chinese Culture University, 122, 123

Chinese Nationalists, 93, 110, 120, 180, 188, 218; Americans and, 97; arrival of, 11, 54, 83, 104, 127, 170; colonization by, 63; criticism of, 95; flight of, 112, 171, 172; governing by, 94, 115–16; penal practice and, 190; POWs and, 79; PRC and, 6; protests and, 7; rule of, 48; treatment by, 98

Chinese People's Political Consultative Conference, 114

Chinese primacy, myth of, 225

"Chinese Restaurant, The" (Zhongguo fandian) (Chen), 123

Chineseness, 114, 124

Ching, Leo T. S.: on China/colonial period, 48

Chin-lung, 185

Chiye/Yoshino Village (Jiye Yimin Cun), 52

Choe Nam-seon, 150

Choebols, 214

Chou Te-wei, 188

Chou Tzuyu, 134–36; apology by, 140; canceling, 139; support for, 137; youth of, 138
Chou Wen-yao, 149
Chou Yu, 188
Christianity, 1, 9, 100, 102, 103, 155, 156, 157; Chinese, 106, 159; conversion to, 62, 104
Chu Fengmin, Mrs.: suicide of, 129–30
Chung Jae-yong, 150
Chung Yi-ren, 114
Chungli, protest at, 188
Churchill, Winston, 79
City of Sadness (film), 75
Civil Aeronautics Administration, 208
civil liberties, 128, 191
civil rights, 128, 132, 154
civil war, 88, 106, 121, 171, 185
"Clinical Notes: A Patient Named Taiwan" (Linchuang jiangyi: Guanyu Taiwan zhege huanzhe) (Chiang), 146, 147
Cohen, Myron, 202
colonial authority, 82, 115–16
colonial government, 54, 157
colonial historical timeline, 3 (table)
colonial period, 50, 63; Japanese, 48, 98, 158
colonialism, 3, 6, 7, 22, 48, 100; effects of, 52–53, 89; Japanese, 11, 54, 62, 63, 150; Manchu, 40. *See also* settler colonialism
colonization, 10, 47, 79, 200; consequences of, 89; farming, 60; history prior to, 3; hybrid, 2, 7; Indigenous peoples and, 70, 219, 220; Japanese, 2, 22, 48, 98, 112, 121, 164, 191, 199; layers of, 3, 9, 232; Manchu, 9, 40, 191; "metropole" forms of, 2; postwar, 63
communism: containing, 204; martial law and, 114
Communists, 80, 104, 175
Community Development Program, 205
Confessions of a Mask (Mishima), 86
Confucianism, 126, 149, 157

Confucius, 32, 36
"Confusion" (Huo) (Chen), publication of, 122
consciousness: non-Chinese national, 98; radical, 89; Taiwanese, 89, 124
Conservative Party, 125
Contemporary Literature (Xiandai wenxue), 122
Control Yuan, 194
copper, 75, 76, 78
Corporate Communications, 79
Council for Economic Planning and Development, 205
Council of Aboriginal Affairs, 221
Council of Hakka Affairs, 128
Council of Indigenous Peoples, 12, 128, 221, 224
Council of Labor Affairs, 194
Country Doctor, A (Kafka), 146
COVID-19, 12, 211, 214, 216, 226, 227
Criminal Code, 116, 191
Cross-Strait Service Trade Agreement, 129
CTBC Financial Holding Company (Zhongxin Jituan), 38
Cultural Revolution, 114, 178
culture, 10, 11, 115, 120, 149, 212, 219; Austronesian, 63; Chinese, 176; Confucian, 126; Dapenking, 9; Indigenous, 9, 62, 63, 200; Japanese, 63; material, 199, 221; political, 126, 187; popular, 139, 219; revitalization of, 200; settler, 9; Taiwanese, 32–33
Curthoys, Ann, 21

Daan District, 112, 133, 187
Dachen Islands (Dachen Zhudao), 178
Dadaocheng, 165, 168, 170, 185, 186, 232; as capital, 23; cultural expression in, 32–33; development of, 151–53, 156; Dodd and, 26; economic/political centrality and, 155; Linn and, 115, 158; marginality and, 155

Dadaocheng Presbyterian Church, 159
Dahe Company (Dahehang),
    establishment of, 36
Dalongdong, 185
Dante, 78
Dapu Self-Help Organization (Dapu
    Zijiuhui), 129
Declaration of Taiwan's Plain Indigenous
    Peoples, 222
democracy: consolidation of, 116, 227; fight
    for, 6, 12, 126, 187; impact of, 135, 209;
    Indigenous peoples and, 217; liberal, 126,
    183; maintaining, 190; sacrifice for, 195;
    self-determining, 159; transformation
    to, 208, 227
Democratic Progressive Party (DPP), 168,
    193, 224; agenda of, 186–87; democracy
    and, 107; formation of, 188; KMT and,
    133; power for, 208; Tsai and, 134, 135,
    228, 229–30, 231; victory for, 127, 227
democratization, 129, 188, 216, 200, 225
Den Kenjirō, 83
Department of Cultural Affairs, 166, 168
Department of Indigenous People, 224
Department of Social Welfare, 194
Diamond, Norma, 201
Diana, Princess, 80
Diary of a Madman (Kuangren riji) (Lu),
    146
dingcuo, 45, 46
Document No. 2701, 79
Dodd, John, 26–27, 155; research by, 24–25;
    tea and, 25, 26
Dodd, John, Sr., 24
Dodd, Margaret, 24
Dodd, Mary Lloyd, 26
Dodd and Company, 26, 155, 156
dōka, 47–48, 63
Douglas, Carstairs, 101, 102
DPP. *See* Democratic Progressive Party
Du Bois, W. E. B., 154

Dulan, 64, 67, 68, 218
Dulles, John Foster, 98
Dumbarton Oaks Conference (1944), 79
DuPont, 127
Dutch, 5, 21, 43, 62; arrival of, 7, 23, 60–61;
    colonization and, 2
Dutch East Indies, 66
Dyer, Samuel, 101

Echo Chen, 121, 122
economic growth, 10, 27, 34, 54–55, 131, 183
economic issues, 204, 209, 218, 221, 224
economic systems, 5, 10, 33
economic transformation, 183–84, 207, 200,
    210
Economist, The, 12
education, 50, 55, 82, 84, 101, 208, 209, 223;
    assimilation and, 83; colonial, 89, 95;
    system, 83, 88
Education Rescript (1919), 82
Edwards, Jack, 72, 74, 77, 78, 81; liberation
    of, 79; youth of, 76
Election Study Center, 6
Elles and Company, 155
Empire of the Sun (Ballard), 81
English Maru (freighter), 76
environmental issues, 60, 127, 130–31
Environmental Protection Administration
    (Huanjing Baohu Shu) (EPA), 131
Eskildsen, Robert, 22
Essentials to Encourage and Reward
    Immigration (Yizhu Jiangli Yaoling), 52
ethnicity, 61–62, 119, 130, 164, 217
E'tolan, 64, 218
Eva Airways Corporation, 208
Ever Given (container ship), 203, 204
Evergreen Group, 208
Evergreen International Hotels, 208
Evergreen Marine Corporation, 203–7
Evergreen Maritime Museum, 208
Evergreen Symphony Orchestra, 208

Executive Yuan (Xingzhengyuan), 128, 131, 221

Ex-Servicemen's Association, 79

Fan Sun-lu, 224

Fan Yun, 125–32

Fanon, Frantz, 89

FCSD (Formosan Christians for Self-Determination), 104, 107

February 28th Incident Handling Committee, 151

Fell, Dafydd, 227

Fengtian/Toyota Village (Fengtian Yimin Cun), 52

First Boys' High School, 36

First Opium War (1839–42), 101

Flying Tigers, 177

food robbery, 158

food shortages, 68, 165

foot binding, 176

Foot Emancipation Society (Buchanzuhui), 158

Foreign Missions Committee, 102

Formosa, 94, 106, 120, 189; mission in, 103; smallness of, 93

Formosa Association (Taiwan Qingnianhui), 111

Formosa Betrayed (Kerr), 98

Formosa: Licensed Revolution and the Home Rule Movement, 1895–1945 (Kerr), 98

Formosa Magazine (Meilidao zazhi), 184, 186

Formosa Research Unit, 97

Formosan Christians for Self-Determination (FCSD) (Taiwan Renmin Zijue Yundong), 104, 107

Francis, Pope, 212

Fujian, 5, 23, 24, 33, 44, 45, 70, 101, 155

Fujita Company, 75

Fukushima Daiichi nuclear disaster, 130

Fuzhou, 24, 26, 159

Gao Gongqian, 40

Garden Centre Association, 203

Gaw Bun-sui (Wu Wenshui), 103

gay pride, 128, 211

"Gods, Ghosts, and Ancestors" (Wolf), 201

gold, discovery of, 74

Golden Horse Awards, 123

Gongyihui, 37

Government House, 85

Graham, Jamie, 81

Great Exodus, 175

Greater East Asia Co-Prosperity Sphere, 71, 83

Green Island (Ludao), 192–95

Green Island (Ryan), 169, 195, 205–6

Green Island Human Rights Culture Park (Ludao Renquan Wenhua Yuanqu), 193

Green Island White Terror Memorial Park (Baise Kongbu Ludao Jinian Yuanqu), 193

Guandi (Kuan-ti), 32

Guangdong, 70, 212, 213

Gutzlaff, Karl, 101

Gwangju massacre, 126

Habermas, Jürgen, 150

Hakka, 10, 34, 171, 200, 228

Hallyu fandom, described, 136

Han Chinese, 49, 52, 115, 200, 220; non-Han (Yi) peoples versus, 218; population of, 5; settlement of, 34, 41, 44

Han River, 204

Hanaoka Ichiro, 59

Hanlim Multi Art School, 138

Hanuabada, 66

Harrell, Stevan, 99, 201

Hatazō Adachi, suicide of, 69

Hayao Miyazaki, 75

healthcare, 55, 76, 210, 215, 216

Heidegger, Martin: existentialism of, 148

Heito, 72

heritage, 4; cultural, 48, 52, 199, 219; Japanese colonial, 232; maritime, 208; sociocultural, 3

Hetou Town, 175

Heylen, Ann, 48

High Bridge Presbyterian Church, 101

High Command of the Armed Forces, 87

Hikawa Maru (ocean liner), 87

Hiraga Kyoko, 112

Hirohito, Emperor, 83, 88, 93, 163

history, 120, 165; Chinese, 149, 173; colonial, 2, 12; Indigenous, 225; national, 148; political, 12, 183; social, 11, 12; sociopolitical, 1–2; Taiwanese, 195; transnational, 21

History of Taiwan, The (Taiwan tongshi) (Lien), 156

Ho Ming-sho, 127–28

homelessness, 53, 157, 159, 172

Hong Kong, 24, 76, 79, 101, 106, 183, 213; Japanese assault on, 105

Hongji Hospital (Hongji Yiyuan), 158

"Honorable Soldier, The" (song), 66

Hoping Hospital, 213, 214

Hou Hsiao-hsien, 75

House of Lin (Wolf), 202

House of Peers, 37

Hsieh Chang-ting, 188

Hsieh Hsueh-hung, 113, 114

Hsieh Tsung-min, 109

Hsinchu, 33, 49, 165

Hsinchu Science Park, 209

Hua Nan Bank (Huanan Yinhang), 36

Huaguang, 129, 130

Huaguang Community (Huaguang Shequ), 130

Hualien, 52, 223

Hualien Harbor Office, 52

Hualien-Taitung corridor, 222

Huang, Mrs., 25

Huang An, 134, 136, 137

Huang Chiau-tong, 116

Huang Chun-ying, 194

Huang Hsin-chieh, 12, 184–86, 188, 192, 193; death of, 187; Tangwai and, 187

Huang Jui-niang, 45

Huang Nanqiu, 156

Huang Shou-li, 167

Huang Xing, 172

Huang Yu-shu, 35

Huang Yujie, 158

Huang Zhanghui, 104

Huguang, 172

Hui-yu Ts'ai, 190

human rights, 217, 230

Human Rights Day, 126, 184, 190

Human Rights Forum, 184

Huntington, Samuel, 126

Ictihad, 147

identity, 89, 108, 154, 232; civic, 2, 227; collective, 99; community, 205; concepts of, 10, 60; crisis, 95, 110; defining, 128; denial of, 139; digital, 137; factionalized, 46; forming, 12, 27, 99, 119, 121, 122; Han, 11; Indigenous, 61, 220, 221, 222; Japanese, 47, 64; national, 88; nativization of, 98; notions of, 3, 119; pan, 62; postcolonial, 227; social, 74; Taiwanese, 87, 113, 153, 170, 171, 225

Ikichi Honda, 85

Imabari Shipbuilding, 204

immigration, 5, 41, 50; Chinese, 63; Indigenous, 47; Japanese, 52–53, 55

Imperial Chinese Maritime Customs, 22

Imperial Comprehensive Geographies, 39

Imperial State, 88

imperialism, 2, 22, 63, 100, 148

imperialization (*kōminka*), 48, 63, 83, 94

Indigenous communities, 26, 41, 50, 62, 101, 200, 219, 221; displacement of, 171; war effort and, 66

Indigenous Historical Justice and Transitional Justice Committee, 224

Indigenous Languages Development Act, 230

Indigenous peoples (*yuanzhumin*), 9, 10, 25, 41, 47, 66; acculturation of, 61, 63, 199, 219; challenges for, 221, 222; Chinese and, 63; colonization and, 70, 219, 220; equality for, 223; evangelization of, 61, 62; history of, 60, 69–70; Japanese army and, 64; Japanese designations for, 8; land purchases and, 52; languages of, 59; legacy of, 217; migration of, 69–70; protests by, 130–31; rights of, 217, 224; shared experiences of, 218; subjugation of, 2, 115; urbanization and, 223

industrial development, 27, 64, 74, 205, 218

industrial workers (*sangyō*), 86, 87

infrastructure, 65, 84–85, 145, 205

Inō Kanori, 62, 199, 200

integration, 60, 61, 64, 153

intermarriage, 34, 60, 83

Internal Security of the State in the Criminal Code, 191

International Military Tribunal for the Far East, 79

Irish Home Rule Movement, 151

Is Time Still on Our Side? (documentary), 108

Jacobs, J. Bruce, 116, 174

Japanese, 5, 60, 62, 172; being, 47; consolidation of power by, 46; invasiveness of, 48; Taiwanese-born, 96

Japanese Army, 11, 76, 206

Japanese Diet, 147

Japanese Eighteenth Army, 67, 69

Japanese Empire, 2, 7, 53, 66, 75, 82, 88, 150, 173, 207; attacks by, 71; colonial expansion by, 48; Taiwan and, 55

Japanese governor-generals (1895–1945), listed, 51

Japanization, 50, 83

Jardine Matheson and Company, 25, 152

Jen-ai Educational Experimental Institute (Taiwan Renai Jiaoyu Shiyansuo), 194

Jhunan Science Park (Zhunan Kexue Yuanqu), 129

Ji Qiguan, 39, 74

Jiang Yuying, 40

jiao system, 33, 34, 38

Ji-Hyun Ahn, 138

Jin Su-qin, 177, 178, 180; marriage of, 179; youth of, 175–76

Jinan Presbyterian Church, 159

Jinguashi, 74–76

Jiufen, 74, 75

John Paul, Pope, II, 212

Joint Declaration by the Representatives of the Indigenous Peoples of Taiwan, 217

Jordon, David, 201

Journal of the Anthropological Society of Tokyo, 199

Juan Mei-shu, 167, 168

Judicial Yuan, 223

Jung Chang, 176

junks, 5, 42, 43

JYP Entertainment, 134–35, 137, 138, 140

Kabayama Sukenori, 157

Kafka, Franz, 146, 147

Kanagawa, 85, 86

Kanaseki Takeo, 199

Kang Ning-hsiang, 186, 187, 188

Kangxi, Emperor, 43

Kao Chun-ming, 107

Kao Yu-shu (Henry Kao), 186

Kaohsiung, 84, 86, 194; army in, 95; migration to, 222; port at, 22, 31, 164; prodemocracy demonstrations in, 192

Kaohsiung Eight, 184, 192, 194

Kaohsiung Incident, 107, 184, 186, 194, 195

"Kapah" (song), 219

Karenko Camp, 79

Keelung, 31, 164, 206; Banka and, 25, 32; landing at, 95, 96; port at, 22, 31, 48, 74, 163, 164; railway at, 156

Keelung Coal Mining Company, 75

Keelung River, 74, 185

Kerr, George H., 93, 94, 169; identity and, 99; KMT/nationalism and, 98; 228 Incident and, 97; youth of, 97

Kierkegaard, Søren: existentialism of, 148

Kikuchi Kan, 53

Kinkaseki (Jinguashi) Camp, 71, 72, 74, 77, 79

KMT. See Kuomintang

Knapp, Ronald G., 34

Kobayama Sukenori, 49

Kobayashi Seizō, 63, 83

Koo, Jeffrey, Sr., 38

Koo (Ku) Kwang-ming, 112

Koos Group (KGI), 37–38

Korean Declaration of Independence, 150

Korean Independence Movement, 150

Korean War, 178

Korean Wave (Hallyu), 136

Koza, 85, 87, 89

Ku Chin, 35

Ku Fu-sheng, 122

Ku Hsien-jung, 37, 156, 159; birth of, 35; prominence for, 36, 38

Ku Jui-yun, 114

Kukutsu Camp, 72, 78

Kung, H. H., 104

Kuo Yu-hsin, 193–94

Kuomintang (KMT), 75, 94, 185–86, 195; brutality of, 187; communist ideology and, 114; desertion from, 179; DPP and, 133; flight of, 97; government by, 126; joining, 180, 208; loss of control for, 191–92; nationalism and, 98; opposition to, 112, 184, 190, 192, 193–94; Presbyterian Church and, 107; rule of, 111; secret agencies/tribunals of, 191; social engineering and, 119, 121; support for, 128; victory for, 128; women/labor market and, 205

K-pop fandom, 135, 136, 138

Kyoto Prefectural Second Girls' High School (Suzaku High School), 53

La Jeunesse, 149

labor, 183–84, 223; child, 12, 82, 86; Chinese, 77; foreign, 225; migrant, 9, 41; skilled, 25; women and, 205

Lai Ching-te, 228

Lake, Marilyn, 21

Lan Yinding, 152

Landsborough, David, 105, 106

language: Austronesian, 3, 4, 8–9; complexities of, 137; Formosan, 26; Hokkien, 166, 168, 170, 171, 180, 208; Indigenous, 115; Japanese, 64, 82, 168, 170; Mandarin, 94, 168, 170, 185, 208; migratory, 59–60; revitalization, 231; Sirayan, 61; Southern Min, 101, 103; Taivoan, 61

laoyuzai, 168–69

League for Self-Determination of Formosans (Taiwan Zhumin Zijue Lianmeng), 111

Lee Teng-hui, 126–27, 183, 186, 187, 195; Article 100 and, 116

Legislative Yuan (Lifayuan), 128, 129, 131, 133, 139, 186, 224

Leo Ching, 47

LGBTQ rights, 129, 132, 230

Li Chi, 199

Li Chunsheng, 25, 32, 153, 154, 155, 156, 159; philanthropy of, 158

Li Dazhao, 173

Li Desheng, 155

Li Fu-chun, 186

Li Hsien-wen, 167
Li Mei-yu, 207
Li Wenliang, 211, 212
Li Ye-Isi, 153
Liang Qichao, 173
Liao Chinlin, 121
Liao Wen-I, 111, 112
Liberty Times, 167, 168
Lien Chan, 159
Lien Chen-tung, 159
Lien Hao, 185
Lien Heng, 156
Lien Wen-ching, 147, 185
Lim Chông-gī (Lin Zongyi), 104, 107
Lim Iong-iong, 108
Lin Chao-hsuan, 46
Lin Chao-hui, youth of, 112
Lin Chao-tung, 46
Lin Cheng-tang, 36
Lin Chia-yin, 45
Lin Chiang-mai, 165, 166, 167, 170; bullying
 of, 168; 228 Incident and, 168; wounding
 of, 169
Lin Ching-wu, 95–96
Lin Chiung-yao, 45
Lin family, 44; Manchus and, 45–46
Lin Hsien-tang (Huang Deshi), 36, 149, 151
Lin Hsiung-cheng, 157, 159
Lin Hung-hsuan, 184, 192
Lin Lantian, 151–52
Lin Ming-chu, 166–69
Lin Pao-lo, 167, 168
Lin Qianguang, 39
Lin Qingyue, 158
Lin Shih, 44, 45
Lin Shuang-wen, 45
Lin Shuguang, 121
Lin Sun, 45
Lin Tien-kuo, 45
Lin Tin-pang, 45
Lin Weiyuan, 156

Lin Wen-cha, 45
Lin Wen-chin, 46
Lin Wen-ming, 45, 46
Lin Wen-shan, 165
Lin Xiong-zheng, 36
Lin Yi-hsiung, 131, 184
Ling Shung-sheng, 200
Lingjing Township, 175
linguistic issues, 8, 60, 62, 98
Lintian/Hayashida Village (Lintian Yimin
 Cun), 52
Liu Chieng-hung, 129
Liu Mingchuan, 152, 156, 158
Liu Yongfu, 49
Living Rooms as Factories (Keting Ji
 Gongchang), 205
Lloyd, John, 27
Lo Fong-pin, 212
Lo-Sheng (Lesheng) Sanatorium, 139
Loa Daera, 66, 67
Lohok family, 223
London Missionary Society, 101
London School of Economics (LSE), 200,
 229
Longyu, Empress Dowager, 173
*Looking for the Silent Mother of the 228
 Incident* (Xunzhao ererba de chenmo
 muqin), 166
LSE (London School of Economics), 200,
 229
Lu Hsiu-lien, 184, 190, 191
Lu Xun, 146, 149
Lugouqiao, 174
Lukang, 35, 36, 45, 127
Lung Ying-tai, 95

Ma Ying-jeou, 136, 166, 209, 224, 229;
 apology by, 195; election of, 128, 132;
 environmental issues and, 130; Hoping
 Hospital and, 213
Ma Yung-cheng, 132

MacDonald, Mr., 105

Mackay, George Leslie, 102, 103, 158, 159

Mackenzie, H. L., 101

Malinowski, Bronislaw, 199

Manchu Empire, 6, 21, 39, 41, 48, 95, 156, 172; Taiwan and, 61

Manchukuo, 229

Manchus: annexation by, 40; foreign encroachment and, 172; Lin family and, 45–46; migration and, 41, 43; prisons and, 191; settler colonialism of, 7, 60; Taiwan and, 32, 39–40, 49; war with, 21, 22, 48

Mandated Territory of New Guinea, 66

manufacturing, 55, 205; labor-intensive, 222

Mao Zedong, 173

March First (Sam-il) Movement (Samil Undong), fallout of, 150–51

Marco Polo Bridge, 174

Marriage and Adoption in China, 1845–1945 (Wolf and Huang), 201

martial law, 8, 106, 184, 208, 227; communism and, 114; imposition of, 7, 191; lifting of, 11–12, 106, 107, 127, 183, 186; success for, 119; White Terror and, 232

Marxism, 114, 149

Mattau (Madou), burning of, 61

Maxwell, James Laidlaw, 102, 103, 110

May Fourth Movement, 121, 149

Mazu, 4–5, 11, 32

Medhurst, Walter, 101

medicine, 101, 102, 210, 214, 215

Memorial Hall Plaza (NTU), 126, 131

"Mezheb-i BahauIlah-Din-i Umem" (Cevdet), 147

migration, 46, 69–70, 148, 224; changes in, 23, 34, 35; government-run, 50; growth of, 10; Han, 40; history of, 200, 225; illegal, 41, 42; impact of, 31; motivation for, 9; non-Indigenous, 47; place of, 232; routes of, 60

Milne, William, 101

Minami Nippon Kisen Kabushiki Gaisha, 206

Ming dynasty, 7; overseas trade and, 41; transition from, 42

Ming-sho Ho, 128

mining, 55, 74–80

Ministry of Health, 213

Ministry of Justice Investigation Bureau, 165

Ministry of Labor, 194

Ministry of National Defense Green Island Reform and Reeducation Prison, 192

Ministry of Revenue (Hubu), 34

Mishima Yukio, 86

missionaries, 100–103

Mitsui, 75

Miyamoto Nobuhito, 199

MNET (radio station), 138

modernization, 24, 204, 218; colonial, 199; cultural, 220

Mongols, 6, 41

Monopoly Bureau, 169–70

Montgomery, W. E., 105

Moody, Campbell, 100

Morals Monthly, 208

Mori Ushinosuke, 199

Morrison, Robert, 101

Mother's Workshops (Mama Jiaoshi), 205

Mukden Incident, 174

MUSE Performing Arts Workshop, 138

Musha Incident (Wushe Shijian), 50

My Little Television (Mai liteul telebijeon), 134

Nagashima Hatsu, 206

Nakano School (Rikugun Nakano Gakkō), 64

nation-building, 5–6, 12, 164

National Alliance for the Rescue of the Tamsui River (Quanmin Qiangjiu Danshuihe Xingdong Lianmeng), 131

National Assembly, 126, 133, 191, 192
National Chengchi University (NCU), 6, 229
National Chung Hsing University, 185
national language family (*kokugo katei*), 206
National Taiwan Normal University, 105
National Taiwan University (NTU), 126, 187, 199, 212, 223; Chen at, 123; College of Medicine, 151; Hospital, 213; sit-in at, 131; Student Association, 132; Student Association Autonomous Region (Guoli Taiwan Daxue Xuesheng Zizhi Guizhang), 132; Tsai at, 230
National Yang-Ming University Hospital, 213
nationalism, 22; Chinese, 48, 115, 120, 172, 173, 228; civic, 127; community and, 89; creole, 113; elite, 112; ethnic, 8, 127; Japanese, 48, 53; KMT and, 98; postcolonial, 115; self-determining, 159; start-again, 7–8, 89, 113, 115, 124, 170; Taiwanese, 6, 116, 188
nationality (*gukjeok*), 119, 140
Naval Ministry, 85
NCU (National Chengchi University), 6, 229
Near Oceania, colonization of, 60
Neolithic people, 9
Netherlands East Indies, 64
netizens, Taiwanese, 134, 135, 137, 139
networks, 5, 32, 34, 35, 130, 153, 210, 213; kin, 10, 33; social, 139; trade, 27, 33
New Army, 172
New Britain Island (Papua), 66
New Cultural Movement (Xinwenhua Yundong), 149, 173
New Gourmet (Shinchinmi), 112
New Guinea, 64–67
New Life Correction Center (NLCC), 192
New Party (Xindang), 131

New Taipei City, 202, 206
New Youth (Xin qinqnian), 149
Ng Bu-tong (Huang Wudong), 104, 107
Ng Leng-kiat (Huang Nenjie), 104
Ni Jianghui, 152
Niles, D. T., 107
Ningbo, 101, 175, 177
Nobosuke, Kishi, 185
North Gate, 156
Northern Taiwan, map of, 15
NTU. *See* National Taiwan University
nuclear power, 130

Oasis Villa, 192
Occupy Movement, 139
October Revolution (1917), 149
"One China, One Formosa" policy, 107
Orchid Island, 131
Order of Martial Law (Jieyan Ling), 132
Ottoman Empire, 145, 147
Overseas Alliance of Taiwan Democracy Movement, 194
Overseas Mission Committee, 105
overseas trade (*haijin*), ban on, 41

Pacific Islanders, 9, 60
Pacific Ring of Fire, 4
Pacific War, 11, 66, 67, 83, 175
Pagoda Park, 150
Pai Hsien-yung, 122
Paiwan, 65, 228
Palau, 65
Pan-Blue, 128, 168
Papua New Guinea, 66–67; hostilities/casualties on, 68
Papuan Infantry Battalion (PIB), 66–67
Paris Peace Conference, 146, 149
Park, Robert Ezra, 154
Park Chung-hee, 204
Park Shin-Eui, 136
Parker, Peter, 101

Parod, Icyang, 224, 225; youth of, 223
PCE (Presbyterian Church of England), 101
PCT (Presbyterian Church in Taiwan), 103, 106, 107
Pearl Harbor, 71, 85, 105
Peking University, 149, 173, 185
penal track, 191
Peng Ching-kao, 95
Peng Ming-min, 95, 104, 106, 116; asylum for, 109; placelessness for, 110
People First Party (Qinmindang), 131
People's Republic of China (PRC), 6, 13, 119, 175, 188, 202, 227, 232; diplomatic relations with, 191; UN Security Council and, 120
Petition Movement for the Establishment of a Taiwanese Parliament, 37, 46, 151
Philippines, 8, 59, 60, 64, 98
Pijun Irrigation Region, 52
piracy, 4, 42
Placeless People (Stonebridge), 171
placelessness, 110, 164, 172
Police Security Bureau, 174
political economy, 209
political issues, 54, 129, 187
political transition, 126, 183
politics, 136, 139, 140, 187, 231; equal participation in, 164
Port Moresby, 66, 67
postcolonialism, 8, 116, 219
Potsdam Declaration, 88
poverty, 82, 127, 205
POW camps, 71, 72, 77; in Taiwan, 73 (table)
POWs, 11, 72, 77–81; Chinese, 178. *See also* prisoners
PRC. *See* People's Republic of China
Presbyterian Church, 62, 102, 159; KMT and, 107; as moral compass, 104; nativization of, 156
Presbyterian Church in Canada, 102

Presbyterian Church in Taiwan (PCT), 103, 106, 107
Presbyterian Church of England (PCE), 101
Presidential Office, 130
prisoners, 72, 74, 76, 77, 79, 191, 192; political, 116, 190, 193; supervision of, 78; treatment of, 71. *See also* POWs
protests, 130–31, 132, 188; grassroots/student, 130; policing, 127–28
Provincial Assembly, 187, 191
Provisional Government of the Republic of Formosa (Taiwan Gongheguo Linshi Zhengfu), 111
PTT, 137, 211; Bulletin Board System, 209
public health, 214, 215, 216
Public Health Specialist Act, 215, 216
Pudu (Universal Salvation Festival), 158
Puyi, Emperor, 173, 174

Qian *jiao*, 33
Qianlong period, 74
Qing army, 49
Qing dynasty, 6, 62, 74, 172–74; expansion of, 2, 40; Taiwan and, 23, 34, 70; transition to, 42
Qing government, 22, 34, 41, 75, 147, 172; administration by, 43; colonialism and, 10, 40
Qiu Fengjia, 49
Qualcomm, 209
Quan *jiao*, 33
Quanzhou, 33, 35, 46, 151; kin networks, 10, 152
Quero y Ruíz, José María, 122, 123

Rabaul, 66, 69
Reagan, Ronald, 125
Recollections and Reflections (Shoki), 106
Red Dust (Gungun Hongchen) (film), 123
refugees, 106, 110, 130, 171, 172, 175, 230

INDEX *279*

Religion and Ritual in Chinese Society (Wolf), 201

Remote Oceania, colonization of, 60

Republic of China (ROC): Air Force, 177; claim of, 6; establishment of, 172; flight to, 175; foot binding and, 176; PRC and, 119, 174; recolonization by, 88; 228 Incident and, 191; UN Security Council and, 80, 120

Republic of Formosa, 49

Republic of Taiwan, 46, 111

Research Institute of Painting (Huihua Yanjiusuo), 152

resistance, 36, 46, 49, 61, 62, 78, 150, 195; antigovernment, 41; Han, 50; Indigenous, 11, 33, 34, 50, 63; systematic, 2, 63

Ricci, Matteo, 157

rice, 43, 52, 55, 156; deficiency, 40

Righteous Harmony Society, 49

Ritchie, Hugh, 102

rituals, 176, 218, 220

River Dajia, 102

River Tamsui, 23, 25, 185, 187

ROC. *See* Republic of China

Ro'eng, 64–68, 70, 74; arrival of, 69

Roman Catholic Church, 1

Rooney, Maurice, 71, 72

Roosevelt, Franklin, 79

Rotary International, 54

Royal Asiatic Society, 26

Royal Corps of Signals, 76

Royal Geographical Society, 24

Rudao, Mona, 59

Ruey Yih-fu, 200

Ruicheng, 172

Russo-Japanese War (1904–5), 50

Ryan, Shawna Yang, 163, 169, 195, 205–6, 232

Said, Edward, 109, 180

Saint Mary's Church, 27

Saint Thomas à Becket, 1

Sanchao River, 74

Sangren, Steven, 201

sanjiaozai (*Sann-kha-á*), 78

Sanmao, 119, 121, 123, 124

Sanmao craze (Sanmaore), 124

Sanyi clan, 152

SARS, 12, 211–15

Sartre, Jean-Paul, 148, 155

Sawai, Hideo, 85

School of Oriental and African Studies (SOAS), 105

SDP (Social Democratic Party), 133

Sebastian, Elsa, 134

Second Industrial Revolution (1870–1914), 27

self-determination, 7–8, 63, 104, 111–12, 113, 116, 150; pursuit of, 98; Wilsonian ideals of, 98

self-government, 146, 222

selfhood, 49, 83, 104

self-interest, economic, 9–10

self-realization, social fact of, 218

semiconductor companies, 209

Sepik River, 67

settlement, 41; Chinese, 2, 33, 40, 70; colonial, 227; Indigenous, 34, 220; Japanese, 52–53; pioneer, 38; urban, 34

settler colonialism, 2, 5, 7, 8, 10, 43, 61, 116, 225; metropole, 62; narrative of, 21; site of, 21; stages of, 50

715 Announcement (Qiyiwu Shengming), 132

Seventieth Army, 96

Shanghai, 105, 145, 149, 173, 176, 178

Shenyang, 174

Shih Chao-tzu, 53, 55

Shih Chien, 53, 159

Shih Chiutuan Incident (Shi Jiuduan Shijian), 36

Shih Hsin University, 193

Shih Hsiu-feng, 53

Shih Ming-teh, 184, 192

Shih Wu-ching, 54

Shih You, 151

Shimizu Teruko, 53, 55–56, 124, 159; death of, 54; 228 Incident and, 54

Shoei Kisen Kaisha, 204

Shoki Coe (Huang Zhanghui, Shōka), 104; death of, 107–8; mission work of, 105, 107; transnationality of, 106

Shonan Maru (submarine chaser), sinking of, 207

shōnenkō, 83, 84, 86–89, 229

sijiaozai (*Sì-kha-á*), 78

silk, market for, 5

silver, discovery of, 75

Singapore, 24, 26, 183; fall of, 76; POWs from, 72

Sino-American Joint Commission on Rural Reconstruction, 183

Sino-French War, 46

Sino-Japanese War (1894–95), 22, 48, 49

Sixteen (Sikseutin), 138

Sixty-Second Army, 95

small and medium enterprise (SME), 204

Smith, Gunner J. M. M., 71

smuggling, 4, 42

Social Democratic Party (Shehui Minzhu Dang) (SDP), 133

social development, 113, 130

social engineering, 48, 119

social environment, 34, 127

social interaction, 27, 35

social issues, 10, 34, 127, 129, 139, 140, 146

social justice, 230

social media, 135, 137, 139, 214

social mobility, 152, 183–84

social movements, 127–31, 133, 140

social transformation, 140, 146, 207, 210

Solomon Islands, 64, 68

Sommers, Scott, 48

Sòng Chôan Sēng (Song Quansheng), 104, 107

Song Jiaoren, 172

"Song of the Taiwanese Soldiers, The," text of, 66

Songshan Airport, 95, 97

Soochow University School of Law, Tsai at, 229

Soong Ai-ling, 104

Soong May-ling, 98, 104

Southbound Policy, 230

Southern Warehouse Company (Nanyang Cangku Zhushi Huishe), 36

Spanish, 5, 43

Spirited Away (anime), 75

Stalin, Josef, 79

#StandByYu, 137

Starlux Airlines, 207

Statute to Prevent Espionage, 191

stereotyping, 26, 218

Stonebridge, Lyndsey, 171

Stonequist, Everett, 154

Stories of the Sahara (Sahala de gushi) (Chen), publication of, 123

student movements, 111, 126, 132

Studio Ghibli, 75

Su Beng, 112–16, 147; culture and, 115; nationalism and, 113

Su Tseng-chang, 185, 228

Suao (Suō Town), 206

Suez Canal, 203

sugar, 36, 43, 52, 55

Sui-Rin Grade School, 84

Suming, 219

Sun Yat-sen, 88, 153, 172, 174–75, 228

Sunflower Movement (Taiyanghua Xueyun), 8, 127–33, 139, 140

Suzhou Internment Camp, 82

Swinhoe, Robert, 23, 24, 25

Tadashi, Yoshimura, 65

Taehwagwan Restaurant, 150

Tai Chao-chuen Incident (Diachaochun Shijian) (1862–65), 45

Taian Hospital (Daan Yiyuan), 153

Taichung (Taichū, Dali), 23, 36, 44, 45, 72, 85, 102, 114, 222

Taihoku College of Commerce (Taihoku Kōtō Shōgyō Gakkō), 206

Taihoku Industrial School (Taihoku Kōgyō Gakkō), 159

Taihoku University, 200

Tainan, 7, 22, 41, 85, 102, 105, 156; as capital, 23; capitulation of, 49

Tainan Municipal Fusing Junior High School, 138

Tainan Theological College, 105

Taipei, 74; bombing of, 88; elite in, 121; evictions from, 130; Japanese surrender and, 94; as provincial capital, 23, 120

Taipei Commercial High School, 206

Taipei Confucius Temple, 32–33

Taipei First Girls' School, 121

Taipei Jen-Chi Relief Institution (Renjiyuan), 157, 159

Taipei Natural Foot Association (Taibei Tianranzu Hui), 158

Taipei Veterans General Hospital, 124

Taisho democracy, 50

Taitung Development Company, 52, 65

Taitung Harbor Office, 52

Taitung Sugar Manufacturing Company, 52

Taiwan, map of, 14

Taiwan Administration Junior College (Taiwan Xingzheng Zhuanke Xuexiao), 185

Taiwan Army Volunteer System, 87

Taiwan Assembly, 153

Taiwan Bank, 185

Taiwan Campaign, 49

Taiwan Citizen Union (Gongmin Zuhe), 133

Taiwan Democratic Self-Governing League, 114

Taiwan Garrison Command, 192, 195

Taiwan Gold and Copper Mining Bureau (Taiwan Jintong Kuangwuju), 76

Taiwan Governor's Office, 52

Taiwan High School, 105

Taiwan Human Rights Commission (Taiwan Renquan Weiyuanhui), 111

Taiwan Independence Armed Corps, 113

Taiwan Indigenous Languages Development Act, 224

Taiwan Medical College, 151

Taiwan Metal Mining Company (Taiwan Jinshu Kuangye Gongsi), 76

Taiwan Miracle, 183

Taiwan Museum, 199

Taiwan Politics (Taiwan zhenglun), 186, 187

Taiwan Provincial Council, 193

Taiwan Provincial Government, 191

Taiwan Provincial Self-Governing Body of Koza, 87

Taiwan Public School Decree, 82

Taiwan Semiconductor Manufacturing Company (TSMC) (Taiwan Jiti Dianlu Zhizao Gufen Youxiangongsi), 209

Taiwan Silk Industry Bureau, 156

Taiwan Strait, 7, 38, 42, 96, 120; cargo route across, 208

Taiwan War (1895), 22, 48

Taiwan's 400-Year History (Su), 112, 113, 115, 116

Taiwanese, 55; Japanese and, 96

Taiwanese Communist Party, 113

Taiwanese Cultural Association (Taiwan Wenhua Xiehui) (TCA), 12, 113, 149, 151, 153, 185

Taiwanese Nationalism, 138

Taiwanese People's Party, 113, 153

Taiwaneseness, 48, 55

Taiyang Gold Mine Office (Taiyang Kuangye Shiwu Suo), 75

Takao, 85, 102

Takasago Volunteers (Takasago Giyutai), 64, 70

"Tall Nose Road" (Zhuobizailu), 77

Tama Tulum, 223

Tamaki, Lieutenant, 72

Tamsui, 23, 25, 101–2; port at, 22, 24, 31, 152

Tanaka Company, 75

Tandao Yimen (Entry Door to the Heavenly Way), 157

Tang, Audrey (Tang Fang), 212

Tang Jia Bao, 195

tang *jiao* (sugar guild), 33

Tang Jingsong, 49

Tang Yu, 76, 77, 78

Tangwai (Dangwai), 114–15, 184, 189, 192, 194, 195, 230; described, 187; moderates in, 188; political discussion groups and, 188

Tangwai's Tale, 12

Taoism, 104

Taoyuan City (Humaozhuang), 35, 165, 168, 190, 204, 222

Tapani Incident (Jiaobanian Shijian) (1915), 49, 50, 150

Tatu River, 72

Taylor, James Hudson, 101

TCA (Taiwanese Cultural Association), 12, 113, 149, 151, 153, 185

tea, 55, 156; Formosan, 24, 25, 26

technology: adoption of, 27; advances in, 125; future, 210; green, 209; innovative, 209

Telluride Fellowship, 200

temples, 36; building, 31–32, 35

Territorial Army, 76

Thatcher, Margaret, 125, 203

Theological Education Fund, 107

Three Principles of the People, 174–75

Three Principles of the People (Sun), 88, 153, 228

Tiananmen Massacre (1989), 79, 127

Tianma Tea House (Tianma Chafang), 165

Tien-en Lin, 138

Titherington, Arthur, 77, 78

Tobacco Monopoly Bureau, 165

Tokyo, 86, 105, 112, 185

Tongan clan, 152

Torii Ryūzō, 199

trade, 27, 33, 34; Dutch, 61; international, 5, 22, 23, 31, 32; local, 25; monopoly, 43; overseas, 41

tradition, 200, 218–19, 224; literary, 121; modern concepts of, 220; political, 23

Traitors' Punishment Act, 191

Treaty of Shimonoseki, 48

Treaty of Versailles, 146, 173

treaty ports, 22–24, 27, 32, 38, 62, 152

"Truths and Lies of Lin Chiang-mai, The" (Lin Jiangmai de zhenzhen jiajia), 167

Tsai Chieh-sheng, 228–29

Tsai Hui-ping, 168, 169

Tsai Ing-wen, 1, 12, 134, 135, 194, 224, 226, 232; birth of, 228; consensus and, 136; politics and, 229–31

Tsai Pei-huo, 147

Tsinghua University, 149

Tu, Ethan, 209, 210

Tudigong, 11, 32

27 Brigade, 113, 114

TWICE (girl band), 134, 135, 138

two-China policy, 106

228 Incident, 54, 97, 106, 113, 151, 165, 170; exodus following, 111; investigation of, 167, 168; literature after 120; martial law and, 7, 183, 191; nationalism and, 170; Presbyterian Church and, 104; Taiwanese identification and, 12, 99

Ueno High School, 185

UNICEF, 82

Union for Formosa's Independence in Europe, 111

United Daily News, 123, 168

United Formosans in America for Independence (Quanmei Taiwan Duli Lianmeng), 111

United Nations, 80, 89, 98, 120, 171

United Nations General Assembly, 184

United Nations Security Council, 80, 120

United Young Formosans for Independence (Taiwan Qingnian Duli Lianmeng), 111

Universal Declaration of Human Rights, 184

Upper House of the Japanese Diet (Kizoku-in), 37

US Air Force, 88

US Army Air Forces, 79

US Department of War, 97

US Fifth Air Force, 67

US Marine Corps, 79

US Naval Reserve, 97

US State Department, 120

Vatican, 212

violence, 150, 225; ethnic, 10, 34

waishengren, 98, 167, 180; *benshengren* and, 166, 168; ethnic divisions of, 130, 164; identification and, 99; prejudices against, 169, 179

Wan Hsi-chi, 178

Wang family, 180

Wang Hsi-chi, 178, 179

Wang Hsu-kang, 179

Wang Kuei-jung, 167

War of Resistance against Japanese Aggression (Zhongguo Kangri Zhanzheng), 95

Waseda University, 112

"We Refugees" (Arendt), 110

Wedemeyer, Albert C., 94

Wei Hwei-lin, 200

Wei Lien-chih, 212

Wei Tao-ming, 191

Wei Te-sheng, 113

Wei Ting-chao, 109

Weller, Robert, 201

Wenzhou people, 77

Wewak, 66, 67

White Shirt Army (Baishanjun), 139

White Terror (Baise Kongbu), 116, 119, 167, 193, 195, 232

WHO (World Health Organization), 211, 215, 227

Wild Lily student movement (Ye Baihe Xue Yan), 126, 127, 132, 187, 223

Wild Strawberries (Ye Caomei), 128

Wildlife Conservation Law, 130

Wisteria Tea House (Zitenglu), 112, 187, 188

Wolf, Arthur P., 12, 200–201, 202

Wolf, Margery, 201, 202

Women and the Family in Rural Taiwan (Wolf), 202

World Health Organization (WHO), 211, 215, 227

World United Formosans for Independence (WUFI) (Taiwan Duli Jianguo Lianmeng), 111, 112

World War I, 148, 150, 154

World War II: children and, 81, 82; end of, 160, 171; impact of, 106; Papua and, 69; Taiwan and, 74

Wu Den-yih, 129–30

Wu Feng, myth of, 218

Wu San-lien, 185

Wu Zhenchen, 39

Wuchang Uprising, 172

Wufeng Lin, 36, 44, 46

WUFI. *See* World United Formosans for Independence

Wylie, Iain, 203

Xia *jiao*, 33
xiacuo, 45, 46
Xiamen, 24, 33, 41, 114, 155
Xiatang village, 175
Xindian, 23
Xinhai Revolution, 172
Xintai Marine Corporation (Xintai Haiyun Gongsi), 207
Xu Huaizu, 39
Xuchun, 78

Yamamoto Isoroku, 85
Yang, Dominic, 175
Yang Du, 166, 167
Yang Nan-chun, 86
Yang Sanlang, 152
Yanqi Tong, 130
Yao Chia-wen, 184, 185
Yasuji, Okumura, 94
Yen Yun-nian, 75
Yilan, 151, 193, 206, 213

Young, James, 101
Yu Qingfang, 49
Yu Teng-fa, 189
Yu Yonghe, 39, 42
Yuan Yu Shyi-kun, 213
Yuanzhumin Zhengming Yundong (Indigenous Name Rectification Movement), 224
Yung-Fa, 206
yutingtang (orphanages), 159

Zealandia theme park, 113
zhanbao, 224
Zhang Jingguang, 151
Zhang Leping, 124
Zhang Zhaoze, 177, 179
Zhangzhou, 10, 44, 45
Zhejiang, 121, 123, 176
Zheng Chenggong (Koxinga), 7
Zhongshan District, 229
Zhuluo, 43

Milton Keynes UK
Ingram Content Group UK Ltd.
UKHW040612130924
448159UK00002B/13